PAPER

TRAILS

GLOBAL INSECURITIES

A series edited by Catherine Besteman and Darryl Li

PAPER TRAILS

Migrants, Documents, and Legal Insecurity

EDITED BY SARAH B. HORTON AND JOSIAH HEYMAN

Duke University Press   *Durham and London*   2020

Designed by Courtney Leigh Richardson
Typeset in Minion Pro and Helvetica Neue by Westchester
Pub-lishing Services

Library of Congress Cataloging-in-Publication Data

Names: Horton, Sarah Bronwen, [date] editor. | Heyman,
    Josiah McC. (Josiah McConnell), [date] editor.
    Title: Paper trails : migrants, documents, and legal
  insecurity / Sarah B. Horton and Josiah Heyman, editors.
    Other titles: Global insecurities.
Description: Durham : Duke University Press, 2020. | Series:

    Global insecurities | Includes bibliographical references
    and index.
Identifiers: LCCN 2019047825 (print)
LCCN 2019047826 (ebook)
ISBN 9781478007944 (hardcover)
ISBN 9781478008453 (paperback)
ISBN 9781478012092 (ebook)
Subjects: LCSH: Identification cards—Law and legislation—
    United States. | Identification cards—Law and legislation—
    Great Britain. | Emigration and immigration law—United
    States. | Emigration and immigration law—Great Britain.
Classification: LCC KF4840. P37 2020 (print) |
    LCC KF4840 (ebook) | DDC 342.7308—dc23
LC record available at https://lccn.loc.gov/2019047825
LC ebook record available at https://lccn.loc.gov/2019047826

COVER ART: Form I-821D, DACA

Contents

SARAH B. HORTON

Introduction. **PAPER TRAILS**
Migrants, Bureaucratic Inscription, and Legal Recognition

New developments have made identity documents an increasingly revealing site at which to examine the power dynamics between migrants and
the state in traditional immigrant-receiving countries. First, in the United
States, Canada, and the European Union, new forms of temporary and provisional legal status are proliferating, even as states are less likely to grant
permanent legal status.[1] In Canada, for example, the number of nonimmi-
grants the state admits through its guest worker program has only increased
since the 1970s, even as those admitted as legal permanent residents have declined.[2] In Spain, new immigration laws passed in the 1990s admit migrants
only as temporary workers on one-year renewable permits,[3] while in the
United Kingdom, only the wealthiest investors and highly skilled migrants
are granted a chance at permanent settlement.[4] Finally, in the United States,
provisional forms of lawful presence—such as Temporary Protected Status
and the "stays of deportation" offered by the Deferred Action for Childhood
Arrivals program—multiplied during the Obama administration even as
opportunities for regularization for unauthorized migrants stalled.[5]

These temporary and provisional statuses may be seen as the bureaucratic
manifestation of a broader phenomenon of "global apartheid"—that is, of a
system of heightened immigration restrictions in more prosperous nations
that increasingly deny foreigners the stability of permanent legal status in

the receiving country. We follow Nandita Sharma in conceptualizing "global apartheid" as a system of restrictive immigration and citizenship controls that admit foreigners only on a temporary or "illegal" basis.[6] As Sharma observes, global apartheid is not about keeping people of different citizenship statuses apart, but rather about incorporating foreigners into the nation on unequal terms via the denial of legal permanent status. In Sharma's formulation, therefore, legal distinctions on the basis of citizenship status have replaced those made on the basis of race, creating a highly vulnerable class of foreign workers who serve as an "efficient, flexible, and globally competitive workforce."[7]

This volume focuses on documents as a window onto the power dynamics between migrants and states in high-income countries that have been traditional destinations for South-to-North migration. Although we recognize that documents have become an increasingly important site through which states manage South-to-South migration and migration in transit states, we focus on South-to-North migration here due to space limitations.[8] Because the new immigration statuses created in the North are only temporary, they have profound, and understudied, implications for migrants' relationships to state bureaucracies. They more intensively subject migrants to state bureaucratic surveillance. That is, migrants must request frequent renewals and meet a battery of requirements to prolong these already-"liminal" legal statuses.[9]

The expansion of these temporary statuses has occurred against the backdrop of a moment of growing uncertainty for migrants in traditional receiving countries—one in which the pressures of national securitization appear to be trumping the impulse toward humanitarianism. These developments disrupt the old certainties migrants had come to expect in their interactions with the state. On the one hand, the old bureaucratic firewalls are coming down. U.S. government agencies formerly kept separate in the name of humanitarianism—such as the U.S. Department of Health and Human Services and ICE—are now changing policy to share information about migrants, facilitating the criminal prosecution of asylum seekers and of parents who enable their children's unauthorized passage.[10] On the other hand, government officials are collaborating with new bureaucratic agents in immigration control. In the United States, debates continue over the role of the police, probation officers, and even Department of Motor Vehicles officials in collaborating with immigration enforcement. Meanwhile, in the United Kingdom, the government is increasingly devolving responsibility for immigrant policing to landlords, professors, and truck drivers.[11] This environment of insecurity intensifies the stakes for migrants when interacting with state bureaucracies—even with the very arms of the state charged with extending legal status rather than enforcing immigration controls.[12] Migrants reluctantly and fearfully submit to state scrutiny because they seek the privileges and security identity documents confer, even as they have reason to fear that becoming "legible" to the state may lead to their eventual deportation.

Finally, official identification documents are proliferating, as local branches of government and even foreign governments are newly providing official identifications to unauthorized migrants. In the United States, for example— and to a lesser extent in Europe and Canada—municipal and state governments are themselves extending official identity documents to migrants. Predicated on the affirmation of unauthorized migrants' membership in local communities and on the knowledge that lacking accepted forms of identification leads to myriad forms of social exclusion,[13] these local-level identity documents are an increasingly popular means of acknowledging unauthorized migrants' "social personhood."[14] Indeed, municipal IDs represent attempts by local governments to establish membership policy at the local rather than the national level.[15] In addition, foreign governments— including Mexico, Guatemala, Colombia, Senegal, Mali, and Nigeria—now extend consular IDs to their expatriates to provide them with official verification of their identity; they even campaign to expand local acceptance of such documents in order to stabilize their expatriates' situation abroad.[16] Diverse identification documents have varying levels of legitimacy for different purposes, and they interact in complex, unpredictable ways with formal immigration documentation and statuses.[17] Most importantly for our purposes, even inclusive forms of bureaucratic inscription at the local level—such as municipal IDs and driver's licenses—may unintentionally expose unauthorized migrants to the risk of immigration enforcement, as we discuss below.

This volume brings together anthropologists, sociologists, geographers, and political scientists to examine these practices of what we call "bureaucratic inscription" and migrants' resistance to them.[18] By "bureaucratic inscription," we refer to the social and material dynamics through which migrants are inscribed into official bureaucratic systems at various scales of government. We hold that bureaucratic inscription entails discrete—and sometimes prolonged—moments of visibility to a field of power. We use state practices of documentation as a lens to explore how they transform migrants' subjectivities and conceptualization of their place in the nation, as well as how they reveal contradictions in governance created by the contested and changing form of "the state" itself.[19] In this volume, then, we ask the following questions: How do the processes entailed in applying for legal status and local-level forms of documentation alter migrants' behaviors and attitudes toward "the state" in its varied forms? In what ways are migrants able to exercise agency when applying for legal statuses and when using official documents to achieve various aims, and in what ways do these paper trails capture or entangle migrants? How is legal status made concrete through documentation, and how does examining the bureaucratic processes of documentation reveal techniques of state power and the power asymmetries between migrants and the state? What is omitted when the particularities of individual biographies are compressed into standardized legal categories through bureaucratic processes, and what happens when individuals' narratives of identity and state bureaucratic identifications conflict?[20] We keep in mind that identity (held by the self) is not the same as identification (emplaced from outside); important questions occur at their intersection.[21] In that regard, how do documents, and the practices and statuses linked to them, become an important site for action, both individual and collective?

Our Approach

We suggest that documents—the tangible evidence of bureaucratic inscription—constitute a particularly useful site at which to analyze the power relationship between migrants and the state. First, migrants primarily encounter the state through everyday practices of documentation. "The state" often appears distant and faceless to those it governs; it is through documents and the process of entering state bureaucracies that the state takes concrete form. Indeed, migrants not only encounter the state during processes of *inscription* (that is, when they submit to government surveillance by applying for identity documents, benefits, or legalization), but also during *validation* (that is, when they receive documentary proof of legal status, benefits, or identity) or *verification* (that is, when they submit their documents for verification, either by the state or by third parties). Second, documents are concrete distillations of state power; through documents, the state strives to identify and enumerate its population and separate it by legal status. Yet because documents are the result of practices of inscription, they are simultaneously a potent site of resistance; as forms of writing, documents may be forged, mimicked, and subverted.[22] Divorced from the authority they are intended to represent, after all, documents are merely material artifacts. Thus migrants may appropriate some of the power of the state by engaging with documents as objects: by separating them from their lawful bearers, by deploying them to alternative ends, or by exchanging, pooling, and "renting" them.[23] And finally, as material objects, documents are crystallizations of the law at a particular historical and social moment.[24] While the law is a "living document," subject to change, identity documents are concrete distillations of the law in time and space. Therefore, attention to bureaucratic inscription and the materiality of documents brings into sharp relief the law as human artifact. It reveals changing state policies regarding migrants' rights and the contradictory policies of localities and foreign governments that have devised their own documentary practices.

Placing documents at the center of our study of immigration controls underscores the fact that legal status is fundamentally conferred in *writing*. Many scholars have identified writing as key to the administrative capacity of modern states, suggesting that the documents provided by state bureaucratic systems serve as forms of surveillance and control.[25] As James Scott has argued, a central concern of modern states is ensuring that their populations are *legible*—that is, enumerated and categorized in standardized ways—so that they can be governed effectively.[26] Yet we recognize that bureaucratic inscription exceeds writing as well—individuals are inscribed into state bureaucracies through fingerprints, retina and iris scans, voice recognition, and photos that may be read by facial recognition technologies.[27] Thus we use the term *bureaucratic inscription* in an expansive sense to refer to the various processes and technologies through which information about individuals and their immigration status is incorporated into official state registers. These are socio-material processes enacted by a variety of actors—not only state bureaucrats and the street-level bureaucrats who assist them, but also legal advocates[28] and migrants themselves.

Similarly, we use the term *documents* to refer not only to official immigration papers bestowed by the nation-state, such as passports and visas, but also to the myriad documents now extended to denizens at subnational levels. Little attention has been devoted to how documents granted by other levels of government—driver's licenses, municipal and NGO IDs, consular IDs—interact with the official immigration documents granted by national governments. In some cases, policy makers seek to prohibit unauthorized migrants' access to documents provided by other levels of government out of a fear that they may serve as "breeder documents"—ingeniously parlayed by migrants for the rights and privileges associated with legal status.[29] In other cases, policy makers aim to extend valid forms of identification to unauthorized migrants in order to grant them the everyday privileges of local denizenship—such as picking children up from school or requesting library privileges. Thus the struggle over whether to include unauthorized migrants in the national body plays out at different levels of the state in the form of contests over documentation.

Recent volumes have used historical and sociological approaches to examine the key role that official documents and state bureaucratic systems play in the ability of states to distinguish between citizens and noncitizens and therefore to control mobility.[30] They have also examined the complex relationship between state practices of identification and how individuals conceive of their own identities.[31] Yet less scholarship examines how the complicated power dynamic between migrants and the state unfolds through bureaucratic interactions and the documents that concretize them—especially at a moment in which legibility to the state entails heightened risks. This volume's contribution lies in examining how migrants on the ground experience, accept, and resist state bureaucratic practices in a time of increasing securitization. This introduction highlights four main themes related to processes of bureaucratic inscription that run through the chapters assembled here: (1) the tension inscription raises for migrants, as they seek the security documents offer yet fear visibility to the state; (2) how new forms of bureaucratic inscription (that is, municipal IDs and driver's licenses) attempt to include migrants in local communities but simultaneously extend the power of the state; (3) the dynamics of inscription as state power and migrant resistance; and (4) the different subjectivities created by varying intensities and durations of bureaucratic inscription.

The Tension between Legibility and Security

Inscription generates "paper trails" that follow migrants. That is, state-issued identity documents may grant security by verifying migrants' identity and conferring legal status. However, in rendering migrants not only known to the state but *legible*—that is, locatable through the information tied to migrants' identities—documents also make migrants more vulnerable.[32] Indeed, recent developments in the United States and Europe have thrown this tension between legibility and security into sharp relief.

First, the United States and nations in Europe increasingly offer temporary and provisional forms of immigration status in lieu of legal permanent residency. The Deferred Action for Childhood Arrivals (DACA) program in the United States, for example, offers its bearers only a temporary and contingent reprieve from deportation and must be renewed every two years.

Temporary Protected Status (TPS), a form of legal status granted immigrants fleeing "extraordinary and temporary conditions,"[33] must also be renewed in the same time frame. The temporary work visas that have proliferated in Spain, France, and the United Kingdom also require renewals.[34] Because these temporary statuses may be rescinded at any moment, and none of them provides a pathway to legal permanent residency, they leave bearers suspended in a prolonged state of "liminal legality."[35]

Asylum seekers in Europe and the United States occupy a similar legal limbo. They may wait years for a decision on their cases; if they lodge an appeal, their cases may drag out even further.[36] As they await a resolution, they remain visible to the state, their presence "lawful" but their status "unlawful" as their cases are pending. Meanwhile, domestic workers in the United Kingdom and those on EB-3 visas in the United States endure a kind of "probationary" or "conditional" lawful status in that they must remain with their employers in order to receive legal permanent residency.[37] The bearers of these provisional and temporary statuses in the United States and the United Kingdom share an ambivalent relationship to the documents that bestow on them their lawful presence. Their stays of deportation, temporary authorizations, or asylum claims leave a paper trail that makes them locatable by the state.

The increase of these provisional statuses in the United States and Europe comes amid a growing emphasis on securitization that only amplifies uncertainty for migrants. In this context, the risk entailed by bureaucratic inscription—of being known to an arbitrary and often punitive central state authority—may outweigh the risk of remaining unknown. For migrants facing stringent and punitive immigration systems, illegibility to the state may serve as a shield. Changes to immigration laws in the United States since the 1990s, for example, have eroded the security once offered by legal status. On the one hand, the boundary between legal and "illegal" status has become more permeable, as the frequent renewals, high administrative fees, and arcane rules governing temporary legal statuses have made it easier to "fall out of status."[38] On the other hand, changes in immigration law in 1996 have rendered legal permanent residents deportable for a greater number of offenses, brightening the line between "citizens" and "noncitizens."[39] Thus, those unauthorized migrants who have never interacted with state bureaucratic systems may ironically feel safer from punitive immigration enforcement than even legal immigrants who are deeply embedded within bureaucratic systems. As a result, even those unauthorized migrants eligible to adjust their legal status may opt out in order to preserve their invisibility and security.[40]

Yet, in other cases, migrants already captured within the system may find benefits to disappearing from it, even at the risk of apprehension and deportation. That is, some U.S. migrants with legal status may voluntarily give up that status in order to remain safe from an immigration regime they view as arbitrary and punitive.[41] Similarly, migrants from certain countries that remain largely excluded from legitimate entry to Europe have been known to destroy their national documentation in order to seek relief through the asylum system instead. This illustrates the way documents may constrict migrants' possibilities, highlighting the profoundly *"disqualifying*, rights-*limiting* character of a passport as a marker of nationality."[42] In short, entering state bureaucratic systems entails significant risk at this moment of punitive immigration enforcement and heightened national securitization.

Local-Level Bureaucratic Inscription

It is not only applications for status adjustment that make migrants legible to the state; bureaucratic inscription is carried out at multiple levels. Indeed, local-level governments in the United States and Europe are increasingly issuing their own identity documents to unauthorized migrants in the form of municipal IDs or driver's licenses. Because cities must address the practical needs of their residents on the ground, they may be more likely to resist restrictive immigration policies carried out by the national government.[43] Issuing formal identification to unauthorized residents is a means by which municipalities resist national membership policy and attach entitlements to local inhabitance rather than legal status. By framing their efforts around the principle of local residence (or *jus domicile*), policy makers and migrant advocates assert unauthorized migrants' deservingness of the everyday prerogatives of local citizenship.[44]

In the United States, for example, the driver's license serves as a kind of "master identifier," monopolizing the legitimate means to verify identity. Only with this officially validated identifier can one access the everyday privileges that community residents take for granted: the ability to obtain library cards, open bank accounts, rent apartments, and establish utilities.[45] Lacking a driver's license also makes it difficult for unauthorized residents to identify themselves when picking up their children from school or obtaining marriage licenses.[46] Yet due to concerns about national security prompted by 9/11, unauthorized migrants became ineligible for driver's licenses in all but twelve states and the District of Columbia. The unquestioned acceptance of the driver's license as a universal identifier renders unauthorized migrants unidentifiable and therefore excludes them from local bureaucracies. In fact, the refusal of some law enforcement officers to accept any form of official identification other than U.S. driver's licenses poses a particular threat to unauthorized residents. Because the police are required to take any individual they cannot identify into custody, unauthorized migrants who are stopped by the police run the risk of being arrested and, as a consequence, deported.[47]

To grant unauthorized migrants greater security and extend them the everyday privileges of community life, then, migrant advocates in the United States have increasingly focused on expanding the reach of a form of identification based on local inhabitance—municipal IDs.[48] Municipal IDs grant migrants access to the same municipal services as other residents, serving as a symbolic statement of their local belonging. These IDs gained traction in the United States after the failure of comprehensive immigration reform in 2012 and the 2016 Supreme Court stalemate over former President Obama's proposal to legalize the parents of children with legal status.[49] Since 2015, cities such as Baltimore, Chicago, Detroit, Phoenix, Philadelphia, Pittsburgh, and South Bend, Indiana, have begun considering offering municipal IDs to residents;[50] some Midwestern counties (in Michigan and Wisconsin) have followed suit.[51] In their efforts to integrate unauthorized migrants into local communities, some European cities have also created municipal ID cards, including Vienna in 2015 and Madrid in 2016.[52] In contrast, sanctuary measures in Canadian cities—in Toronto, Hamilton, London, and Montreal—have focused on removing identification requirements such that unauthorized migrants may access city services.[53]

Municipal IDs—while an assertion of unauthorized migrants' deservingness of urban citizenship[54]—are still a form of bureaucratic inscription. Thus, ironically, these efforts at inclusion may increase the risk of migrants' apprehension by making them visible to other branches of government. The recent struggle over the confidentiality of records of applicants for New York City's municipal ID (IDNYC) is a vivid example of this. The result of a compromise between migrant advocates and the police, proponents of New York's municipal ID law pledged to maintain applicants' personal data for up to two years in order to enable potential investigations of fraud.[55] More than a million New Yorkers signed up for the IDNYC by the end of 2016, more than half of whom use the card as their primary identification. Yet after the election of President Trump, city officials hastily announced that, starting in 2017, they would no longer retain the records—that is, the copies of the documents applicants had presented as proof of identity and residence—once the IDs were issued. Moreover, they announced they would also jettison the data of former applicants in order to prevent their falling into the hands of the Department of Homeland Security.[56] Citing concerns of "national security," however, two Republican assemblymen sued to force the city to retain the records and lodged a Freedom of Information law request for the personal information of all applicants to make them accessible to the federal government.[57] Thus, as municipalities operate within an increasingly precarious national immigration climate, extending legitimacy to unauthorized migrants through local-level identification also exposes them to the risk of deportation.

The actions of renegade officers in the Vermont Department of Motor Vehicles shortly after the state passed a law allowing unauthorized migrants to obtain "driver privilege cards" further illustrate this tension. Even though Vermont state policy prohibits state employees from carrying out federal immigration enforcement, in 2014 the Vermont DMV forwarded to ICE the information of a Jordanian national, Abdel Rabbah, and even took the extraordinary measure of luring Rabbah to the DMV so that ICE could apprehend him and initiate deportation proceedings.[58] While Rabbah launched a discrimination lawsuit against the DMV, ultimately settling for $40,000, a new investigation reveals that the DMV routinely sent the information of unauthorized migrants to ICE well after the incident and even informed ICE officers of the dates of migrants' appointments.[59] Thus, while driver's licenses include migrants in the everyday life of local communities and grant them greater security from local police, they may unintentionally expand the reach of state power. At this moment of intensified insecurity for migrants, attending to the articulations between local-level forms of identification and state bureaucratic systems, as well as how migrants and their advocates navigate this relationship, is incumbent on us.

The Dynamics of Inscription: State Power and Migrant Resistance

This brings up our third main theme: the interaction between inscription as a form of state power and migrant resistance. Clearly, those seeking official recognition must submit to state power. Whether applying for municipal IDs, state driver's licenses, or formal legal statuses, they must meet a series of evidentiary requirements. In Spain, for example, a 2005 regularization program required that workers demonstrate duration of residence, proof of employment, and evidence of social integration (in the form of proof of family ties or a report from the local town council).[60] Meanwhile, in the United

States, migrants seeking to regularize their status must assemble evidence of positive interactions with local institutions (churches, schools, doctors' offices) to attest to their "good moral character."[61] Ironically, then, migrants must accumulate significant paper trails in order to successfully adjust their legal status. Regularization, then, requires that "undocumented" migrants develop an intimate relationship to bureaucratic records.

Regularization requirements transform the meaning of mundane records to migrants as well as migrants' relationships to local bureaucracies. When migrants regularize, a wide variety of state and non-state records—receipts for medical appointments, check stubs, tax returns, school enrollment records, and utility bills—assume new importance. For example, Don Pablo is an unauthorized farmworker who had missed the last opportunity for regularization in the United States in 1986 because he threw out his back and was recuperating in Mexico. His employer had sent him a letter informing him that he was eligible and urging him to apply, and Don Pablo kept that letter ever since. Aware that the 1986 "amnesty" had required farmworkers to supply proof of duration of residence and work history, for thirty years Don Pablo had diligently collected all the "official"-seeming documents he could in three plastic bags under the cot in his apartment. One held his tax returns; another bills, medical documents, and receipts; and the third his check stubs. Regularization requirements therefore mean that ordinary paperwork assumes new currency to migrants, as it becomes valuable evidence of one's duration of residence, work history, or "moral character" (diligence, civic responsibility, compliance with the authorities). For these reasons, some have observed that "the state"—whether the local branches of government that issue these myriad documents or a centralized government authority—often assumes a greater presence in the lives and imaginations of precariously positioned migrants than it does in those of its citizens.[62]

The state's unilateral authority to enact immigration laws and interpret bureaucratic records illustrates the arbitrariness of the state—a principal attribute of state power.[63] On the one hand, the state has largely unquestioned authority over immigration policies; in the United States, for example, the doctrine of plenary power places control over the disposition of noncitizens residing in the nation and those entering from abroad squarely in the hands of the executive branch and Congress. This allows the state to suddenly expel foreigners in the name of national security, to ban the entry of particular nationalities, and to exclude at whim those previously included in the national body.[64] On the other hand, "the state" is not a single entity; it is made up of myriad bureaucrats who differ in their interpretation and enactment of "state" policies across bureaucracies and localities;[65] the discretionary power of these individuals to enact state policy only exacerbates the state's arbitrariness. Finally, state policies regarding immigration are often ambiguous and open to interpretation;[66] they are almost always complicated, changeable, and so inaccessible to the layperson that few dare approach them without legal representation.[67] Thus a profound asymmetry in power between the state and migrants lies at the heart of bureaucratic inscription; the very opacity of the state and its inscrutability to those it governs helps uphold its power.

The very foreignness of the logics of immigration law to ordinary individuals helps illustrate this asymmetry. Indeed, because of the discretionary power given to officials in applying immigration law, as well as changes in law and procedure, state officials may accord documents a different value and significance depending on the time and place. For example, even expired documents or supposedly "negative" documentation—that is, evidence of a migrant's unlawful entry—may become valuable for regularization. Expired work permits may be useful evidence of a migrant's duration of residence in the United States.[68] A bail receipt for release from immigration detention may also serve as evidence of duration of residence by providing an official time stamp. On the other hand, seemingly "positive" documentation may also be interpreted in such a way as to facilitate removal. For example, a migrant may present his visitor's visa at the U.S.-Mexico border only to find himself deported, branded as a potential visa overstayer due to his prior trips to the United States.[69] The shifting significance of documentation, and its interpretation in erratic ways, reveals the unpredictability of state power and of the agents who enact it each day.

Yet even as the state exerts control over migrants through its arbitrariness in granting and interpreting documents, migrants do not submit passively to state power. Some actively assert control over their fates by attempting to disrupt government identification schemes. Failed asylum seekers in Europe may destroy their original passports or identity cards in order to avoid government identification and delay their return, preventing their countries of origin from promptly issuing travel documents to authorize their deportation.[70] In the era of voluntary departure, Central American migrants crossing into the United States also ditched their passports and official documents so that if they were apprehended, they would be released into Mexico rather than flown back to El Salvador or Guatemala.[71] Similarly, those with deportation orders—whom federal authorities are actively seeking—may evade legibility by working under the documents of others, preventing the generation of any paper trail of their whereabouts.[72] When deportation is imminent, illegibility is often migrants' only remaining source of power.

Others may submit to bureaucratic scrutiny yet refuse to buy into the state's logics. Migrants may agentively and creatively engage with official documents and those who bestow, verify, and check them. Indeed, migrants are acutely aware that valid documents are a scarce form of capital in migrant communities; they open the doors to other forms of capital, such as the ability to travel, to access driver's licenses, to find a job, or to access public benefits. In both Europe and the United States, then, official work authorization documents may be exchanged, rented, and sold.[73] In marginalized communities with scarce access to formal documentation, migrants may treat legal status as a fungible commodity.

Migrants also deploy their knowledge of the blind spots and prejudices of the state agents charged with document verification. As Ordóñez shows in this volume, Otavalo migrants from Ecuador take advantage of border officials' inability to distinguish among indigenous individuals in order to use the travel documents of others to cross international borders. By pooling and exchanging "papers," migrants treat documents as a communitarian resource. Thus, migrants have developed ingenious practices of document circulation in resistance to a global system in which the privileges of mobility are unevenly distributed.[74]

Bureaucratic Inscription and Subjecthood

As a technique of power, bureaucratic inscription may shape migrants' subjectivity and sense of self. Modern processes of classification and documentation may be seen as a means by which the state "knows," enumerates, and surveils its population, and therefore as key to ensuring and maintaining state control.[75] As instantiations of state power, documents and bureaucratic requirements may be viewed as biopolitical technologies that help transform migrants into particular kinds of subjects.[76] Indeed, as the chapters here show, state bureaucratic processes shape individuals' behaviors and forge their ideas of their relationship to the state—sometimes even before migrants enter the state's ambit.

In the United States, for example, unauthorized migrants from Central America and Mexico often learn to diligently save both official and informal records in case they should have the opportunity to apply for legalization. Because of these groups' duration of migration to the United States and their networks' knowledge of legal requirements, they often assemble their own paper trails *in anticipation* of their applications for legal status. As Abarca and Coutin show, for example, noncitizens attending a legal advocacy clinic in Southern California knew in advance that recordkeeping was a vital practice in their efforts toward legalization; they already knew the names of official immigration forms and had emplotted possible pathways toward legalization.[77] They carried shopping bags or binders full of a variety of mundane and bureaucratic records to meet state evidentiary requirements; even those who remained ambivalent about applying for an adjustment of status had meticulously saved their records. Thus, Abarca and Coutin's data suggests that the intensity and duration of Central Americans' exposure to U.S. practices of bureaucratic inscription have an enduring effect on the ways they view documents and their relationship to state power. Noncitizens' very anticipation of future interactions with an unpredictable state yields compulsively careful recordkeeping practices.

If Central American migrants may anxiously collect documents in advance of opportunities for legalization, the effects of such anticipation may also last well after they have adjusted their status. For example, Menjívar has shown that because of the long and unpredictable duration of their TPS status as well as a hostile local environment, liminally legal Central Americans in Phoenix often live "hyperaware" of the law.[78] Not only does their legal instability shape the life decisions they make regarding family unification; it also shapes their everyday actions such as deciding which supermarket is "safe" to visit. However, as she describes in this volume, this vigilant attitude toward the state is not unique to unauthorized or temporarily authorized migrants. Because of the racialized nature of requests for documents in a state and county in which law enforcement is a visible presence, even Latinx legal permanent residents and citizens continue to arm themselves with "their documents" as they go about their daily business. As they are constantly reminded of their racialized outsider status in their everyday interactions, then, Latinx immigrants of all statuses avoid the state because they have internalized the implication that their presence is "illegitimate."

These examples, then—along with the chapters in this volume by Boehm and Coutin—attest to the power of the state and the efficacy of state disciplinary practices in shaping migrants' behaviors. As Cris Shore and Susan Wright argue in their volume on governmentality, we may see state bureaucratic practices in a Foucauldian sense as "political technologies" that shape individuals' conduct "so that they themselves contribute, not necessarily consciously, to a government's model of social order."[79] And yet in other cases, state bureaucratic processes appear to have minimal efficacy in shaping migrants' behaviors and subjectivities in ways congruent with state objectives. As Ordóñez shows for the indigenous Ecuadorian migrants who make their lives as itinerant merchants and musicians in Colombia and Europe (this volume), this group's long-standing existence on the margins of the Ecuadorian state has instilled a deeply skeptical and pragmatic attitude toward state institutions. Indigenous Ecuadorians strategically pool and exchange official IDs and letters of invitation to achieve particular purposes, regard deportation and imprisonment as minor inconveniences, and flexibly adapt their documentary strategies to suit different regimes. Therefore, Ordóñez makes the important point that migrants' attitudes toward the immigration controls of the European states they enter were fundamentally shaped by their experiences with the state in Ecuador, and by their position of marginality. Perhaps because of their long-standing evasion of state bureaucratic control, these migrants exhibit a markedly flexible—and almost cavalier—attitude toward documentation when compared with the Central American and Mexican migrants discussed above. In short, the success of state disciplinary projects in different locations remains an ethnographic question. Migrants' differing relationships with their home states, in combination with the relative intensity and duration of surveillance in their receiving states, shapes differing attitudes toward documentation and the state power it embodies.

Conclusion

This volume outlines why the study of documentation is a particularly fertile ground for examining the relationship between migrants and the state, and an especially important one at this political juncture. Identity documents stand at the intersection between legitimacy and legibility, identity and identification, and security and insecurity. Even as states increasingly restrict the kinds of identification noncitizens may receive, a variety of governments at the subnational level—swayed by the concerns of migrants and their advocates—have extended identity documents to unauthorized and liminally legal migrants in order to stake their claims to local citizenship. Yet as these nations enter an ever more xenophobic and nativist phase, in turn emboldening immigration agents, the paper trails left by migrants in even local bureaucracies have become a renewed focus of concern. If documents position migrants at the fulcrum between legitimacy and legibility, the current political moment has decidedly shifted the balance toward the latter. As scholars, we must attend to new contestations of migrants' rights that occur at the material level of identity documents. Moreover, we must be alert to the new struggles emerging over local-level forms of documentation that once seemed secure (such as state driver's licenses), over who has the right to access to such paper trails, and over the new forms of legibility they create.

As temporary, provisional, and liminal statuses proliferate in traditional receiving countries and in transit states, this not only ensnares migrants in a web of bureaucratic relations with the state that creates new vulnerabilities; it also yields a plethora of contradictory and inconsistent implications for migrants' eligibility for government programs, for ordinary privileges, and even for immigration status adjustments. The arbitrariness of such rules and the disjunctures they create across governments—and even across different scales of single governments—testifies to the limitations of enacting local citizenship policy in the absence of comprehensive immigration reform. It also highlights the inconsistency of "the state" itself as a fragmented and ever-shifting entity. By documenting these inconsistencies, we aim to demystify the state and the proliferating paper trails it creates.

Notes

I would like to thank my research assistants, Lorena Cannon and Lucia Terpak, for their help with this project.

1   See Ruth Gomberg-Muñoz, *Becoming Legal: Immigration Law and Mixed-Status Families* (Oxford: Oxford University Press, 2016); Cecilia Menjívar, "Liminal Legality: Salvadoran and Guatemalan Immigrants' Lives in the United States," *American Journal of Sociology* 111 (2006): 999–1037; Cecilia Menjívar and Daniel Kanstroom, eds., *Constructing Immigrant "Illegality": Critiques, Experiences, and Responses* (New York: Cambridge University Press, 2014); Nandita Sharma, *Home Economics: Nationalism and the Making of "Migrant Workers" in Canada* (Toronto: University of Toronto Press, 2006); Nandita Sharma, "Global Apartheid and Nation-Statehood: Instituting Border Regimes," in *Nationalism and Global Solidarities: Alternatives to Neoliberal Globalisation*, ed. James Goodman and Paul James (New York: Routledge, 2007), 71–90. There is evidence that countries of transit—that is, nontraditional migrant-receiving countries—may also be creating more provisional legal statuses to cope with increased immigration. In the face of growing criticism over its handling of Central American migration and its low rate of approval of asylum cases, for example, Mexico has increasingly created new temporary and short-term visas. Article 52 of Mexico's 2011 Nueva Ley de Migración grants a stay of deportation to those who have witnessed a "grave crime" and report it to the authorities—a stay that ends once the crime has been investigated. Similarly, after a delegation of disabled Honduran train victims paid a high-profile visit to Mexico in April 2014, the Mexican government promised to issue humanitarian visas to all train victims—visas that would be valid for a year,

may lead to legal residence, and are renewable. Nevertheless, a full examination of how countries of transit are responding to immigration through the creation of temporary and provisional legal categories is outside the scope of our analysis. See Jasmine Gersd, "Beast Victims Finally Start Getting Rights," *Fusion News*, April 22, 2014, accessed November 3, 2014, http://www.fusion.net/section/news; Sonia Wolf, "Migrantes Víctimas de Delito: ¿Detectar y Deportar o Detectar y Proteger?," *Insyde AC* 10 (2013): 1–3.

2 Sharma, *Home Economics*; Sharma, "Global Apartheid and Nation-Statehood."

3 Kitty Calavita, *Immigrants at the Margins: Law, Race, and Exclusion in Southern Europe* (New York: Cambridge University Press, 2005).

4 See Anderson, this volume.

5 Gomberg-Muñoz, *Becoming Legal*; Menjívar, "Liminal Legality"; Menjívar and Kanstroom, eds., *Constructing Immigrant "Illegality."*

6 Sharma, *Home Economics*; Sharma, "Global Apartheid and Nation-Statehood."

7 Sharma, "Global Apartheid and Nation-Statehood," 80; see also Josiah Heyman, "Capitalism and US Policy at the Mexican Border," *Dialectical Anthropology* 36 (2012): 263–77; Sharma, *Home Economics*; David Spener, *Clandestine Crossings: Migrants and Coyotes on the Texas-Mexico Border* (Ithaca, NY: Cornell University Press, 2009).

8 While the pattern of exclusions due to citizenship status that is characteristic of global apartheid began with increased South-to-North migration, it has recently spread to new migrant-receiving countries. These include richer and safer countries in the South that are receiving more migrants from other countries in the South as well as transit countries that have adopted policies and practices similar to those in the North that obstruct migration. Here we focus on the implications of temporary and provisional immigration statuses for migrants in traditional immigrant-receiving countries as the process of global apartheid is the most developed and entrenched in these regions.

9 Menjívar, "Liminal Legality." In this volume, we use the term *migrant* as opposed to *immigrant* to highlight the "intrinsic incompletion and consequent irresolution" of migration rather than a unidirectional and purposeful movement; Nicholas P. De Genova, "Migrant 'Illegality' and Deportability in Everyday Life," *Annual Review of Anthropology* 31 (2002): 419–47. Critics have argued that the term *immigrant* itself describes new arrivals from the perspective of the nation-state, often connoting a linear process of assimilation. Nevertheless, we acknowledge that the current political moment has raised the real-world stakes of claiming migrants as "immigrants"—that is, as people who intentionally entered a country in order to settle permanently—rather than as temporary interlopers. Therefore, we have allowed our contributors to choose which term they prefer; Gomberg-Muñoz and Menjívar (this volume) both prefer the term *immigrant* to signal their interlocutors' intent to remain in the United States. Similarly, for the sake of consistency, we use the term *unauthorized* to refer to migrants without official permission to enter a nation-state. As Heyman, Talavera, and Núñez note, the common term *undocumented immigrants* is a misnomer as many unauthorized migrants do in fact have

various forms of documentation. Indeed, migrants are "undocumented" only from the state's perspective; they often have various forms of documentation, including expired visas through which they once entered and then overstayed. See Josiah Heyman, Victor Talavera, and Gina M. Núñez, "Healthcare Access and Barriers for Unauthorized Immigrants in El Paso County, Texas," *Family and Community Health* 32 (2009): 4–21.

10 Dara Lind, "The Trump Administration's Separation of Families at the Border, Explained," *Vox*, June 11, 2018; Franco Ordóñez, "Trump Administration Targets Parents Who Paid to Smuggle Children into US," *Charlotte Observer*, June 29, 2017.

11 See Anderson, this volume.

12 Asad L. Asad, "On the Radar: System Embeddedness and Latin American Immigrants' Perceived Risk of Deportation," preprint draft (Ithaca, NY: Center for the Study of Inequality, Cornell University, 2017).

13 Els De Graauw, "Municipal ID Cards for Undocumented Immigrants: Local Bureaucratic Membership in a Federal System," *Politics and Society* 42 (2014): 309–30; Helen Marrow, "Deserving to a Point: Unauthorized Immigrants in San Francisco's Universal Access Healthcare Model," *Social Science and Medicine* 74 (2012): 846–54; Juan Thomas Ordóñez, *Jornalero: Being a Day Laborer in the USA* (Oakland: University of California Press, 2015).

14 Susan Bibler Coutin, *Legalizing Moves: Salvadoran Immigrants' Struggle for US Residency* (Ann Arbor: University of Michigan Press, 2000).

15 Monica Varsanyi, "Interrogating 'Urban Citizenship' vis-à-vis Undocumented Migration," *Citizenship Studies* 10 (2006): 229–49.

16 Over two dozen countries currently offer consular IDs, and their requirements vary. For example, a Matrícula Consular de Alta Seguridad from Mexico verifies that the bearer is a Mexican citizen living abroad (usually in the United States). To obtain such a card, one must produce a birth certificate, a form of photo identification, and proof of address in one's country abroad; the cards contain a photo and give the migrant's birthplace and residence.

17 Local law enforcement's acceptance of consular IDs as valid identification is not uniform, just as not all banks accept municipal IDs. See Monica Varsanyi, "Documenting Undocumented Migrants: Matrículas Consulares as Neoliberal Local Membership," *Geopolitics* 12 (2007): 311.

18 This volume is the end result of a Wenner-Gren Foundation–sponsored workshop, "Migrants and Documents: A View of the Nation-State from Below," which was held at the University of Colorado, Denver, in August 2017, with Sarah B. Horton and Josiah Heyman as principal investigators.

19 Veena Das and Deborah Poole, "State and Its Margins: Comparative Ethnographies," in *Anthropology in the Margins of the State*, ed. Veena Das and Deborah Poole (Santa Fe, NM: School of American Research Press, 2004).

20 As Yngvesson and Coutin astutely note: "Paper trails, which ought to substantiate truth, sometimes plunge their referents into a reality that is incommensurable with their sense of self." See Barbara Yngvesson and Susan Bibler Coutin, "Backed by Papers: Undoing Persons, Histories, and Return," *American Ethnologist* 33 (2006): 184.

21 Josiah M. Heyman, "Class and Classification on the U.S.-Mexico Border," *Human Organization* 60 (2001): 128–40.

22 Veena Das, *Life and Words: Violence and the Descent into the Ordinary* (Berkeley: University of California Press, 2006); Das and Poole, "State and Its Margins"; Madeleine Reeves, "Clean Fake: Authenticating Documents and Persons in Migrant Moscow," *American Ethnologist* 40 (2013): 508–24.

23 See Apostolous Andrikopolous, "Argonauts of West Africa: Migration, Citizenship, and Changing Kinship Dynamics in a Changing Europe" (Ph.D. diss., Amsterdam Institute for Social Science Research, 2017); Sarah Horton, "Identity Loan: The Moral Economy of Migrant Document Exchange in California's Central Valley," *American Ethnologist* 42 (2015): 55–67; Ordóñez, this volume. Campbell and Heyman use the term *slantwise* for diagonal maneuvers that interact with power relations but cannot easily be classified as either domination or resistance. The tripartite set of domination, resistance, and slantwise maneuver seems useful in understanding the play of action around documentation. Howard Campbell and Josiah M. Heyman, "Slantwise: Beyond Domination and Resistance on the Border," *Journal of Contemporary Ethnography* 36 (2007): 3–30.

24 Susan Coutin, "Falling Outside: Excavating the History of Central American Asylum Seekers," *Law and Social Inquiry* 36 (2013): 569–96.

25 Das, *Life and Words*; Das and Poole, "State and Its Margins"; James Scott, *Seeing Like a State: How Certain Schemes to Improve the Human Condition Have Failed* (New Haven, CT: Yale University Press, 1998).

26 Scott, *Seeing Like a State*.

27 David Lyon calls these techniques "the co-opting of the body itself as a means of identification," noting, "Information can now be extracted from the body that can override the person's own claims to a particular identity." David Lyon, "Under My Skin: From Identification Papers to Body Surveillance," in *Documenting Individual Identity: The Development of State Practices in the Modern World*, ed. Jane Caplan and John Torpey (Princeton, NJ: Princeton University Press, 2001), 291.

28 See Coutin, this volume.

29 See Provine and Varsanyi, this volume.

30 Jane Caplan and John Torpey, eds., *Documenting Individual Identity: The Development of State Practices in the Modern World* (Princeton, NJ: Princeton University Press, 2001); Ilsen About, James Brown, and Gayle Lonergan, eds., *Identification and Registration Practices in Transnational Perspective: People, Papers and Practices* (London: Palgrave Macmillan, 2013); John Torpey, *The Invention of the Passport: Surveillance, Citizenship and the State* (Cambridge: Cambridge University Press, 2000).

31 About, Brown, and Lonergan, eds., *Identification and Registration Practices in Transnational Perspective*; Heyman, "Class and Classification."

32 Deborah Boehm, *Returned: Going and Coming in an Age of Deportation* (Oakland: University of California Press, 2016); Coutin, *Legalizing Moves*; Cecilia Menjívar, "The Power of the Law: Central Americans' Legality and Everyday Life in Phoenix, Arizona," *Latino Studies* 9 (2011): 377–95. See also Yngvesson and Coutin, "Backed

by Papers," 184, for a different definition of "paper trails." Yngvesson and Coutin examine the temporal aspects of paper trails in both referencing a past origin and compelling future movement. They note that official papers "do not merely document prior moments and movements but also have the potential to redefine persons, compel movement, alter moments, and make ties ambiguous."

33 USCIS, "Temporary Protected Status," last updated May 13, 2019, https://www.uscis .gov/humanitarian/temporary-protected-status#What%20is%20TPS?.

34 Calavita, *Immigrants at the Margins*; Stephen Ruszcyczk, "Local Governance of Immigrant Incorporation: How City-Based Institutional Fields Shape the Cases of Undocumented Youth in New York and Paris," *Comparative Migration Studies* 6 (2018); see also Anderson, this volume.

35 Menjívar, "Liminal Legality." The Trump administration has placed the future of migrants with temporary legal status in doubt. It announced the end of DACA in 2017 and in 2018 rescinded the eligibility for TPS of nationals from El Salvador, Haiti, Honduras, Nepal, Nicaragua, and Sudan. Adding to the uncertainty, both moves have been temporarily blocked by the courts. As those with DACA and TPS await adjudication of their fate, they live with the uncertainty of knowing that these liminal legal statuses render them visible to the state.

36 Camila Ruz, "What Happens to Failed Asylum Seekers?," *BBC News Magazine*, August 23, 2015.

37 See Anderson, this volume.

38 Menjívar, "Liminal Legality."

39 Asad, "On the Radar"; Juliet Stumpf, "The Crimmigration Crisis: Immigrants, Crime, and Sovereign Power," *American University Law Review* 56 (2006): 367–419.

40 Asad, "On the Radar."

41 Asad, "On the Radar."

42 Torpey, *The Invention of the Passport*, 155, emphasis in the original.

43 R. Penninx et al., *European Cities and Their Migrant Integration Policies: A State-of-the-Art Study for the Knowledge for Integration Governance (KING) Project, University of Amsterdam*, 2014, https://pure.uva.nl/ws/files/4504632/167659_496057 .pdf.

44 Varsanyi, "Interrogating Urban Citizenship vis-à-vis Undocumented Migration"; Varsanyi, "Documenting Undocumented Migrants."

45 Varsanyi, "Documenting Undocumented Migrants."

46 Ordóñez, *Jornalero*, 198.

47 Varsanyi, "Documenting Undocumented Migrants," 311.

48 Center for Popular Democracy, "Who We Are: Municipal ID Cards as a Local Strategy to Promote Belonging and Shared Community Identity," 2013, accessed January 30, 2019, https://populardemocracy.org/news/who-we-are-municipal -id-cards-local-strategy-promote-belonging-and-shared-community-identity; Center for Popular Democracy, "Promoting Equality: City and State Policy to Ensure Immigrant Safety and Inclusion," 2016, accessed January 30, 2019, https:// populardemocracy.org/news/publications/promoting-equality-city-and-state -policy-ensure-immigrant-safety-and-inclusion; De Graauw, "Municipal ID Cards

for Undocumented Immigrants." To obtain a municipal ID, an applicant must present photo identification (in the form of a foreign birth certificate, driver's license, passport, or consular ID card) as well as proof of address (such as a utility bill, insurance bill, or check stub).

49 This is the now-defunct Deferred Action for Parents of Americans and Lawful Permanent Residents program.

50 CPD, "Promoting Equality," 5.

51 See Lauren Slagter, "First County Issued ID Card in Midwest Proves Popular with Immigrants," *MLive*, April 27, 2017, http://www.mlive.com/news/ann-arbor/index.ssf/2017/04/washtenaw_county_id_projects.html. In conservative and swing states, however, municipalities offering such IDs may be constrained by hostility of the broader political units within which they must operate. For example, Pittsburgh and Philadelphia began entertaining the prospect of municipal IDs in 2015 but stalled in the face of state legislation rendering "sanctuary cities" liable for any personal or property damage by unauthorized immigrants. See Joel Mathis, "PA 'Sanctuary Cities' Could Face Crackdown," *Philly Mag*, February 18, 2016, http://www.phillymag.com/citified/2016/02/18/philadelphia-sanctuary-city/. Thus, the continuing struggle over municipal IDs illustrates the contestation of localities' rights to determine local membership policy and the limitations of subnational citizenship.

52 Center on Migration, Policy, and Society, "European Cities and Migrants with Irregular Status," 2017, accessed January 30, 2019, https://www.compas.ox.ac.uk/wp-content/uploads/City-Initiative-on-Migrants-with-Irregular-Status-in-Europe-CMISE-report-November-2017-FINAL.pdf; Platform for International Cooperation on Undocumented Migrants (PICUM), *Cities of Rights: Ensuring Health Care for Undocumented Residents* (Brussels: PICUM, 2017).

53 Dan Goffin, "Toronto Not Truly a 'Sanctuary City,' Report Says," *Star*, February 17, 2017, accessed May 2, 2017, https://www.thestar.com/news/gta/2017/02/17/toronto-not-truly-a-sanctuary-city-report-says.html.

54 Varsanyi, "Interrogating 'Urban Citizenship' vis-à-vis Undocumented Migration."

55 Liz Robbins, "New York City ID Holders Aren't a Threat, NYPD Official Says in Court," *New York Times*, January 5, 2017, accessed May 2, 2017, https://www.nytimes.com/2017/01/05/nyregion/new-york-id-program-immigrants.html.

56 Robbins, "New York City ID Holders Aren't a Threat."

57 Jarrett Murphy, "Can New York's Mayor Do More to Protect Immigrants from ICE?," *Nation*, March 14, 2017, accessed May 2, 2017, https://www.thenation.com/article/can-new-yorks-mayor-protect-immigrants-from-donald-trumps-deportation-machine/.

58 Gabe Ortiz, "ACLU Documents Show Vermont DMV Colluded with ICE to ID Undocumented Immigrants," *Daily Kos*, April 11, 2017, accessed May 10, 2017, http://www.dailykos.com/story/2017/4/11/1652189/-ACLU-documents-show-Vermont-DMV-colluded-with-ICE-to-ID-undocumented-immigrants.

59 Migrant Justice, "ICE to Vermont DMV: 'We're Going to Have to Make You an Honorary ICE Officer!,'" Migrant Justice, October 12, 2016, accessed May 1, 2017,

https://migrantjustice.net/news/ice-to-vermont-dmv-were-going-to-have-to-make
-you-an-honorary-ice-officer.

60 Sébastien Chauvin, Blanca Garcés-Mascareñas, and Albert Kraler, "Working for Legality: Employment and Migrant Regularization in Europe," *International Migration* 51 (2013): 118–31.

61 Gomberg-Muñoz, *Becoming Legal.*

62 Das, *Life and Words*; Das and Poole, "State and Its Margins: Comparative Ethnographies."

63 Akhil Gupta, *Red Tape: Bureaucracy, Structural Violence, and Poverty in India* (Durham, NC: Duke University Press, 2012); Miriam Ticktin, "Where Ethics and Politics Meet: The Violence of Humanitarianism in France," *American Ethnologist* 33 (2006): 33–49.

64 Gray Abarca and Susan Coutin, "Sovereign Intimacies: The Lives of Documents within US State-Noncitizen Relationships," *American Ethnologist* 45 (2018): 7–19; Hiroshi Motomura, "Immigration Law after a Century of Plenary Power: Phantom Constitutional Norms and Statutory Interpretation," *Yale Law Journal* 100 (1990): 545–613; see also Coutin, this volume.

65 Gupta, *Red Tape*; Ticktin, "Where Ethics and Politics Meet."

66 Ticktin, "Where Ethics and Politics Meet."

67 Menjívar, "Liminal Legality"; see also Coutin, this volume.

68 See Coutin, this volume.

69 See Boehm, this volume.

70 Ruz, "What Happens to Failed Asylum Seekers?"

71 Sarah Mahler, *American Dreaming: Immigrant Life on the Margins* (Princeton, NJ: Princeton University Press, 1995), 72.

72 Horton, "Identity Loan," 60–62.

73 Andrikopolous, "Argonauts of West Africa"; Horton, "Identity Loan"; Ordóñez, *Jornalero.*

74 Josiah M. Heyman, "Ports of Entry as Nodes in the World System," *Identities: Global Studies in Culture and Power* 11 (2004): 303–27.

75 Michel Foucault, *Security, Territory, Population: Lectures at the Collège de France, 1977–1978* (New York: Palgrave Macmillan, 2004).

76 Cris Shore and Susan Wright, "Policy: A New Field of Anthropology," in *Anthropology of Policy: Critical Perspectives on Governance and Power*, ed. Cris Shore and Susan Wright (New York Routledge Press, 1997).

77 Abarca and Coutin, "Sovereign Intimacies."

78 Menjívar, "The Power of the Law."

79 Shore and Wright, "Policy: A New Field of Anthropology," 6.

Bibliography

Abarca, Gray, and Susan Coutin. "Sovereign Intimacies: The Lives of Documents within US State-Noncitizen Relationships." *American Ethnologist* 45 (2018): 7–19.

About, Ilsen, James Brown, and Gayle Lonergan, eds. *Identification and Registration Practices in Transnational Perspective: People, Papers and Practices*. London: Palgrave Macmillan, 2013.

Andrikopolous, Apostolous. "Argonauts of West Africa: Migration, Citizenship, and Changing Kinship Dynamics in a Changing Europe." Ph.D. dissertation, Amsterdam Institute for Social Science Research, 2017.

Asad, Asad L. "On the Radar: System Embeddedness and Latin American Immigrants' Perceived Risk of Deportation." Preprint draft. Ithaca, NY: Center for the Study of Inequality, Cornell University, 2018.

Boehm, Deborah A. *Returned: Going and Coming in an Age of Deportation*. Oakland: University of California Press, 2016.

Calavita, Kitty. *Immigrants at the Margins: Law, Race, and Exclusion in Southern Europe*. New York: Cambridge University Press, 2005.

Campbell, Howard, and Josiah M. Heyman. "Slantwise: Beyond Domination and Resistance on the Border." *Journal of Contemporary Ethnography* 36 (2007): 3–30.

Caplan, Jane, and John Torpey, eds. *Documenting Individual Identity: The Development of State Practices in the Modern World*. Princeton, NJ: Princeton University Press, 2001.

Center for Popular Democracy (CPD). "Promoting Equality: City and State Policy to Ensure Immigrant Safety and Inclusion." Center for Popular Democracy, October 25, 2016. Accessed January 30, 2019. https://populardemocracy.org/news/publications/promoting-equality-city-and-state-policy-ensure-immigrant-safety-and-inclusion.

Center for Popular Democracy (CPD). "Who We Are: Municipal ID Cards as a Local Strategy to Promote Belonging and Shared Community Identity." Center for Popular Democracy, December 2013. Accessed January 30, 2019. https://populardemocracy.org/news/who-we-are-municipal-id-cards-local-strategy-promote-belonging-and-shared-community-identity.

Center on Migration, Policy, and Society. "European Cities and Migrants with Irregular Status." Oxford: COMPAS, University of Oxford, November 2017. Accessed January 30, 2019. https://www.compas.ox.ac.uk/wp-content/uploads/City-Initiative-on-Migrants-with-Irregular-Status-in-Europe-CMISE-report-November-2017-FINAL.pdf.

Chauvin, Sébastien, Blanca Garcés-Mascareñas, and Albert Kraler. "Working for Legality: Employment and Migrant Regularization in Europe." *International Migration* 51 (2013): 118–31.

Connor, Phillip, D'Vera Cohn, and Ana Gonzalez-Barrera. "Chapter 2: Migrant Destinations." In *Changing Patterns of Global Migration and Remittances*. Washington, DC: Pew Research Center, 2013. Accessed January 29, 2019. http://www.pewsocialtrends.org/2013/12/17/chapter-2-migrant-destinations/.

Coutin, Susan Bibler. "Falling Outside: Excavating the History of Central American Asylum Seekers." *Law and Social Inquiry* 36 (2011): 569–96.

Coutin, Susan Bibler. *Legalizing Moves: Salvadoran Immigrants' Struggle for US Residency*. Ann Arbor: University of Michigan Press, 2000.

Das, Veena. *Life and Words: Violence and the Descent into the Ordinary*. Berkeley: University of California Press, 2006.

Das, Veena, and Deborah Poole. "State and Its Margins: Comparative Ethnographies." In *Anthropology in the Margins of the State*, edited by Veena Das and Deborah Poole, 3–34. Santa Fe, NM: School of American Research Press, 2004.

De Graauw, Els. "Municipal ID Cards for Undocumented Immigrants: Local Bureaucratic Membership in a Federal System." *Politics and Society* 42 (2014): 309–30.

Foucault, Michel. *The Birth of Biopolitics: Lectures at the Collège de France, 1978–1979.* New York: Palgrave Macmillan, 2004.

Foucault, Michel. *Security, Territory, Population: Lectures at the Collège de France, 1977–1978.* New York: Palgrave Macmillan, 2004.

Gersd, Jasmine. "Beast Victims Finally Start Getting Rights." *Fusion News*, April 22, 2014. Accessed November 3, 2014. http://www.fusion.net/section/news.

Gomberg-Muñoz, Ruth. *Becoming Legal: Immigration Law and Mixed-Status Families.* Oxford: Oxford University Press, 2016.

Gomberg-Muñoz, Ruth. "Inequality and US Immigration Reform." *Anthropology News* 54 (2013): e11–e37.

Gomberg-Muñoz, Ruth. "The Punishment/El Castigo: Undocumented Latinos and Immigration Processing." *Journal of Ethnic and Migration Studies* 41 (2015): 2235–52.

Gupta, Akhil. *Red Tape: Bureaucracy, Structural Violence, and Poverty in India.* Durham, NC: Duke University Press, 2012.

Heyman, Josiah M. "Capitalism and US Policy at the Mexican Border." *Dialectical Anthropology* 36 (2012): 263–77.

Heyman, Josiah M. "Class and Classification on the U.S.-Mexico Border." *Human Organization* 60 (2001): 128–40.

Heyman, Josiah M. "Ports of Entry as Nodes in the World System." *Identities: Global Studies in Culture and Power* 11 (2004): 303–27.

Heyman, Josiah M., and Alan Smart, eds. *States and Illegal Practices.* New York: Bloomsbury Academic, 1999.

Heyman, Josiah, Victor Talavera, and Gina M. Núñez. "Healthcare Access and Barriers for Unauthorized Immigrants in El Paso County, Texas." *Family and Community Health* 32 (2009): 4–21.

Horton, Sarah. "Identity Loan: The Moral Economy of Migrant Document Exchange in California's Central Valley." *American Ethnologist* 42 (2015): 55–67.

Lyon, David. "Under My Skin: From Identification Papers to Body Surveillance." In *Documenting Individual Identity: The Development of State Practices in the Modern World*, edited by Jane Caplan and John Torpey, 291–310. Princeton, NJ: Princeton University Press, 2001.

Mahler, Sarah. *American Dreaming: Immigrant Life on the Margins.* Princeton, NJ: Princeton University Press, 1995.

Marrow, Helen. "Deserving to a Point: Unauthorized Immigrants in San Francisco's Universal Access Healthcare Model." *Social Science and Medicine* 74 (2012): 846–54.

Mathis, Joel. "PA 'Sanctuary Cities' Could Face Crackdown." *Philly Mag*, February 18, 2016. Accessed May 2, 2017. http://www.phillymag.com/citified/2016/02/18/philadelphia-sanctuary-city/.

Menjívar, Cecilia. "Liminal Legality: Salvadoran and Guatemalan Immigrants' Lives in the United States." *American Journal of Sociology* 111 (2006): 999–1037.

Menjívar, Cecilia. "The Power of the Law: Central Americans' Legality and Everyday Life in Phoenix, Arizona." *Latino Studies* 9 (2011): 377–95.

Menjívar, Cecilia, and Daniel Kanstroom, eds. *Constructing Immigrant "Illegality": Critiques, Experiences, and Responses.* New York: Cambridge University Press, 2014.

Migrant Justice. "ICE to Vermont DMV: 'We're Going to Have to Make You an Honorary ICE Officer!'" Migrant Justice, October 12, 2016. Accessed May 1, 2017. https://migrantjustice.net/news/ice-to-vermont-dmv-were-going-to-have-to-make-you-an-honorary-ice-officer.

Morawetz, Nancy. "Understanding the Impact of the 1996 Deportation Laws and the Limited Scope of Proposed Reforms." *Harvard Law Review* 113 (2000): 1936–62.

Motomura, Hiroshi. "Immigration Law after a Century of Plenary Power: Phantom Constitutional Norms and Statutory Interpretation." *Yale Law Journal* 100 (1990): 545–613.

Murphy, Jarrett. "Can New York's Mayor Do More to Protect Immigrants from ICE?" *Nation*, March 14, 2017. Accessed May 2, 2017. https://www.thenation.com/article/can-new-yorks-mayor-protect-immigrants-from-donald-trumps-deportation-machine/.

Ordóñez, Juan Thomas. *Jornalero: Being a Day Laborer in the USA.* Oakland: University of California Press, 2015.

Penninx, R., T. Caponio, B. Garcés-Mascareñas, P. Matusz Protasiewicz, and H. Schwarz. *European Cities and Their Migrant Integration Policies: A State-of-the-Art Study for the Knowledge for Integration Governance (KING) Project.* University of Amsterdam, 2014. Accessed January 30, 2019. https://pure.uva.nl/ws/files/4504632/167659_496057.pdf.

Platform for International Cooperation on Undocumented Migrants (PICUM). *Cities of Rights: Ensuring Health Care for Undocumented Residents.* Brussels: PICUM, 2017. Accessed January 30, 2019. http://picum.org/picum.org/uploads/publication/CityOfRights_FINAL_WEB_EN.pdf.

Reeves, Madeleine. "Clean Fake: Authenticating Documents and Persons in Migrant Moscow." *American Ethnologist* 40 (2013): 508–24.

Ruszcyczk, Stephen. "Local Governance of Immigrant Incorporation: How City-Based Institutional Fields Shape the Cases of Undocumented Youth in New York and Paris." *Comparative Migration Studies* 6 (2018): 32.

Ruz, Camila. "What Happens to Failed Asylum Seekers?" *BBC News Magazine*, August 23, 2015. Accessed May 2, 2017. http://www.bbc.com/news/magazine-33849593.

Scott, James C. *Domination and the Arts of Resistance.* New Haven, CT: Yale University Press, 1992.

Scott, James C. *Seeing Like a State: How Certain Schemes to Improve the Human Condition Have Failed.* New Haven, CT: Yale University Press, 1998.

Sharma, Nandita. "Global Apartheid and Nation-Statehood: Instituting Border Regimes." In *Nationalism and Global Solidarities: Alternatives to Neoliberal Globalisation*, edited by James Goodman and Paul James, 71–90. New York: Routledge, 2007.

Sharma, Nandita. *Home Economics: Nationalism and the Making of "Migrant Workers" in Canada*. Toronto: University of Toronto Press, 2006.

Shore, Cris, and Susan Wright. "Policy: A New Field of Anthropology." In *Anthropology of Policy: Critical Perspectives on Governance and Power*, edited by Cris Shore and Susan Wright, 3–42. New York: Routledge, 1997.

Spener, David. *Clandestine Crossings: Migrants and Coyotes on the Texas-Mexico Border*. Ithaca, NY: Cornell University Press, 2009.

Stumpf, Juliet. "The Crimmigration Crisis: Immigrants, Crime, and Sovereign Power." *American University Law Review* 56, no. 2 (2006): 367–419.

Ticktin, Miriam. "Where Ethics and Politics Meet: The Violence of Humanitarianism in France." *American Ethnologist* 33, no. 1 (2006): 33–49.

Torpey, John. *The Invention of the Passport: Surveillance, Citizenship and the State*. Cambridge: Cambridge University Press, 2000.

USCIS. "Temporary Protected Status." Washington, DC: U.S. Citizenship and Immigration Services. Updated May 13, 2019. Accessed January 2, 2016. https://www.uscis.gov/humanitarian/temporary-protected-status#What%20is%20TPS?.

USCIS. *USCIS Policy Manual*, vol. 7: *Adjustment of Status*. "Part B-245(a) Adjustment." Washington, DC: U.S. Citizenship and Immigration Services. Updated May 10, 2019. Accessed May 7, 2017. https://www.uscis.gov/policymanual/Print/PolicyManual-Volume7-PartB.html.

Varsanyi, Monica. "Documenting Undocumented Migrants: Matrículas Consulares as Neoliberal Local Membership." *Geopolitics* 12 (2007): 299–319.

Varsanyi, Monica. "Interrogating 'Urban Citizenship' vis-à-vis Undocumented Migration." *Citizenship Studies* 10 (2006): 229–49.

Varsanyi, Monica, ed. *Taking Local Control: Immigration Policy Activism in U.S. Cities and States*. Palo Alto, CA: Stanford University Press, 2010.

Varsanyi, Monica, Paul Lewis, Marie Provine, and Scott Decker. "Multilayered Jurisdictional Patchwork: Immigration Federalism in the United States." *Law and Policy* 34 (2012): 138–58.

Wolf, Sonia. "Migrantes Víctimas de Delito: ¿Detectar y Deportar o Detectar y Proteger?" *Insyde AC* 10 (2013): 1–3.

Yngvesson, Barbara, and Susan Bibler Coutin. "Backed by Papers: Undoing Persons, Histories, and Return." *American Ethnologist* 33 (2006): 177–90.

PART I

FOUNDATIONS
Controlling Space and Time

The chapters in this section delineate the basic features of identification and documentation in bounded, territorial states, the situation encountered throughout the book. Two relationships are central. First, the sovereign state claims to identify all individuals directly and to use documents to "know" who they are. This contrasts with other forms of social relations, in which individuals are known through hierarchical statuses (e.g., aristocrats), membership in communities (e.g., religious and ethnic groups), and certification by powerful sponsors.[1] Second, mobility control and rights to work, residence, social distributions, and so on are governed within discrete state territories. Borders have a notable role in such governance.[2] This segment of the book, then, identifies through particular case studies the fundamentals of modern state identification and documentation. It looks at spatial controls over presence and mobility, the time spans of statuses, and diversity and contestation within states that render statuses complex and changeable.

Sharma's chapter sets the table by examining the historical construction of the category of migrant, as opposed to that of citizen. It identifies the pivotal role of documents, in this case signed labor contracts, in controlling the mobility of subordinate temporary labor migrants. The contracts regulated entry and exit across zones of the British Empire, from South Asia to Mauritius, bounded territories where people had not previously been subject to spatial mobility control. The restricted movement of South Asian temporary contract workers contrasted with freely mobile white European citizens of the empire, some of them settler immigrants. Temporary contract workers also supplanted an earlier social formation, chattel slaves—humans forcibly moved and documented as commodities, not people. Constituting a new hierarchy within "free" labor, key forms of stratification between citizens and immigrants begin to emerge, marked by borders, infused with racial distinctions, and documented by paper trails.

While Sharma's chapter focuses on space, it also implies a temporal dimension to both immigration statuses and the documents that codify them. Contract laborers were temporary migrants, limited to specific periods of entry and exit in their contracts, thus distinguished temporally as well as spatially from free migrant settlers and travelers. Nevertheless, as Anderson points out, analyses of immigration controls frequently neglect the way they regulate time, so her chapter explores this theme. For example, in the United Kingdom, recent policy has aimed to reduce immigration by restricting the number of permanent settlers. In practice, this has shifted immigration statuses toward temporary worker and visitor roles that do not provide permanent settlement rights, temporally bounding and redocumenting rather than reducing the number of migrants per se. States impose temporal controls on citizens as well, as eligibility for public programs may be tested according to time of residence in localities. Her chapter raises the provocative question of how and why states distinguish among residents, immigrants, migrants, visitors, students, and so forth. Taken-for-granted distinctions, such as those between new internal migrants, global tourists, and temporary workers from abroad, are hardly natural and obvious; rather, they are constructed in law and power in spatial and temporal terms. Documents offer an important window onto these distinctions.

Anderson principally analyzes a bounded, territorial state, though a complicated one (at the time of her writing, the United Kingdom was part of the European Union, and internally divided). Yet, as her example of residence time–tested citizenship shows, subnational policies modify national frameworks. Provine and Varsanyi take up political struggles around driver's licenses in Arizona and New Mexico during a period when the U.S. federal government sought to make these local documents into de facto national identification cards, even though the ability to drive and immigration status are largely unrelated. Arizona and New Mexico have very different histories and political formations, and the outcomes of legislative struggles over licenses remained distinctive. In the culture of automobility typical of the United States, one can hardly find a more crucial form of spatial regulation of everyday lives than driver's licenses. Driver's licenses illustrate an important point: identification documents are used for many purposes, private and public; they are issued by many authorities, organizations, and businesses—at national and local levels—and they interrelate in unexpected and sometimes powerful ways. Documents not only confer status and identity; they compose much of the texture of our lives.

Notes
1 John Torpey, *The Invention of the Passport: Surveillance, Citizenship and the State* (Cambridge: Cambridge University Press, 2002).
2 Adam McKeown, *Melancholy Order: Asian Migration and the Globalization of Borders* (New York: Columbia University Press, 2008); Joseph Nevins, *Operation Gatekeeper: The Rise of the "Illegal Alien" and the Making of the U.S.-Mexico Boundary* (New York: Routledge, 2002).

Bibliography
McKeown, Adam. *Melancholy Order: Asian Migration and the Globalization of Borders*. New York: Columbia University Press, 2008.
Nevins, Joseph. *Operation Gatekeeper: The Rise of the "Illegal Alien" and the Making of the U.S.-Mexico Boundary*. New York: Routledge, 2002.
Torpey, John. *The Invention of the Passport: Surveillance, Citizenship and the State*. Cambridge: Cambridge University Press, 2002.

1

THE "PEOPLE OUT OF PLACE"

State Limits on Free Mobility and the Making of (Im)migrants

I historically situate the work done by state documents to restrict people's mobility by examining the first enactment of immigration controls within the British Empire in the 1830s. In so doing, we see that, far from being a timeless and integral element of state sovereignty, as is often supposed, immigration controls were implemented as part of the early nineteenth-century effort to find new ways to discipline labor in the absence of slavery. In this process the contract of indenture attached to individual workers was crucial. By the late nineteenth century, such contracts as well as immigration controls had become central to a growing number of states' efforts to subsume—and obfuscate—capitalist class relations within the increasingly popular politics of nationalism. As the subjectification of people as national citizens became globally hegemonic by the late twentieth century, so too did immigration controls. Indeed, such controls came to *define* the national form of state sovereignty. In all of these processes, state documentary practices were a crucial part of gaining control over people's entry to a given sovereign territory.

Contracts of indenture, acting as a form of immigration control, not only added to the arsenal of state power, but they also significantly enabled the continued profitability of capital investments, particularly, but not only, in plantation agriculture. Indeed, from the beginning, such controls were a crucial link between state and capital. Having already outlawed the slave trade in 1807, the British Empire first enacted immigration controls only after slave labor relations themselves began to be abolished, starting in 1834. The need not only to find replacements for a highly profitable labor force of enslaved people but also to design alternative systems of labor discipline of ostensibly "free" workers became critical. The new labor system for recruiting people pejoratively known as "coolies," mostly from British-colonized Asia, through contracts of indenture was the main alternative settled upon.[1] The coolie labor system rested on a legal requirement for workers to labor for a contracted period of time (usually five years). During this period, they were tied to the contracting employer and could not change either their employer or their place of work without the employer's permission.[2] The coolie system of labor recruitment acted as a bridge between what Radhika Mongia terms the imperial state's "logic of facilitation" of human movement and the nation-state's "logic of constraint."[3] In this, the document of the contract of indenture played a starring role. It provided a powerful mechanism for disciplining workers, while appeasing many slavery abolitionists through the fiction that coolie laborers were "free."

By examining the emergence and growth of regulations and restrictions on human mobility within the politics of antislavery, labor control, and the growing power of nationalist discourses, we can better understand the historic emergence of the state's growing interest in documentary practices to secure and control a labor force. We are also able to see the significance of discourses of "protection" to states' implementation of immigration controls and to the politics of rescue engaged in by those speaking on behalf of (Im)migrants.[4]

The Making of the (Im)migrant

The first restrictions on mobility within the British Empire were enacted in 1835 in its colony of Mauritius. They were first enacted against coolie laborers—and only coolies—moving from one part of the empire (British India) into another (British Mauritius). These first immigration controls were instituted as a result of numerous concerns, some of which were conflicting and contradictory, but most of which centered on the desire to maintain the profitability of sugar plantations on Mauritius once the end of slavery took effect on February 1, 1835. Planters and colonial officials on Mauritius were desperate to secure a new labor force, while the London Colonial Office, not uninterested in the continued profitability of the colony, also wanted to ensure that the labor recruitment system that replaced slavery *not* be portrayed as slavery by ever-vigilant abolitionists. With the impending end of slave labor relations, the key question would be how to control and discipline the new labor force in the absence of the enormous coercion that was slavery. Meanwhile, antislavery campaigners signaled their intent to protect the new workforce from their would-be slavers. Recruiting workers from British India through the institution of coolie labor, each governed by the contract of indenture and required to pass through both emigration and immigration controls, solved both their problems.

No one working in the British imperial state's wide and dispersed apparatus in the early 1830s would have known of the long-term consequences of regulating the entry of British subjects from one of its territories to another. Instead, these early regulations were piecemeal strategies responding to the economic and political crises of the moment. Nonetheless, their formulated response to the end of slave labor relations in the empire precipitated a new world order of nation-state regulations and restrictions of human mobility, one that has created many crises for people trying to move ever since, most especially those seeking new livelihoods. It also created the new state category—and figure of approbation—the (Im)migrant.

Imperial Logic of Human Mobility

In examining the importance of documentary controls to the emergence of the figure of the (Im)migrant, it is important to note the significant differences between how imperial states and nation-states operated. Imperial states ruled by making those affected by their powers of taxation, levies, and forced labor into imperial subjects. Generally speaking, the more subjects the state had, the more people whose labor it could exploit, the more wealth it could amass, and the more power it could command. This was a major motivation for the expansion of imperial territories. Consequently, imperial states' concerns about borders and boundaries were primarily about restricting people exiting their territories. Holding people within imperial territories was, indeed, the sine qua non of imperial projects of "civilization" (which, as James Scott notes, is always an effect of state power[5]). This was never an easy task. Many would-be imperial subjects, keen on making their escape, practiced what Scott aptly terms "the art of not being governed." Escapees carved out non-state spaces for themselves wherever, whenever, and for as long as they could. Thus, in contrast to the Hobbesian story of sovereignty, in which states were purportedly created by people to protect themselves from the violent chaos of an "uncivilized" (i.e., stateless) life, historically the violence took place at the point of state formation and the transformation of people into state subjects and their land into territory.

Imperial states were actively engaged in moving people, often on a massive scale. For example, various European empires after the late fifteenth century moved people through systems of slavery, impressment, debt bondage, penal transport, servitude, and, in late imperialism, the coolie labor trade. Each system of movement was at the same time a system of labor discipline. Indeed, facilitating human mobility was crucial for the profitability of empires, particularly where colonialism resulted in high death rates among the colonized, often as a result of their enslavement.[6] Across the imperial system, in the Americas and the Caribbean, Europe, Africa, and Asia, there was a continuous and urgent need to replenish the imperial supply of labor power. European imperialism thus created a world market for labor power.[7]

One of the first systems for moving large numbers of people within the rapidly globalizing space of imperialism was the trade in enslaved people from Africa, a system dramatically altered with the introduction of capitalist market imperatives. The British Empire, the first to impose capitalist social relations on the colonized, became both the most powerful of the European empires and the largest slave-trading empire after the 1760s, the period in which the Atlantic slave trade peaked. Slightly more than half of the people enslaved in Africa and transported to the Americas each year were carried on slave ships owned by British subjects and protected by the imperial state's navy. By 1780, at the height of the Atlantic slave trade, a slave ship left Britain practically every other day. Over the course of the British slave trade, approximately 12.5 million people were transported from Africa. Almost 2 million people perished at some point in the murderous Middle Passage, while the survivors were put to work in British colonies in the Caribbean, in South America, and, to a much lesser extent, in North America. In the eighteenth century, the movement of people as slaves from Africa into the British Empire was the richest part of Britain's trade. While the movement of slaves was well documented—in ship captains' ledgers, in insurance company actuarial tables, in government tallies, and more—and as enslaved people themselves were marked (e.g., by torturous branding), slaves were not documented; that is, they were not required by states to carry documents in the process of their movement.

The end of the "evil trade," indeed the world-historical shift that came with the delegitimization of slavery, was undoubtedly the result of the centuries-long, countless acts of rebellion of the enslaved as well as those who joined them in organized movements to abolish slavery. These latter efforts began in the late eighteenth century and from within the center of the British Empire itself—the City of London.[8] With its March 25, 1807, Abolition of the Slave Trade Act, the British Empire outlawed the slave trade. Yet, due to the heavy reliance on slave labor by plantation owners and the imperial treasury, the institution of slavery itself (the slave labor relation) was maintained within the empire for several decades afterward, indeed in some imperial territories even for several years after Britain passed its Slavery Abolition Act of 1833. The main reason for the decades-long gap between the end of the British slave trade (1807) and the end of slave labor relations (1834–43), was the search for a system of labor recruitment that could replace it in a manner that met investors' demands for a cheapened and weakened workforce. The central issue was that of rights. What rights, if any, would the workers recruited to replace enslaved workers have after the abolition of slavery? And from where would these workers be recruited? To these questions there were no uniform answers.

The post-abolition period saw a dramatic increase in people recruited from Europe to other imperial territories for a variety of work.[9] They faced no immigration controls when entering these territories until well into the early part of the twentieth century (e.g., in 1921 in the United States). However, while many of these workers were held in some kind of bondage to their employers (or masters, in the parlance of the day), by the early nineteenth century the numbers of people arriving from Europe were less and less likely to be employed in unfree employment relations.[10] Moreover, already by the seventeenth century—and certainly by the end of the eighteenth century—a racialized division of labor had been established, resulting in, among other things, a highly differential pay scale between workers racialized as white and those racialized into various categories of nonwhites. This was especially the case in the various British "white settler" colonies (e.g., the United States, Canada, Australia, New Zealand), where the ratio of whites to nonwhites had been reversed early on. However, the higher "wages of whiteness" meant that the search to replace enslaved workers did not end with the increased movement of people from Europe.[11] Moreover, the newfound freedom of white male workers had substantially lessened employers' ability to exercise control over them. Free labor relations, economically, socially, and politically empowering to (mostly white male) workers, were seen by employers as too costly to their bottom line. In any case, outside of the white settler colonies, white people did not in the main migrate in large numbers *as workers.*

The Abolition of Slavery and the Start of Coolieism

The more effective "solution" to capital's problem with the end of slavery was the coolie system: the system of recruitment and exploitation of already negatively racialized people—mostly men and mostly from British-controlled China and India—to work in conditions of indentured servitude.[12] From approximately 1830 to the 1920s, coolieism was the dominant system through which workers were moved within the world market for labor power.[13] While there is no definitive figure for the number of coolies recruited—some estimate a low of 12 million, while some argue that "an estimate of 37 million or more would not be entirely without foundation"—the scale of the coolie system was, even at the lowest estimates, comparable to those of slavery.[14] The intensity of the coolie system, with its movement of millions of workers from Asia within the space of slightly less than a hundred years, surpassed African slavery, during which period approximately 12.5 million people were moved over a period of 450 years.[15]

Significantly, the end of slavery in the British Empire had an effect on the *supply* of coolies as well. Slaves in territories controlled by the East India Company (as well as Ceylon) were freed in 1843, thus expanding the number of available coolies enormously. Yet, even before then, the introduction of capitalist social relations in British India had led to the existence of a "surplus population" (i.e., a "reserve army of labor") left devoid of land and livelihood and desperate for both. Under British imperialism, most people were forced to engage in capitalist markets, including labor markets, for their continued survival. After 1833, successive famines throughout British India—in 1837 and 1861 in Bengal and northern India, and in 1877, 1878, 1889, 1892, and from 1897 to 1900 in other parts of India—exacerbated this situation.

Some of these famines were a result of British insistence that its colonial subjects grow cash crops so that the empire could accrue hard currency in the international trading market. One of these cash crops was opium, which was sold in China in an effort to reverse the British imbalance of trade. The resultant Opium Wars (1839–42 and 1860–62) between the British and Chinese (Qing) imperial states expanded British control over territory and people in mainland China and structured a growing dependency upon global capitalist markets for the people located there. In short, starting in the early nineteenth century, tens of millions of people across British India and British-controlled China were ripe candidates to be exploited as coolies throughout the globally operative British Empire (and to be traded to other empires as well).

As they were moved throughout the space of empire(s), the relationship of coolies to the former—or soon-to-be former—slaves, and to the institution of slavery, was called into question. The main political question was whether coolieism was a new form of slavery or whether it represented free labor. It was the effort to distance coolieism from slavery that formed the foundation for establishing documentary controls on immigration in the British Empire. In other words, it was the impending end to slave labor relations that led to the enactment of the very first documentary controls on the entry of imperial subjects into that imperial state's territory. And it was against coolies from Asia, required to carry documents ensuring they were contractually indentured, that growing numbers of regulations to monitor the mobility of people were first ordered.[16]

Specifically, as Radhika Mongia's study shows, it was on the British colony of Mauritius, an island in the Indian Ocean about 2,000 kilometers off the southeast coast of continental Africa, where the first efforts to regulate the in-migration of workers into the territories of the British Empire took place.[17] It was a monumental shift, one that generated much heated discussion at the time. The effort by the local colonial government of Mauritius to regulate and restrict the entry of people who were then *co-British subjects* marked a historic shift from imperial concerns about exit to new concerns about workers' entry. In retrospect, it was the beginning of the end of the regime of unrestricted entry of British subjects within its empire.

People from the African continent had been enslaved on Mauritius since the Dutch Empire first colonized it (1638–1710). Slavery continued there under the French (1710–1810), and on the eve of the British takeover of Mauritius in 1810, there were some 63,000 enslaved workers there.[18] Sugar plantations reliant on slave labor from Africa remained the mainstay of the colonial economy once Mauritius came under British control. As the date for the abolition of slave labor relations on Mauritius (in 1835) drew near, however, plantation owners were highly concerned about their profits and sought an alternative labor supply. Local British colonial officials were likewise concerned. However, given the harsh working conditions prevalent on sugar plantations, they did not believe that the planters' intent to recruit workers from India to replace the soon-to-be-freed slaves would secure the necessary labor force. This led the colonial government to formulate a measure to immobilize the new workforce. Forcing enslaved people over the age of six to work for another three to five years as "apprentices" temporarily accomplished this in regard to enslaved people,[19] but the same measure did not solve the problem of the freedom of workers from British India.

In 1835, the same year that slaves were freed on Mauritius, two ordinances regulating the entry of people from British India were passed by the local British council (and ratified by the British Parliament in 1837).[20] These ordinances, meant to regulate the mobility—and discipline the labor—of coolie workers from India, required that coolies entering Mauritius had to have documented permission to do so from the governor of the colony. It was thought that this measure would allow the colony to select a workforce it felt was appropriately docile. This restriction limited the hitherto free mobility of coolie laborers within the British Empire who, theoretically, were on par with all other British subjects. The Mauritius ordinances thus made a break with previous British imperial practice concerning migration. Indeed, such interventions were viewed as wholly novel and lacking in legal precedent. The imperial office admitted as much when it stated that "this practice [of regulating migration] has no foundation in any existing law."[21]

The shock of such mobility restrictions affected planters in Mauritius as well. They feared that these would be used to limit the number of workers they could recruit from British India. One planter, Hollier Griffith, used the argument that any intervention into the movement of workers from India was unprecedented. Writing to G. F. Dick, the colonial secretary for Mauritius, Griffith noted that the imperial state might prohibit the departure of a British subject from British territory (but even then only in "*exceptional cases*"); however, he maintained, the state's sovereignty did "not extend so far as to prohibit the *entrance* into his dominions of any of his subjects."[22] In other words, he argued that regulations and restrictions on immigration were not the purview of the British imperial state. In response, Prosper D'Epinay, the newly appointed protector general of Mauritius, defended the right of local Mauritian authorities to impose entrance restrictions on recruited coolies, and argued that the ordinances were "a measure of foresight and of internal police," without which there would be "tumult and disorder [rather] than [an] increase in [the] industry of the country."[23] He added that, "it is . . . necessary to proceed with caution in the new order of things."[24]

His claims for a "new order" were not hyperbolic. In retrospect, the Mauritius ordinances marked a world-historical shift in British policies regarding movement of its subjects. Significantly, while bowing to the still dominant (and formal) notion that British Indian subjects had the same rights as "those who reside in any possession, territory, or dependency of Great Britain," D'Epinay defended the elimination of this formal equality when he asked whether "the term British subject, and the privileges attached to it, are not according to places and circumstances, susceptible of important division and modification."[25] In the negotiations between colonial authorities on Mauritius and in London, the view in favor of regulating and restricting the movement of people from British India to British Mauritius won out and was the start of juridical distinctions between who could and who could not freely move across the British Empire. The fact that from 1835 to 1838, approximately 25,000 coolie laborers from India were shipped to Mauritius—of whom 7,000 died—alleviated planters' concerns that these new ordinances would curtail the supply of labor.

Yet, although the Mauritius colonial officials became enthusiastic about the effects of entrance controls, both the British Indian government and the London Colonial Office remained unconvinced. The political success of the slavery abolition movement led them to believe that it was crucial that the new coolie labor recruitment system *not* be viewed as a new form of slavery. Nonetheless, realizing the singular importance of a coolie labor force for planters, both sets of colonial authorities came to support the Mauritius colonial government's regulations and restrictions on free mobility. They did so by expanding the limits placed on the mobility of coolies by adding documentary emigration controls to the immigration controls imposed by the Mauritius colonial government.

Importantly, both sets of controls were carried out in the name of protecting coolies. The British presented them as necessary to ensure both that the movement of coolie workers from British India was "voluntary" and that the sale of their labor power on Mauritius plantations was "free." With no sense of irony, it was declared that people's free mobility across British imperial territories had to end in order to ensure that British subjects were free waged labor. In the process, the coercion inherent in the making and reproduction of a capitalist labor force was obfuscated, something that was also a legacy of these first (im)migration controls.

Adding to the new regime of "paper walls," in 1837 British Indian government regulations laid down specific conditions for the lawful movement of people leaving British India from Calcutta, a main port in the coolie labor trade.[26] The would-be emigrant and his (or, less often, her) newly established emigration agent were required to appear before an officer designated by the colonial British government of India with a written statement of the terms of their labor contract. Under coolie contracts of indenture, the length of work (service) was to be five years, renewable for further five-year terms. The emigrant was to be returned at the end of his or her service to the port of departure. Each emigrant vessel was required to conform to certain standards of space, diet, and so on and carry a medical officer. In 1837 this scheme was extended to the city of Madras. Without actual signed contracts of indenture, workers from British India were not permitted to leave British India or to enter British Mauritius. Having documents attesting that coolies had approval from both British Indian emigration and British Mauritius immigration officers to move was a necessary part of getting coolies to labor on the sugar plantations of British Mauritius. Together, contracts of indenture and the documents attesting to the state's permission to move ensured the indentured labor relationship coolies worked under.

Contracts of indenture, often written in English, which coolies signed (or, most often, marked with an *X*) and, after the introduction of fingerprinting technology in India in 1858, marked with their fingerprint, allowed the imperial state to make the case that coolies had voluntarily indentured themselves. Labor contracts thus provided the British colonial administration the documentary proof they needed to claim that the coolie system was not slavery. So central was the contract of indenture to the operation—and legitimation—of the coolie labor trade that those recruited from British India referred to one another as a fellow *girmit* (for "agreement"). Of course, these contracts of indenture also disciplined the labor coolies. Indeed, the power—and effects—of mobility restrictions lay in the ability of states not only to restrict people's exit from and entrance into increasingly fragmented imperial territories but also to restrict the rights and freedoms of workers in the labor market. Employers had much more power to enforce the contracts' terms than did the coolie workers bound by them. This was a result of not only the economic power that employers held over workers under capitalism but also the extra-economic coercive power of the imperial state, whose courts, judges, and prisons punished and disciplined coolie workers accused of not fulfilling their part of a contract. In addition, as occurred under slavery, employers (still called masters) were legally empowered to use corporal and other forms of violence as punishment to enforce their commands.

Not only were conditions inhumane and dangerous in this new Middle Passage; mortality rates where coolies labored were very high. "Coolies," Lisa Lowe notes, "would be shipped on the same vessels that had brought the slaves they were designed to replace; some would fall to disease, die, suffer abuse, and mutiny; [and those] who survived the [often] three-month voyage would encounter coercive, confined conditions upon arrival."[27] Unsurprisingly, then, as soon as knowledge of the new trade in coolie labor became widely known, antislavery campaigns reignited across the British Empire, both in its metropole and in its colonies, especially in British India, challenging the claim that coolies were moving "voluntarily" and were working "freely." A report in the *Anti-Slavery Reporter* stated, "It should be observed, that, of all the thousands who have hitherto gone to Mauritius, or other colonies, there is no proof afforded that any of them went voluntarily; but, on the contrary, decisive evidence that they were either kidnapped for that purpose, and by force put on board vessels employed in transporting them, or were obtained by the most fraudulent statements."[28]

While these campaigns unwittingly contributed to the imposition of mobility restrictions, the requirement that coolies carry—and be inspected for—their contracts of indenture was in no small way a response to these campaigns. Indeed, by focusing on physical force and potential fraud, campaigners valorized a particular notion of freedom, one defined by the absence of direct violence. Many of the campaigners were not averse to all forms of immobilizing people. However, while some coolie laborers were undoubtedly pressed into labor, most were recruited into the coolie labor system through a process that began with their displacement and dispossession by colonial practices. Most coolies sought to replace what they had lost under colonialism with new livelihoods. Yet, while alluding to the "helplessness" of the laborers caused by poverty, campaigners avoided discussion of the source of their impoverishment. In particular, the vast majority of antislavery campaigners paid scant attention to existing imperialist conditions, precisely the conditions that might make moving preferable to staying. Instead, comments focusing on the difficulties caused by the departure of an indentured coolie laborer were deployed by abolitionists: "At present their families for want of food, are begging from door to door"; "family is in great distress for maintenance"; "starving for want of food"; "their families have taken menial service [become slaves?] for maintenance." Yet the costs of staying were not discussed.

Most campaigners concerned with the coolie labor system argued that the only way to ensure the freedom of workers from India and prevent their abuse was to further reduce their freedom to move. In other words, a worker's "freedom" from slavery in British India depended on their being immobilized within the British colony of India. Their lack of freedom to move was presented as a "protection" for these workers, many of whom were trying to survive the colonial transformation of the rural economy in India. Antislavery activists represented this immobilization as the emigrants' own preference. Indeed, campaigners argued that mobility was anathema to people in India. For example, the *Anti-Slavery Reporter* (October 20, 1841) argued, the "population, so far from desiring to emigrate from their native land to distant and foreign parts, are utterly averse to it. They even object to go to distant and unknown sections of their own country."[29] That this flew in the face of actual events on the ground, where tens of millions of people were on the move as part of their survival strategies, did not seem to matter.

Initially, the efforts of antislavery campaigners were successful. Convinced that British Indian government regulations were insufficient to protect those recruited through the coolie system, campaigners successfully pressured the government to appoint a special committee in 1838 to inquire into the issue. Campaigners' success was evidenced in the committee's subsequent report, which concluded that "we conceive it to be distinctly proved beyond dispute that the Coolies and other natives exported to Mauritius and elsewhere, were, generally speaking, *induced* to come to Calcutta, by *misrepresentation* and *deceit*, practiced upon them by native crimps[30] . . . employed by European and Anglo-Indian undertakers and shippers, who were mostly cognizant of these *frauds*, and who received a very considerable sum per head for each Coolie imported."[31] Thus, on May 29, 1839, citing fraud and misrepresentation—not the conditions of British imperialism—as the source of workers' immiseration, the movement of workers engaged in manual labor from British India was prohibited. Any person effecting their emigration could be fined the substantial sum of two hundred rupees or jailed for three months. While a few people continued to move to Mauritius via the French enclave of Pondicherry in southern India, most workers' movement out of India was effectively halted.

Unsurprisingly, the planters in Mauritius and, now, also the Caribbean worked hard to overturn the ban. And the antislavery committee worked just as hard to uphold it. Ultimately, the planters' views held sway. Under their intense pressure, on December 2, 1842, the governors of the East India Company reversed their earlier decision, and the emigration of coolies was again permitted from the ports of Calcutta, Bombay, and Madras to Mauritius. That year, almost 35,000 persons were shipped as indentured coolies from British India to British Mauritius. Indeed, it was precisely to deflect challenges from antislavery campaigners that coolies were required to sign state-authorized contracts of indenture.[32] Likewise, "protectors" of emigrants were appointed at each departure point, largely to avoid coolieism's comparisons with slavery. An office of the protector of immigrants in Mauritius was established for the same purpose. Each came into existence to provide documentary proof that coolies were voluntarily moving and freely signing their contracts of indenture.

As the coolie trade was legally secured, it soon expanded to become part of the global supply chain of workers for the expanding British Empire. By 1844, coolies were shipped to British colonies in the West Indies, including Jamaica, Trinidad, and Demerara. Eventually, coolie laborers from Asia were transported throughout the British Empire and, to a lesser extent, to the French, German, Dutch, Danish, Spanish, Portuguese, Belgian, and U.S. colonies.[33] Everywhere, sugar production expanded rapidly. On Mauritius alone, by the mid-1850s, sugar production surpassed 100,000 tons a year.[34] By 1867, it is estimated that around 366,000 indentured laborers from India had entered Mauritius. There, a ship transporting coolie laborers arrived every few days. And because of the documentary controls now required to land them, a backlog in processing resulted.

Early imperial state regulation of the movement of labor represented as "free" thus took place in the historical conjuncture of the end of slavery and the continued need of capital investors for a cheapened and legally disciplined workforce. While campaigners were unsuccessful in shutting down the coolie labor trade, they did contribute enormously to the portrayal of workers engaged in migration as "simple," "ignorant," and "vulnerable," and thus in need of the "protection" of both contracts and controls to limit their mobility. In this sense, the first effort to exert state sovereignty over the mobility of imperial subjects into the state's territories took place in order to limit their power, all in the guise of protecting them.

The Logics of Constraining Free Mobility

While documentary immigration controls were initiated by the British imperial state in the 1830s and 1840s, it was under what Mongia calls the nation-state's "logic of constraint" that the (Im)migrant was cemented as a crucial state—and labor market—category. It was after the rise of nationalism, and the formation of the world's first nation-states in the late nineteenth and early twentieth century, when pressure to enact more and more regulations and restrictions intensified. The first national controls on immigration began in the Americas, where former colonies successfully transformed themselves into "self-governing" states, and some of them nationalized their sovereignty by the late nineteenth century. With the institutionalization of the idea that "nations" were discrete units of homogenous "races," each new nation-state regulated and restricted the movement of negatively racialized people into their claimed territories. Many further regulated the sexual "respectability" of the women. Unsurprisingly, then, each new nation-state announced its newfound national sovereignty by enacting racist and often gendered immigration controls. Peru was the first, in 1853, followed in quick succession by other states across the Americas. By the period between the two world wars, each "independent" state in the Americas had nationalized its sovereignty.

From the start, such immigration controls were not intended only to keep "undesirables" out of state spaces undergoing the process of nationalization. Instead, while negatively racialized people were indeed regarded by the law as "unwanted" in the nation, their labor power was very much in demand. Immigration regulations and restrictions, thus, not only worked to deny certain negatively racialized and gendered people entry (which they certainly did at particular moments in various national histories); they also placed people from these groups who did enter into highly differentiated and hierarchical state immigration categories. Their immigration status (including the relatively new one of "illegal" or "undocumented" entrant) shaped both the price of their labor power and their everyday realities of life.

Attesting to the global significance of the coolie labor system, many of the first national controls on immigration often concerned those who were recruited as coolies, just as they had in the first British imperial documentary controls on mobility. For example, the first constraints against people's free entry to the United States—the 1875 Page Act—expressly barred the entry of two categories of people: "coolies" from China and women deemed to be "prostitutes." Not unlike the antislavery campaigns' argument to restrict the mobility of working people in British India to "protect" them, U.S. trade unions, whose membership was largely limited to white male workers, came to represent coolie labor as a "relic of slavery" and sought to limit their entry.[35] By the late nineteenth century, white male workers had largely escaped the unfree employment relations established by various Masters and Servants Acts. In winning their freedom, they insisted on the exclusion of all those who were still laboring under unfree employment relations.

The figure of the coolie, the person indentured for his (and, increasingly, her) labor, remains highly relevant to present-day efforts to impose documentary controls on people's entry into nation-state territories. Contemporary immigration controls, far from outlawing unfree labor relations, have merely shifted the burden of unfreedom onto those people categorized as "noncitizens." As I've discussed elsewhere, freedom and unfreedom in nationalized labor markets have been constituted through the establishment of differential (im)migration categories.[36] In the United States, throughout the twentieth century and into the twenty-first, the largest number of

(Im)migrants living and working there are often those categorized as "un-lawful" and "unauthorized" because they are "undocumented." In regard to the lawful migration of people specifically recruited to work in the formal labor market, the numbers of people entering the United States in any given year as permanent residents are extremely low in comparison with those who enter with a temporary status. Indeed, the largest category of work-specific entry to the United States is that of "guest worker."

In 2003, only about 82,000 persons were granted employment-based "green cards" (permanent residency visas), while 360,000 persons came as guest workers with various H-visas.[37] In other words, in 2003, only 19 percent of all persons legally granted permission to work in the United States were given the rights of permanent residency. In contrast, 81 percent were admitted and tied to their employers through the requirements of various H-visa programs. H-visa workers are tied to their employers as a condition of legal entry and continued legal residence in the United States. The category of guest workers could potentially become much larger. This is because an important approach to programs of regularization of "undocu-mented" people would transfer them into the category of guest worker. And, of course, after the election of Donald Trump, the policy changes are largely having the effect of further closing off lawful means of entry and intensify-ing the demonization—and therefore the precarity—of the lives and labor of undocumented (Im)migrants.

Importantly, in the United States, where the politics of immigration en-genders significant controversy, the category of guest workers is more or less unpolitical. There is barely a word about there being hundreds of thousands of people being recruited to work in the United States as largely unfree labor, even as the movement of many fewer people—say, as asylum claimants—are regularly portrayed as highly problematic, even "dangerous," and dominate media attention. Not only are employers and state authorities implicated in such processes; so are the governments of the places whose nationalities guest workers hold. Today's guest worker systems are as globally operative as the previous labor recruitment systems they were designed to replace.

Recently in the United States, a federal lawsuit alleged that U.S. immigra-tion authorities worked closely with Signal International, a marine oil-rig company in Mississippi, to discourage protests by guest workers from India over their job conditions. Signal International, having received a multimillion-dollar contract to repair offshore oil rigs after Hurricane Katrina in 2005, hired about five hundred metalworkers who were Indian nationals in 2006. In a de-position filed in federal district court in New Orleans, Signal's chief operating officer said he grew frustrated with Indian workers who were "chronic whiners." In early 2007 he decided to fire several who were encouraging protests. Those workers, he said, "were making impossible demands" for the company to secure green cards for them or to repay the high fees they had paid recruitment agents.

Signal managers consulted with agents from Immigration and Customs Enforcement for advice on how to fire troublesome workers. According to sworn testimony, the "direction" they received from an immigration enforcement agent was this: "Don't give them any advance notice. Take them all out of the line on the way to work; get their personal belongings; get them in a van, and get their tickets, and get them to the airport, and send them back to India." In an internal email message ten days later, this same witness reported that another immigration official had told him in a meeting that day that the agency would pursue any Indian workers who left their jobs, "if for no other reason than to send a message to the remaining workers that it is not in their best interests to try and 'push' the system."

In the United States, the conditions of its guest worker programs would be considered unconstitutional were they to be applied to those with permanent residency or national citizenship status. With the exception of those who are incarcerated (and in the United States that is not a small exception!), it is unconstitutional to tie U.S. permanent residents or citizens to employers and subject them to conditions whereby either their labor market or their physical freedom is limited. Immigration controls and the documentary realities they produce are, thus, central to the organization of unfree employment relations. International law allows nation-states to determine the membership of their "national communities." This means that states are able to exercise power over those deemed "aliens" much more so than over those deemed "citizens" or "permanent residents."

Conclusion and Implications for Today

It was when the coolie recruitment system replaced the slave labor system that the figure of the (Im)migrant came into being. The (Im)migrant was the person whose movement into state territory was *regulated*. This was begun in the early nineteenth century by the British imperial state, eager to facilitate and legitimate the availability of a highly disciplined and therefore cheapened workforce of coolies and, by the end of the nineteenth century, by states intent on legitimizing a racialized view of the now-national political community, while simultaneously cheapening a negatively racialized workforce. Again, many of the workers whose movement was being restricted through documentary controls were—or were portrayed as—"coolie" labor. Regulations against coolies therefore were often the first contemporary interstate regulations on immigration. Thus, a system of immigration controls came into being with the regulation of workers largely from various parts of Asia, the vast majority of whom were recruited through the coolie labor system.

Importantly, the regulation of (im)migration arose alongside the growing nationalization of states from the late nineteenth/early twentieth and into the twenty-first centuries. In the process, ideas about mobility and people's movements changed profoundly. Obscured in efforts to regulate and restrict human mobility was, as Ellen Meiskins Wood cogently states, the fact that "the distinctive and dominant characteristic of the capitalist market is not opportunity or choice but, on the contrary, compulsion. Material life and social reproduction in capitalism are universally mediated by the market, so that all individuals must in one way or another enter into market relations in order to gain access to the means of life."[38] The immobilization of persons seeking a livelihood, all the while maintaining—indeed intensifying—capitalist market practices that entailed expropriation and exploitation, therefore, was (and remains) the height of hypocrisy.

The (Im)migrant was from the outset a negatively racialized and gendered figure. That this figure was deemed "undesirable" and "unassimilable" by newly nationalized states demonstrates the centrality of nationalism to the racialization and gendering of immigration controls. Crucially, then, it was through the regulation of the international mobility of "undesirables" that states nationalized their sovereignty. Also nationalized were the subjectivities of those who believed they "belonged" to the "nation" that each nation-state purported to rule for. Yet neither regulations on emigration nor restrictions on immigration were meant to fully stop the movement of workers, but only to ensure that the labor of those who entered state territories was sufficiently disciplined. State regulations and restrictions were not only about limiting numbers but also about limiting the rights accorded by the state to various groups of immigrant workers.

Today, we have a globalized system of immigration controls in which it is nearly impossible to move freely across now thoroughly nationalized borders, particularly for those left with little but their labor power to sell in the capitalist marketplace. As François Crépeau has well noted, "We have established all the barriers we could think of to prevent refugees [and other categories of (Im)migrants] from coming: imposition of visas for all refugee-producing countries, carrier sanctions, 'short stop operations,' training of airport or border police personnel, lists of 'safe third countries,' lists of 'safe countries of origin,' readmission agreements with neighbouring countries forming a 'buffer zone,' immigration intelligence sharing, reinforced border controls, armed interventions on the high seas . . . , military intervention," and, as recently announced, even efforts by the European Union to launch attacks against ships used to carry people attempting to move from northern Africa to Europe.[39] Notably, this last—but also many other—border control measure has been rationalized as an effort to "protect migrants" and to "end trafficking" or "modern-day slavery."[40] In this we see part of the legacy of the earliest imperial efforts to regulate and restrict free human mobility. Now, as then, the trope of "rescuing" (Im)migrants is a powerful one in legitimating even murderous actions against those on the move. Now, as then, those with the most to gain from their immobilization—states and capital investors—are perceived to be the "protectors" of (Im)migrants.

Indeed, the abuse and exploitation immigrants face today is organized through the logics of the global system of national sovereignties and the equally global system of capitalist social relations that governs and is governed by them. In particular, the restriction of people's ability to enter now-nationalized state territories results in the vast majority of people on the move being unable to gain full legal status in the places they seek to work and live. The coercion of the state as represented in its immigration regulations is part and parcel of how the coercion of the market is enforced against those denied the possibility of moving freely. It is this, beyond all other facts, that results in their overwhelming reliance on private-market intermediaries to facilitate their clandestine migrations.

In short, the greatest danger to people trying to cross national borders is the documentary controls imposed by the immigration policies and policing of nation-states. At the same time, such controls allow nation-states to manipulate the world market for labor power to shape the supply of labor power in their national territories. The categories that nation-states slot most migrating people into—"unlawful" entrant or "guest worker" being two of the largest—are the greatest threats to their liberty. Being documented as unlawful or a guest worker is precisely what entraps a growing number (and proportion) of people on the move into substandard working and living conditions while severely limiting their rights and mobility. Quite simply put: without national immigration policies, there would be no such group as those we know of as immigrants who could be subordinated, scapegoated, and abused—or rescued.

Notes

1 The term *coolie* has, from the start, connoted deeply racist meanings. I feel it remains significant to use the term, however, as it well reminds us of the close relationship between racism and class.

2 Lydia Potts, *The World Market for Labor Power: A History of Migration* (London: Zed, 1990), 79.

3 Radhika Mongia, "Historicizing State Sovereignty: Inequality and the Form of Equivalence," *Comparative Studies in Society and History* 49, no. 2 (2007): 384–411.

4 I use the term *(Im)migrant* to recognize that the state category of immigrant is attached to those with permanent residency status in the state's territory, while the term *migrant* captures all those whose mobility is regulated and restricted by the state. It is capitalized to signify that the (Im)migrant is one who is controlled by the legal category one is placed in by the state, as well as a socially constructed figure, largely of approbation.

5 James C. Scott, *The Art of Not Being Governed: An Anarchist History of Upland Southeast Asia* (New Haven, CT: Yale University Press, 2009).

6 Andrés Reséndez, *The Other Slavery: The Uncovered Story of Indian Enslavement in America* (Boston: Houghton Mifflin Harcourt, 2016); Bret Rushforth, "'A Little Flesh We Offer You': The Origins of Indian Slavery in New France," *William and Mary Quarterly* 60, no. 4 (2003): 777–808; Larissa Behrendt, interviewed in Steven McGregor, director, *Servant or Slave* (DVD) (Sydney: No Coincidence Media, 2016); Merze Tate and Fidele Foy, "Slavery and Racism in South Pacific Annexations," *Journal of Negro History* 50, no. 1 (1965): 1–21.

7 Potts, *The World Market for Labor Power*, 204.

8 Adam Hochschild, *Bury the Chains: Prophets and Rebels in the Fight to Free an Empire's Slaves* (New York: Houghton Mifflin, 2005); Peter Linebaugh and Marcus Rediker, *The Many-Headed Hydra: Sailors, Slaves, Commoners, and the Hidden History of the Revolutionary Atlantic* (Boston: Beacon, 2000).

9 Until the abolition of the slave trade in 1807, the number of Africans throughout the Americas outstripped the combined total of Europeans by a ratio of 3:4, or even 5:1. Between 1492 and 1820, while approximately 10 to 15 million Africans were forcibly brought to the New World, only 2 million or so people from Europe had made the journey. This began to change only after the abolition of the African slave trade and, even then, only in the 1820s. See Robert J. Steinfeld, *The Invention of Free Labor: The Employment Relation in English and American Law and Culture, 1350–1870* (Chapel Hill: University of North Carolina Press, 1991); Dudley Baines, "European Emigration, 1815–1930: Looking at the Emigration Decision Again," *Economic History Review* 47, no. 3 (1994): 525–44.

10 It is estimated that more than half of all persons moving from Europe to the English colonies of North America during the seventeenth and eighteenth centuries came as indentured servants. Potts, *The World Market for Labor Power*.

11 David R. Roediger, *The Wages of Whiteness: Race and the Making of the American Working Class* (London: Verso, 1999).

12 The India Act of 1858, inaugurating the period of British rule referred to as the Raj (or British India), transferred authority over most parts of the South Asian subcontinent from the British East India Company (which had ruled it from 1757) to the British Crown. Under the 1842 Treaty of Nanking, the British gained direct control over Hong Kong and Canton, while Shanghai, Amoy, Fuzhou, and Nigbo were opened up as nodes in the British-organized and -controlled trade in opium.

13 Potts, *The World Market for Labor Power*, 69.

14 Potts, *The World Market for Labor Power*, 71–73.

15 Potts, *The World Market for Labor Power*, 73.

16 Potts, *The World Market for Labor Power*, 68–71.

17 Mongia, "Historicizing State Sovereignty."

18 Richard B. Allen, *Slaves, Freedmen, and Indentured Laborers in Colonial Mauritius* (Cambridge: Cambridge University Press, 1999), 13.

19 Across the British Empire, the apprenticeship system was ended only on August 1, 1840.

20 Mongia, "Historicizing State Sovereignty," 399.

21 Quoted in Mongia, "Historicizing State Sovereignty," 399.

22 Quoted in Mongia, "Historicizing State Sovereignty," 400.

23 Quoted in Mongia, "Historicizing State Sovereignty," 401.

24 Quoted in Mongia, "Historicizing State Sovereignty," 401–2.

25 Quoted in Mongia, "Historicizing State Sovereignty," 401.

26 David S. Wyman, *Paper Walls: America and the Refugee Crisis, 1938–1941* (Amherst: University of Massachusetts Press, 1968).

27 Lisa Lowe, "The Intimacies of Four Continents," in *Haunted by Empire: Geographies of Intimacy in North American History*, ed. Ann Laura Stoler, 191–212 (Durham, NC: Duke University Press 2006), 339.

28 British Foreign Anti-Slavery Society, *Emigration from India: The Export of Coolies, and Other Labourers, to Mauritius* (London: T. Ward, [1842] 2014), 47.

29 Quoted in British Foreign Anti-Slavery Society, *Emigration from India*, 46.

30 The term *crimps* appears to have first been used in the Atlantic slave trade and also in eighteenth-century British Navy and merchant marine shipping to designate a subcontractor who secured slaves, seamen, or, in this case, coolies for contracted indentured labor.

31 Quoted in British Foreign Anti-Slavery Society, *Emigration from India*, 41.

32 Contracts for labor (or service) were, of course, not exclusively used against coolie labor from British India. An 1823 UK act that bound workers to their employers through labor contracts described its purpose as "the better regulations of servants, laborers and work people." This particular act influenced employment law in Australia (an 1845 act), Canada (1847), New Zealand (1856), and South Africa (1856). As with contracts of indenture applied to coolies, these acts were designed to discipline workers and required their obedience and loyalty to their contracted employer. Infringements of the contract were punishable by the courts, and the punishment was often a jail sentence of hard labor. Such statutes remained in effect in England until 1875, when criminal sanctions for premature departure from a

contracted place of employment were eliminated. Steinfeld, *The Invention of Free Labor*, 115, 160.

33 Potts, *The World Market for Labor Power*, 67.

34 Allen, *Slaves, Freedmen, and Indentured Laborers*, 12.

35 Lowe, "The Intimacies of Four Continents," 202.

36 Nandita Sharma, *Home Economics: Nationalism and the Making of "Migrant Workers" in Canada* (Toronto: University of Toronto Press, 2006).

37 Nandita Sharma, "Freedom to Discriminate: National State Sovereignty and Temporary Visa Workers in North America," in *Citizenship Immigrant Incorporation: Comparative Perspectives on North America and Western Europe*, ed. Gökçe Yurdakul and Y. Michal Bodemann (New York: Palgrave Macmillan, 2007), 163–84.

38 Ellen Meiskins Wood, *The Origin of Capitalism: A Longer View* (London: Verso, 2002), 7.

39 François Crépeau, "The Fight against Migrant Smuggling: Migration Containment over Refugee Protection," in *The Refugee Convention at Fifty: A View from Forced Migration Studies*, ed. Joanne van Selm et al. (Lanham, MD: Lexington, 2003), 174. As Tardy notes, the EU Council established "Operation Sophia" on May 18, 2015. "The operation's mandate," he documents, "is to contribute to the 'disruption of the business model of human smuggling and trafficking networks in the Southern Central Mediterranean' by 'efforts to identify, capture and dispose of vessels used or suspected of being used by smugglers.' The operation focuses on smugglers rather than on the rescue of the migrants themselves." Thierry Tardy, "Operation Sophia: Tackling the Refugee Crisis with Military Means," European Union, Institute for Security Studies, September 30, 2015, accessed December 14, 2016, https://www.iss.europa.eu/content/operation-sophia-tackling-refugee-crisis-military-means.

40 Ian Traynor, "EU Draws Up Plans for Military Attacks on Libya Targets to Stop Migrant Boats," *Guardian*, May 10, 2015, accessed May 10, 2015, http://www.theguardian.com/world/2015/may/10/eu-considers-military-attacks-on-targets-in-libya-to-stop-migrant-boats?CMP=share_btn_fb.

Bibliography

Allen, Richard B. *Slaves, Freedmen, and Indentured Laborers in Colonial Mauritius.* Cambridge: Cambridge University Press, 1999.

Baines, Dudley. "European Emigration, 1815–1930: Looking at the Emigration Decision Again." *Economic History Review* 47, no. 3 (1994): 525–44.

British Foreign Anti-Slavery Society. *Emigration from India: The Export of Coolies, and Other Labourers, to Mauritius.* London: T. Ward, [1842] 2014.

Crépeau, François. "The Fight against Migrant Smuggling: Migration Containment over Refugee Protection." In *The Refugee Convention at Fifty: A View from Forced Migration Studies*, edited by Joanne van Selm, Khoti Kamanga, John Morrison, Aninia Nadig, Sanja Spoljar-Vrzina, and Loes van Willigen, 173–85. Lanham, MD: Lexington, 2003.

Hochschild, Adam. *Bury the Chains: Prophets and Rebels in the Fight to Free an Empire's Slaves.* New York: Houghton Mifflin, 2005.

Linebaugh, Peter, and Marcus Rediker. *The Many-Headed Hydra: Sailors, Slaves, Commoners, and the Hidden History of the Revolutionary Atlantic*. Boston: Beacon, 2000.

Lowe, Lisa. "The Intimacies of Four Continents." In *Haunted by Empire: Geographies of Intimacy in North American History*, edited by Ann Laura Stoler, 191–212. Durham, NC: Duke University Press, 2006.

McGregor, Steven, dir. *Servant or Slave* (DVD). Sydney: No Coincidence Media. 2016.

Mongia, Radhika. "Historicizing State Sovereignty: Inequality and the Form of Equivalence." *Comparative Studies in Society and History* 49, no. 2 (2007): 384–411.

Potts, Lydia. *The World Market for Labor Power: A History of Migration*. London: Zed, 1990.

Reséndez, Andrés. *The Other Slavery: The Uncovered Story of Indian Enslavement in America*. Boston: Houghton Mifflin Harcourt, 2016.

Roediger, David R. *The Wages of Whiteness: Race and the Making of the American Working Class*. London: Verso, 1999.

Rushforth, Bret. "'A Little Flesh We Offer You': The Origins of Indian Slavery in New France." *William and Mary Quarterly* 60, no. 4 (2003): 777–808.

Scott, James C. *The Art of Not Being Governed: An Anarchist History of Upland Southeast Asia*. New Haven, CT: Yale University Press. 2009.

Sharma, Nandita. "Freedom to Discriminate: National State Sovereignty and Temporary Visa Workers in North America." In *Citizenship Immigrant Incorporation: Comparative Perspectives on North America and Western Europe*, edited by Gökçe Yurdakul and Y. Michal Bodemann, 163–84. New York: Palgrave Macmillan, 2007.

Sharma, Nandita. *Home Economics: Nationalism and the Making of "Migrant Workers" in Canada*. Toronto: University of Toronto Press. 2006.

Steinfeld, Robert J. *The Invention of Free Labor: The Employment Relation in English and American Law and Culture, 1350–1870*. Chapel Hill: University of North Carolina, 1991.

Tardy, Thierry. "Operation Sophia: Tackling the Refugee Crisis with Military Means." European Union, Institute for Security Studies, September 30, 2015. Accessed December 14, 2016. https://www.iss.europa.eu/content/operation-sophia-tackling-refugee-crisis-military-means.

Tate, Merze, and Fidele Foy. "Slavery and Racism in South Pacific Annexations." *Journal of Negro History* 50, no. 1 (1965): 1–21.

Wood, Ellen Meiskins. *The Origin of Capitalism: A Longer View*. London: Verso, 2002.

Wyman, David S. *Paper Walls: America and the Refugee Crisis, 1938–1941*. Amherst: University of Massachusetts Press, 1968.

2

AND ABOUT TIME TOO . . .

Migration, Documentation, and Temporalities

Migration is strongly imagined as a spatial process, its temporalities figuring as a series of discrete states: the decision, the journey, arrival, and then either settlement and citizenship or return. Thus, underlying much of the research on migration as well as migration policy is an assumption that those people who successfully migrate move from being temporary to permanent (or "settled") and—it is hoped—"integrated" in a linear progress over the course of time.[1] Yet as several contributions to this volume illustrate, in practice not only are the transitions often far from smooth, but many people find themselves in prolonged liminal statuses. A temporal perspective foregrounds the instability of the category of "migrant," and it also exposes the ways in which those deemed "migrants" are subject to temporal controls that can have devastating consequences for their life trajectories.

This chapter begins with a brief discussion of the relevance of temporality to the study of migration. It then focuses on three interrelated areas where a temporal perspective is particularly productive: work, asynchronicities, and citizenship. I will argue that such a perspective can help make new connections between "migrants" and "citizens." It is important to analyze temporal mechanisms in practice and in context, and the chapter uses the case of the United Kingdom to examine these questions more specifically. The empirical material on subjective experiences derives from two research projects with migrant domestic workers, one undertaken in the 1990s and the other in 2017.[2]

Temporality and the Study of Migration and Mobilities

Mobility as a human process occurs in time as well as across space. However, with certain exceptions this has largely remained unexplored.[3] Lack of attention to time is surprising given that time is a critical element in defining who counts as a "migrant." United Nations data on global migration—which are the data usually referred to when it comes to global trends—define a migrant as: "A person who moves to a country other than that of his or her usual residence for a period of twelve months or more so that the country of destination effectively becomes his or her new country of usual residence."[4] Notably, there is no mention of citizenship status. A person who returns to their country of citizenship after being away can still count as a "migrant" for the purposes of this definition. What matters is *time*: time away (from the *usual* residence) and length of time planned to stay (*twelve months or more*).

In contrast, citizenship is critical to whether or not one is a deportable person and in this sense a "migrant" in law. Citizens, unlike many migrants, are not subject to immigration controls. This can be a problem for evidence-based policy, which typically relies on quantitative data from national datasets, but in national datasets the preferred definition of "migrant" tends to be "foreign born." Thus, in national datasets naturalized citizens, or citizens born abroad, count as "migrants," and therefore policy makers find that not all those who are counted as migrants in data are affected by the levers of immigration controls. Furthermore, the social idea of "migrant" exposes racializations that can be obscured in law and in data—"second-generation" migrants may never have crossed an international border in their lives. The question of how long people remain being cast, by law or perception, as "migrants" and "refugees" unsettles the migrant/citizen binary. Who sheds and who retains "migrancy" as a *social* status is bound up with race, class, and gender. These racializations are complex, revealing the instability of whiteness. In the UK in 2017 a white Canadian professor is unlikely to count as a "migrant" for social purposes, even if they do in data and in law; in contrast, pre-Brexit, a white Polish builder will count as a "migrant" for social purposes even if, as far as the law and the European Commission are concerned, they are a "mobile citizen."[5] In many Northern European countries, EU nationals from Central and Eastern European countries continue to be perceived as migrants, exemplifying that not all people who are socially imagined as migrants can have their movements controlled through immigration policy.

The study of migration has only recently started to properly explore the malleability of the subject of the migrant, and how a temporal lens can help better understand how this figure is created and governed. Research on migration has often been insufficiently attentive to the distinction and relation between categories of practice on the one hand, and categories of analysis on the other. The bulk of the research on human mobility has focused on the racialized, minoritized, and low-waged, that is, on the same groups of people who are socially imagined as migrants and who are the "problems" for migration policy. This emphasis in some countries is compounded by social research funding mechanisms that emphasize policy engagement, meaning that certain types of research on migration find it easier to attract both government and philanthropic funding, with the risk that policy has a strong influence on research agendas. The problem for migration studies is that researchers continually risk reifying the figure of the migrant, thereby contributing to making the very difference between "migrant" and "citizen" that is the subject of concern.

Attention to documents, the material expression of status, can be particularly helpful in this context. Migrants are made and unmade by documents. Documentation is not simply a means of regulating noncitizens' movement (including within states), but, as Sharma and Boehm argue in their contributions to this volume, documents are key to constituting the difference between migrant and citizen in the first place. Which documents a person has or can access is a critical distinction between the citizen and the noncitizen, but importantly they mark productive processes. Focusing on documents and status as productive artifacts and processes can help counter the reification of the migrant, and attending to the temporalities of documentation and status can help us reconnect the bifurcated categories of migrant and citizen.

The diversity of the ways in which time has entered social theory is such that, as Barbara Adam's seminal review observed, it is hard to believe that theorists are describing and analyzing the same phenomenon: "Not only are we faced with an incompatible array of definitions, but we also have to cope with incommensurable ideas about the source of experience and concept of time."[6] One of the responses to this incommensurability has been to generate different typologies of time.[7] In the case of the study of human mobilities and time it can be helpful to ground the discussion through attention to different typologies of time, and more particularly in the tension between time and the state on the one hand, and subjective experiences of time on the other.[8] I characterize these as natural/biological time and industrial/bureaucratic time.

The term *natural* describes both biological and astronomical times, and I use it with due regard to the dangers of the idea of the natural.[9] By "natural"

I mean temporal passing that proceeds irrespective of interference by humans: the length of daylight, the seasons, processes of aging, and so on. It is not that this time cannot be bypassed—heavy blinds can shut out daylight, heating can mimic summer, cosmetic surgery alleviates the physical signs of aging—but there is a process that proceeds nonetheless or is ready to take over as soon as intervention ceases. This time is not reversible. One of the ways its passing is experienced by individuals is through aging and the life course.

Biological/natural time is often associated with "tradition" and is contrasted with clock, or industrial time, which is required and facilitated by technologies and bureaucracies.[10] Thompson, Giddens, and others argue that industrial capitalism is ruled by a standardized, homogeneous clock time that is divisible into ever-smaller units and that, as Marx pointed out, it is possible to commodify.[11] By "bureaucratic time" I mean the synchronous time that is imposed by states and that is necessary for states to function.[12] It is the state-standardized time of both the clock *and the date*. In Europe and North America, the day-to-day experience of time is often imagined and experienced as bureaucratic nested in natural/biological, and the bureaucratic gives a certain rhythm to natural time: the milestones of school and retirement, for example, help structure the life course.

Bureaucracies can exert massive control over the time of "noncitizens," and their subjection to certain kinds of control is an element of their noncitizenship. Time can be micromanaged in reporting requirements, for instance, but more structurally those who enter legally are almost always subject to restrictions on their length of stay on a territory, and may also be subject to restrictions on how they spend their time. The temporariness of stay and associated restrictions on access to citizenship move the border ineluctably inward. To police and enforce border controls requires attention to documents, and to their temporalities. "All documents exist in time, their relationship to time being set and reset by those who use and produce them."[13] Documents mark, periodize, and shape the life course of those subject to migration controls. They formally capture the subjection of migrants to a range of temporal regimes, and the temporalities of documents are firmly fixed in bureaucratic time. The time-limitedness of documents, their renewability, and the relation between legal length of stay and access to permanent residence/citizenship is critical to the governing of migration. Documents breed more documents: applications for permanent residence, for example, may require passports, proof of employment, proof of current residence, birth certificates, marriage certificates, and so on. The collection of these documents is a temporal process that captures past actions into a record that enables the prescription of the past and the future. A person becomes, through this temporal process manifest in documentation, a "case," and this case is put forward in the application for another document that summarizes the previous documents, and that may in the future be required as evidence for another document, and so on. The envelopes that encase documents can themselves become documents, demonstrating proof of sending and proof of receipt as applications typically require forensic attention to dates that often have a material bearing on the case. This is the "paper trail" that is established, and it looks both backward as a description of life processes and forward to the potential for a settled future.[14]

While there are commonalities in experiences relating to the relation between time and migration documents, due attention must be paid to national specificities. I shall now consider three expressions of the relation between temporality and documentation: the making of workers, experiences of asynchronicity, and the shaping of citizenship, taking the UK as an example.

The UK Context

The UK is an interesting case for the study of temporality and documentation. The past two decades have seen a shift in emphasis from policing at the border to internal policing, but unlike other European states, where internal policing has been the norm for longer, the UK has no national identity card. National identity cards were proposed in the second half of the 2000s, but proved very unpopular and were dropped by the incoming 2010 coalition government. However, an exception was made for noncitizens; what is now known as the Biometric Immigration Document was rolled out to all categories of noncitizens resident for six months or more. This is now the principal document that evidences a noncitizen's right to work and to welfare benefits. It confirms all restrictions placed on the holder, including the date that their leave to remain in the UK expires. It is the culmination of a series of other documents, and to obtain it a person must submit a passport/travel document, an immigration status document, council tax letters, letters from a doctor, letters from school/college, bank or utility statements, and relevant Home Office letters. Biometric data (digital photograph and fingerprints) are taken by the UK Border Agency, verified, and then sent to the Driver and Vehicle Licensing Agency to produce a card.

In practice, the day-to-day consequences of the temporalities of documents depend very much on enforcement, and in the UK this has been made the responsibility of different groups of people. Immigration enforcement is becoming part of life not only for migrants but also for citizens. A wide range of people are required to check documents, including statutory agencies, employers, registrars, health officials, travel carriers, university lecturers, and bank employees. If people refuse or forget to check documents, they may be subject to civil, and in some cases to criminal, sanctions. In this way, UK citizens, as well as "migrants," can be criminalized through immigration laws.[15] One of the characteristics of citizenship is that citizens are not subject to immigration controls, but in the UK, immigration controls are encroaching deeply into citizens' lives.

Recent UK migration policy is driven by numbers, with the government setting a target of reducing "net migration" (numbers in minus numbers out) down to under 100,000.[16] This means that policy is not only concerned with decreasing numbers entering, but also with increasing the numbers of people leaving.[17] There has been an acceleration in the shift from immigration statuses leading to settlement to immigration statuses that do not lead to any permanent settlement rights (meaning more numbers out and hence, in theory, to lower net migration). Workers are divided into different tiers with temporally distinct rights. Tier 1 is for exceptional ability or investors and high-net-worth individuals. A person who invests more than £10 million is eligible for settlement after two years; someone who invests between £5 and £10 million is eligible after three years (the standard requirement is five years of legal residence for permanent residence). Tier 2 visa holders are recognized as highly skilled, and they too are eligible for settlement if they earn £35,000 or more, but only after a minimum residence period of five years. Tier 3 visas were designed for "low-skilled" temporary workers. This tier was never implemented because the system was designed at the same time as the EU was enlarged and significant numbers of young EU nationals came to work in the UK labor market; the tier was discontinued in 2013. Tier 4 is for students and not eligible for settlement purposes. Tier 5 is for temporary workers and government-sponsored exchanges, and people entering under Tier 5 visas are not eligible for settlement. In summary, among those who enter the UK as "economic migrants," only those constructed as highly skilled will find themselves able to legally remain for more than four or five years. Thus, the UK immigration and asylum systems produce a hierarchy of security. The person of "exceptional talent" is given permission to stay for a maximum of five years (five years and four months if they apply outside the UK), but if they bring their domestic worker with them, she will only be permitted a six-month, nonrenewable stay.

These kinds of gradations of settlement rights are not confined to workers. In 2012, as part of its attempt to reduce net migration, the UK Home Office extended the "probationary period" required before those on spousal/partnership visas could apply for settlement from two to five years. To explain this extension, the Home Office cited statistics that demonstrate that 10 percent of marriages break down after five years, as compared to 3 percent after two years.

It would be incorrect to assume that the increase in precarity of status was driven entirely by the net migration target. In 2003 the settlement rights of asylum seekers were curtailed by the introduction of humanitarian protection, granted for five years to people held to be at serious risk but not qualified as refugees under the Geneva Convention. At the end of that period, settlement was not automatic, and they became subject to a safe return review, and in the case of a "significant and non-temporary change in country situation" they were subject to return. At the same time, discretionary leave was introduced for a nonrenewable maximum of thirty months on the basis of a serious medical condition or instance of modern slavery or trafficking. In March 2017, it became clear that the safe return review was being implemented not only in cases of humanitarian protection, but also when people with full refugee status under the convention were applying for settlement (when, precisely, this expansion was introduced was the subject of dispute).

The important exception to this proliferation of temporary statuses seemed to be EU citizens, who obtain an automatic right to settlement after five years of legal residence. This relative security was reflected in this group's low levels of application for UK citizenship. However, the Brexit referendum removed the security provided by EU citizenship, resulting in a rise in applications for UK citizenship (as well as a rise in numbers of EU nationals leaving the UK, and possibly also contributing to a reduction in numbers of EU nationals seeking to enter the UK). Many EU nationals seeking to stabilize their situation through settlement and naturalization found themselves caught out in a distinction between *residence* and *presence*.[18] The distinction between *presence* and *residence* is temporal: the etymological origin of *residence* is the Latin *residere*—to remain; the etymological origin of *presence* is the Latin *praesentia*, or being at hand, immediate, that is, in the present. Some EU nationals found that they had been in an unrolling present, rather than an emerging residence. They had indeed been legally *present*, but this is not the same as being legally *resident* because of requirements attached to their legal residence. For example, EU citizens classed as belonging to certain categories of nonworker, such as students, were required to have documentary proof that they had taken out comprehensive sickness insurance (CSI). This was not because they needed to rely on CSI, as EU nationals are entitled to access the National Health Service (NHS), and it is scarcely surprising that many people were unaware of this bureaucratic requirement. However, when they applied for settlement, many people who had been living in the UK for what they thought was a period of time that qualified them for permanent residence found that they had not fulfilled the legal residence criteria.[19] This experience was not uncommon for EU citizen academics, whose stay when they were employed in universities counted toward legal residence but who whose stay as students was found to be merely legal presence.

Work and Temporal Constraints

Immigration controls actively construct certain kinds of workers.[20] This is partly through illegalizing workers and applying deportation powers to break organized labor—in the UK there are increasing reports of cases where organizers have been gathered for legitimate purposes such as health and safety briefings, only to be raided by immigration enforcement. But it is also through the temporal constraints that are put on people who are working legally. Visas may restrict migrants to temporary or part-time work; conversely, they may require them to work full time. These kinds of requirements also often mark a period of dependence on sponsors. Thus, migrants on working visas may effectively be on fixed-term contracts that can be terminated at the employer's discretion. For migrants on work permits, then, not only is their employment mobility limited by the state, but employers are handed additional means of control: should they have any reason to be displeased with the worker's performance, or indeed even have a personal grudge against them, not only the worker's job but their presence in the country can be put in jeopardy. The temporality of the sponsorship system means that employers have powers of labor retention without jeopardizing their ability to fire. When asked why they employ migrants, employers have been found to frequently refer to *retention* as an advantage of migrant labor.[21] Other perceived advantages, often racialized by employers, such as reliability, honesty, and work ethic, must also be understood partly in terms of the level of dependence work permit holders have on their employers because their documentation is only temporary.[22] This entangles subjectivities in immigration controls, as uncertainty about temporariness and permanence can help trap people into precarious work. Precarious status, whether temporarily legal or unauthorized, often also means precarious work, as people with no certainty over their time or future continuation in the job are often prepared to accept work that has little structure or regularity. As Neilson and Mezzadra have argued, the role of borders in shaping labor markets is particularly pronounced in the combination of speed and diversity that characterizes supply-chain capitalism.[23] The temporalities of immigration controls intricately relate to capital flexibility in the creation and control of hypermobile workers and new ways of profiting from them.[24]

The policing of these temporalities may be profitable but, as Menjívar points out in this volume, it is also burdensome. Employers have the duty to prevent illegal working and must check documents of all new employees to see that they have the "right to work." They must verify not only whether the documents are genuine or fake but also whether they are timely or whether the person's permission to remain "has ceased to have effect." The documents to be checked must be demonstrably "current documents," that is, "a document that has not expired."[25] Having checked the documents, they must photocopy them and *record the date* when the check was conducted. The importance of time is apparent in the Home Office instructions:

Step 3 Copy

You must make a **clear copy** of each document in a format which cannot later be altered, and retain the copy securely: electronically or in hardcopy. You must also retain a secure record of the date on which you made the check.

You must copy and retain:

1. **Passports**: any page with the document expiry date, the holder's nationality, date of birth, signature, leave expiry date, biometric details, photograph and any page containing information indicating the holder has an entitlement to enter or remain in the UK and undertake the work in question (the front cover no longer has to be copied).
2. **All other documents**: the document in full, including both sides of a Biometric Residence Permit and a Residence Card (biometric format). You must retain copies securely for not less than two years after the employment has come to an end.

This is further complicated by the specificities of visas. For example, students are not allowed to work consistently, but they are permitted to work between ten and twenty hours a week during their terms (depending on their course and the educational provider) and for any duration during vacations. Their employers are required to discover not only the course and where their student employee is studying (different courses and ages are allowed different maximum working hours), but also their academic terms and vacation dates, and must then enforce appropriately. They must "place" their workers in time. The Home Office does recognize that employers may have valid reasons for failing to comply with the law, and extenuating circumstances are laid out in explanatory guidelines. Depending on the document checked, employers can claim either a "continuous statutory excuse" for the full duration of that person's employment (if they have a UK passport, for example) or a "time-limited statutory excuse" that requires a follow-up check when the document expires, or after six months. Those people who fail to enforce and who do not have a statutory excuse may be fined and in some cases even imprisoned.

While these kinds of enforcement requirements were originally made of employers and "carriers" (companies and individuals responsible for transporting goods and people across borders), they have been expanded to a wide range of people in the effort to create what the Home Office has called a "hostile environment" for unauthorized migrants. For example, since 2016, all landlords who lease a private property in England must conduct a right-to-rent check. Here, too, expiration dates, dates of birth, recording dates of checks, and so on are stressed for the provision of continuous or statutory excuses, and follow-up checks are required when certain types of documents are relied on.

Asynchronicities

Due regard to migration temporalities highlights the asynchronicities between subjective experiences of time and administrative requirements. The ordinary temporalities of a lifetime—children growing older, parents dying, the day-to-day experiences that mark the unfolding of a life—proceed in a very different way than the time of immigration applications. The consequences for those experiencing asynchronicities are profound. Temporal uncertainty is deeply destabilizing and can mean people losing a sense of a recursive engagement with an imagined future. Increasing attention has been paid to the processes and effects of "waiting," most notably in relation to asylum, where there is a tension between the desire for a speedy process and the protraction of stay in the event of a negative decision. Research on temporary protection mechanisms for refugees demonstrates how temporary statuses can become so extended that they would be better characterized as "permanent temporariness."[26] It may be conceptualized as an overly powerful present, recalling the Heideggerian distinction between persisting and leading a life. It is reflected in a sense of limbo and "chronic" waiting.[27]

Importantly, waiting can be a draining feature in the lives of people before they move. Craig Jeffrey uses the term *timepass* to explore the lives of young educated men in India, forced to wait indefinitely to find a job, reflecting the sense of having little to do other than spend/waste time.[28] Indeed, the escape from "stuckness" can also be precisely why people become migrants; Reuben Andersson describes how the search for "deliverance from a world of extended youth and lack of fulfilment in reeling home economies" can motivate migration, only for people to find themselves trapped in the distinct temporalities of a camp that produces dystopian asynchronicities.[29]

There are multiple illustrations of the torment of asynchronicities in UK immigration control. It is instructive to consider an example of regularization—when migrants move from being "unauthorized" to being "documented" and are, in the process, subjected to very specific temporal regimes. One little-known such exercise was the regularization process initiated by the UK government in June 1998 after a well-organized ten-year campaign undertaken by unauthorized domestic workers. These were predominantly women who had entered the UK with their employers and been given a visa that tied them to a named employer. Those who left their employers lost their right to stay, even in cases of extreme abuse.[30] The kinds of temporal disjunctures experienced by unauthorized workers are described by Lucy:

> I want to go home, because my Dad died last September and my husband died two days ago and I can't go home. I want to see my children and to be able to support them now because they're very sad. . . . The first thing I will do when I'm legal here is to go to the Philippines. My Mom is still with us and she has high blood pressure. She looks after my daughter and my daughter has a baby. My daughter is only 18 years so it's very hard. . . . Being illegal is very hard in this country. I need to go home to sort out my husband's pension.[31]

In 2004 the incoming Labour government announced that domestic workers accompanying their employers were no longer going to be tied to their employers and that those who had entered under the old system were to be regularized. The requirements at first seemed relatively simple: a valid passport, proof that the applicant was currently employed as a domestic worker and able to support herself, and proof that they entered as a domestic worker and had left an employer due to abuse.

However, applications were given a deadline. The window was set between July 1998 and July 1999. Mass regularizations are usually time limited—an open-ended regularization is regarded as a structural invitation for irregular migration. However, in this case regularization was restricted to those who entered under a now-defunct visa regime, and the deadline was purely for administrative purposes. Moreover, the requirements noted above were only clarified some six months into the process. Applications were further delayed because employers were reluctant to comply until it was officially confirmed that they would not be prosecuted for employing "illegal immigrants." Pressured by the deadline, many workers left their jobs in search of employers who would sign a statement demonstrating they were currently employed. It was only after considerable lobbying that the government permitted a three-month extension—and no more. This illustrates a common but little-commented-on asynchronicity: the temporal latitude afforded bureaucracies in the face of delay is often not paralleled by any such latitude toward applicants (see Coutin, this volume).

Approximately three thousand migrant domestic workers were regularized through this process, and the immediate response was, as Lucy suggests, to visit family:

> When I got my papers I was feeling so great, very delighted. I hadn't seen my children for ten years. I got indefinite leave to remain in 2000.... My first priority was to go home to see my kids. My father had died in 1993 and I couldn't go to the funeral. I didn't even know about it. We don't have phone, no phone calls only letters—only three letters in a year. It was so very stressful and distressing for me. Before I left London I photocopied everything about my situation in this country. I saw my mother and my two children as well. They had grown big by then.[32]

However, having acquired stable status means the requirement for documents of a different type. Mary was a worker regularized under the exercise:

> Four years after living here the Home Office sent me a letter to say that I could now work here. But I needed my documents. I had to write to my MP. Because I didn't have my documents I couldn't do anything. They sent my documents with the wrong name. I had to send them back again. It was so stressful. After two years I finally got papers with

my own name. When I could hold the documents in my hand it was great. I could now go to Africa to apply for my passport and see my family and meet people and feel free. . . . It was a relief but it was also a pain. But the main thing I wanted was to apply for my tax and national insurance. My employer in Stanmore paid national insurance for their daily worker, but they didn't pay mine because until then I didn't have my papers. I told my employer that I wanted to pay my tax and NI and contribute to the country but my employer kept stalling, . . . HM Revenue and Customs [had arranged] that the employer need only pay tax and NI when the worker got their papers. I kept reminding them for nearly a year but they wouldn't do it. Then I applied myself. They sent me a letter, but I found it torn up. I saw that there was a paper trail and could see my name and that it was from HM Revenue. I was horrified, I had slaved for these people for over five years and then they now have torn up my letter. When my employer came home from work I asked her why my letter was torn and in the bin. She had a big tantrum and insisted that I leave her house.[33]

Employers who were prepared to sign documents attesting to immigration status were not necessarily prepared to sign documents on employment status, as these would require them to recognize their worker as an employee with attendant contractual responsibilities. These employment documents also have immigration ramifications, as in many cases they serve as necessary proof for long-term residence/naturalization applications.

Citizenship

Socialities have a momentum that proceeds both in spite of and shaped by bureaucratic time. This is sometimes expressed in the language of "belonging" (an interesting term that conveys a vision of membership that is related to property). As political theorist Joseph Carens has argued, living in a community on an ongoing basis is part of what makes one a member, and moral claims to membership grow stronger over time. Integration, adaptation, and membership in a "community" are strongly felt to be time-sensitive processes, so in many liberal states, after a person has been present on state territory for a prolonged period, they can apply for special permission to regularize their status.[34] For documented people in many states, immigration restrictions are reduced after a specified period of legal residence, when their status becomes permanent/indefinite, signaling a loosening of control.

To avoid claims to membership on the basis of long residence, states often limit visa duration and renewability to prevent possibilities of building up rights to settlement. In contrast to high-net-worth individuals such as those eligible under the UK's Tier 1 visa, low-waged migrant workers in many countries are not able to renew their documents for the number of years required to obtain permanent residence or citizenship status. Immigration controls do the dirty work of citizenship, and they do so through temporal restrictions.

Temporal restrictions not only prevent some migrants from accessing citizenship, but they can also effectively turn citizens into "migrants" through the distinction between presence and residence. In many European states, residence is the gateway to many social benefits, but just as legal presence in a territory is not sufficient to constitute residence for noncitizens, so too it is not sufficient to constitute residence for citizens, and the presence/residence distinction serves as a barrier to accessing social benefits for noncitizens and citizens alike. In the UK, while all citizens have the "right to reside," for citizens to be able to claim certain means-tested benefits, such as income-based Jobseeker's Allowance (unemployment benefits), housing assistance, council tax support, and pension credits, they must pass the habitual residence test. This was introduced in 1994, and prior to its introduction a person was able to access these kinds of benefits or their equivalent no matter how little time they had been resident in the UK. Now, applicants must have a "settled intention" to reside and must also have been resident for an "appreciable period of time." What counts as settled intention and an appreciable period varies from case to case. The government acknowledges that this has the potential to become a significant problem for British citizens who come to the UK after Brexit, as they will indeed be "migrants" as well as British citizens. Thus, citizens are not immune from documentation requirements, and it is not only migrants who find themselves governed through time. The imagined trajectory from migrant status to the haven of citizenship is disrupted when the status of citizenship is itself exposed as multiple and not unitary.

Perhaps one reason for the taken-for-grantedness of the temporalities of immigration controls is that in practice state control over time is normalized for all residents. This is particularly stark in the governing of welfare benefits. There are requirements to report at the welfare office, to demonstrate that one has devoted sufficient time searching for work, to affirm that one is prepared to travel for up to one and a half hours to take up a job offer, and so on. Those who are late or do not attend interviews are sanctioned, and their benefits can be cut or withdrawn entirely for months or even years.

It is necessary to "look within, at and beyond national borders as we survey the history of movement control," and understanding how time functions as a mechanism of differentiation within processes of sorting also indicates new commonalities.³⁵ These become particularly apparent in the case of local government. Other chapters in this volume consider the dispersal of power from national to state level in the United States, and temporal controls may be imposed at the local as well as the national level. Internal mobility is often distinguished from cross-border migration. The connection between internally displaced peoples (IDP) and international migrants is sometimes acknowledged; this is very much in the context of the Global South, and in the Global North the internal mobility of national citizens is viewed as quite different from the cross-border migration of "migrants," even if the European Union's freedom of movement has somewhat complicated the picture. Yet previously, nation-states' restrictions on mobility were within kingdoms rather than between kingdoms.³⁶ It was often the mobility of beggars, serfs, and vagabonds that was restricted, that is, the mobility of the poor. Taking as a perspective the *longue durée*, we can start to connect the control of the movement and labor relations of contemporary migrants (imagined as today's "global poor") with the movement and labor relations of the laboring poor of the past. Moreover, while it is assumed that in contemporary liberal democracies citizens have free internal movement, variations on these restrictions continue to operate. For example, the UK's 2011 Localism Act has meant that English local authorities have jurisdiction over the allocation of social housing, and from 2012 local authorities started to devise social housing allocation policies. These often denounce migrants for all the usual problems: taking housing from "locals," crime, drugs, and so on. However, in some cases it is noteworthy that "By migration we are not just talking about people moving to and from the UK, it also means the movement of people to and from different parts of the country." That is, British citizens on welfare benefits can also be classified as migrants. Local government responses to these "migrants" often bear striking similarities to naturalization requirements, demanding minimum residence periods, sometimes of up to ten years, before it is possible to join the housing waiting list, and sometimes even requiring that time be spent in the right way, for example, stipulating that unemployed people should spend a certain number of hours a week volunteering.

Conclusion

Attention to time highlights that space-time has been unequally compressed, and that its consequences vary; as deportation processes illustrate, fast is not always good. It also exposes the imbrication of the law and time and how the temporalities of visas and bureaucratic and legal processes such as regularizations have very real consequences in the lives of the people wrestling with them, and that it is easy to overlook the violence of certain kinds of asynchronicity and the obstruction of a capacity to plan—whether for next week or the next ten years. This chapter also indicates the relevance of a temporal analysis in the documentation of citizens as well as migrants. We have seen how citizens' social rights are temporally governed at a national scale through the distinction between (lawful) presence and residence, and at the scale of the municipality through requiring periods of residence in specific local areas. Furthermore, citizens' rights as workers are also temporally shaped: a person starting a new job, even in a well-unionized formal sector, does not acquire all employment rights straight away. For example, in the UK a worker must have worked for the same employer for twenty-six weeks before they are eligible to make a claim for maternity pay and for two years before they can claim unfair dismissal. The duration of the qualifying period is typically determined in regulations rather than in law and is thereby buffered from political dispute: for instance, the doubling of the period of employment necessary before eligibility for unfair dismissal received very little attention.

Taken like this, time, and particularly the "bureaucratic time" considered in this chapter, potentially opens the possibility for thinking about new political alliances that trouble the borders between citizens and noncitizens. Managing the temporariness of migration is a key way in which borders are brought into territorial space, and the UK demonstrates how the growth of temporary statuses has led to increasing surveillance and document checking, not only of migrants but also of citizens—after all, one has to be able to prove one is a citizen in order to be exempt from checks. Attention to documents as illustrations of the multiple ways in which labor relations and social rights are governed temporally, and conversely to the temporal implications of how work and social rights are governed, can help us escape the methodological nationalism of the assumed difference between "migrant" and "citizen," enabling us to see the legal construction of both categories. It demands that we focus on the contract and the utility bill serving as "proof of address" as much as the passport, and that we appreciate how the relation between different types of documents shapes migrants' experiences of being a migrant, and citizens' experiences of being a citizen. We can also make connections between how we might analyze the migrant as the subject who illustrates the most extreme susceptibility of state temporal control, as demonstrated in the thorny path to citizenship.

Notes

1 Michael Piore, *Birds of Passage: Migrant Labor and Industrial Societies* (Cambridge: Cambridge University Press, 1979).
2 See Bridget Anderson, *Us and Them? The Dangerous Politics of Immigration Control* (Oxford: Oxford University Press, 2013); Bridget Anderson, *Doing the Dirty Work? The Global Politics of Domestic Labour* (London: Zed, 2000).
3 Russell King et al., "Gender, Age and Generations: State of the Art," IMISCOE *Working Paper* (Sussex: Centre for Migration and Population Studies, University of Sussex, 2004); Torsten Hagerstrand, "What About People in Regional Science?," *Papers in Regional Science* 24 (1970): 6–21; Saulo Cwerner, "The Times of Migration," *Journal of Ethnic and Migration Studies* 27 (2001): 7–36. More recently, see Melanie Griffiths, Ali Rogers, and Bridget Anderson, "Migration and Temporalities: Review and Prospect," COMPAS *Research Paper* (Oxford: University of Oxford, 2013); Elizabeth Mavroudi, Ben Page, and Anastasia Christou, eds., *Timespace and International Migration* (London: Edward Elgar, 2017).
4 UN Department of Economic and Social Affairs, Statistics Division, "Demographic and Social Statistics: International Migration," https://unstats.un.org/unsd/demographic/sconcerns/migration/migrmethods.htm.
5 In 2013, when Austria, Britain, Germany, and the Netherlands wrote a joint letter to the Irish presidency and the Commission to complain that "certain immigrants from other member states . . . avail themselves of the opportunities that freedom of movement provides, without, however, fulfilling the requirements for exercising this right" (http://docs.dpaq.de/3604–130415_letter_to_presidency_final_1_2.pdf), the then Home Affairs Commissioner Cecilia Malmström's response strongly objected to their use of the word *immigrant*. "EU citizens who have the right to travel, live, work and study where ever they want in the Union are put on a par with immigrants from countries outside the EU. For instance, they are being called EU immigrants, a concept that does not exist." Cited in Peo Hansen, "Undermining Free Movement: Migration in an Age of Austerity," *Eurozine*, February 6, 2015, http://www.eurozine.com/undermining-free-movement/.
6 Barbara Adam, *Time and Social Theory* (Cambridge: Polity, 1994), 15.
7 Helga Nowotny, *Time: The Modern and Postmodern Experience* (Cambridge: Polity, 1994); Griffiths et al., "Migration and Temporalities."
8 Griffiths et al., "Migration and Temporalities."
9 Nowotny, *Time*.
10 Adam, *Time and Social Theory*.

11 E. P. Thompson, "Time, Work-Discipline, and Industrial Capitalism," *Past and Present* 38 (1967): 56–97; Anthony Giddens, *The Constitution of Society: Outline of the Theory of Structuration* (Cambridge: Polity, 1984).

12 David Gross, "Temporality and the Modern State," *Theory and Society* 14 (1985): 53–82.

13 Richard Freeman and Jo Maybin, "Documents, Practices and Policy," *Evidence and Policy: A Journal of Research, Debate and Practice* 7 (2011): 160.

14 Barbara Yngvesson and Susan Bibler Coutin, "Backed by Papers: Undoing Persons, Histories, and Return," *American Ethnologist* 33 (2006): 177–90.

15 Ana Aliverti, *Crimes of Mobility: Criminal Law and the Regulation of Immigration* (Abingdon, UK: Routledge, 2014).

16 Notably, the definition of migrant used to count "net migration" figures is the long-term international migration definition, meaning that citizens leaving the UK or returning from abroad count as "migrants" when it comes to reaching this target.

17 In October 2019 the incoming Johnson administration quietly dropped the net migration target and promoted an "Australian-style" points based system.

18 Sara Stendahl, "To Reside: To Live, Be Present, Belong," *European Journal of Social Security* 18 (2016): 232–45.

19 Migration Observatory, "Here Today Gone Tomorrow: The Status of EU Citizens Already Living in the UK," *Migration Observatory Commentaries*, 2016, accessed October 10, 2017, https://www.Migrationobservatory.ox.ac.uk/resources/commentaries/today-gone-tomorrow-status-eu-citizens-already-living-uk/.

20 Josiah Heyman, "Capitalism and US Policy at the Mexican Border," *Dialectical Anthropology* 36 (2012): 263–77.

21 Sally Dench et al., *Employers' Use of Migrant Labour* (London: Home Office Online Report, 2006), accessed November 5, 2018, https://www.academia.edu/23074515/Employers_Use_of_Migrant_Labour_Main_Report; Roger Waldinger and Michael Lichter, *How the Other Half Works: Immigration and the Social Organization of Labor* (Berkeley: University of California Press, 2003).

22 Jennifer Gordon and Robin Lenhardt, "Rethinking Work and Citizenship," UCLA *Law Review* 55 (2008): 1161–238.

23 Brett Neilson and Sandro Mezzadra, *Border as Method, or, The Multiplication of Labor* (Durham, NC: Duke University Press, 2013).

24 Biao Xiang, *Global Body Shopping: An Indian Labour System in the Information Technology Industry* (Princeton, NJ: Princeton University Press, 2007).

25 "Employer's Guide," Home Office Guidance, 2016, accessed November 5, 2017, https://www.gov.uk/government/uploads/system/uploads/attachment_data/file/571001/Employer_s_guide_.

26 Adrian Bailey et al., "(Re)Producing Salvadoran Transnational Geographies," *Annals of the Association of American Geographers* 92 (2002): 125–44; Jennifer Simmelink, "Temporary Citizens: U.S. Immigration Law and Liberian Refugees," *Journal of Immigrant and Refugee Studies* 9 (2011): 327–44.

27 Carolina Kobelinsky, "Waiting: Asylum Seekers in France," paper presented at the 9th European Association of Social Anthropologists Biennial Conference: Migration and Europe Workshop, Bristol, UK, September 18–21, 2006.

28 Craig Jeffrey, "Timepass: Youth, Class, and Time among Unemployed Young Men in India," *American Ethnologist* 37 (2010): 465–81.

29 Reuben Andersson, "Time and the Migrant Other: European Border Controls and the Temporal Economics of Illegality," *American Anthropologist* 116 (2014): 805.

30 Anderson, *Doing the Dirty Work?*

31 Bridget Anderson, Margaret Healy, and Vanessa Hughes, *Better Off with Us!* (London: Unite the Union, 2017).

32 Anderson et al., *Better Off with Us!*

33 Anderson et al., *Better Off with Us!*

34 Joseph Carens, *The Ethics of Immigration Controls* (New York: Oxford University Press, 2013).

35 Robert Pallitto and Josiah Heyman, "Theorizing Cross-Border Mobility: Surveillance, Security and Identity," *Surveillance and Society* 5 (2008): 316.

36 Anderson, *Us and Them?*; John Torpey, *The Invention of the Passport: Surveillance, Citizenship and the State* (Cambridge: Cambridge University Press, 1999).

Bibliography

Adam, Barbara. *Time and Social Theory.* Cambridge: Polity, 1994.

Aliverti, Ana. *Crimes of Mobility: Criminal Law and the Regulation of Immigration.* Abingdon, UK: Routledge, 2014.

Anderson, Bridget. *Doing the Dirty Work? The Global Politics of Domestic Labour.* London: Zed, 2000.

Anderson, Bridget. *Us and Them? The Dangerous Politics of Immigration Control.* Oxford: Oxford University Press, 2013.

Anderson, Bridget, Margaret Healy, and Vanessa Hughes. *Better Off with Us!* London: Unite the Union, 2017.

Andersson, Ruben. "Time and the Migrant Other: European Border Controls and the Temporal Economics of Illegality." *American Anthropologist* 116 (2014): 795–809.

Bailey, Adrian J., Richard Wright, Alison Mountz, and Ines Miyares. "(Re)Producing Salvadoran Transnational Geographies." *Annals of the Association of American Geographers* 92 (2002): 125–44.

Carens, Joseph. *The Ethics of Immigration Controls.* New York: Oxford University Press, 2013.

Cwerner, Saulo. "The Times of Migration." *Journal of Ethnic and Migration Studies* 27 (2001): 7–36.

Dench, Sally, Jennifer Hurstfield, Darcy Hill, and Karen Akroyd. *Employers' Use of Migrant Labour.* London: Home Office Online Report, 2006. Accessed November 5, 2018. https://www.academia.edu/23074515/Employers_Use_of_Migrant_Labour_Main_Report.

Drayton, Richard. "Imperial History and the Human Future." *History Workshop Journal* 74 (2012): 156–72.

Freeman, Richard, and Jo Maybin. "Documents, Practices and Policy." *Evidence and Policy: A Journal of Research, Debate and Practice* 7 (2011): 155–70.

Giddens, Anthony. *The Constitution of Society: Outline of the Theory of Structuration.* Cambridge: Polity, 1984.

Gordon, Jennifer, and Robin Lenhardt. "Rethinking Work and Citizenship." *UCLA Law Review* 55 (2008): 1161–238.

Griffiths, Melanie, Ali Rogers, and Bridget Anderson. "Migration, Time and Temporalities: Review and Prospect." *COMPAS Research Paper.* Oxford: University of Oxford, 2013.

Griggs, Mary. "Time Is Understood Very Differently in Different Cultures." *Popular Science,* September 6, 2017. Accessed November 5, 2017. https://www.popsci.com/what-time-looks-like-to-different-cultures.

Gross, David. "Temporality and the Modern State." *Theory and Society* 14 (1985): 53–82.

Hagerstrand, Torsten. "What about People in Regional Science?" *Papers in Regional Science* 24 (1970): 6–21.

Heyman, Josiah. "Capitalism and US Policy at the Mexican Border." *Dialectical Anthropology* 36 (2012): 263–77.

Jeffrey, Craig. "Timepass: Youth, Class, and Time among Unemployed Young Men in India." *American Ethnologist* 37 (2010): 465–81.

King, Russell, Mark Thomson, Anthony Fielding, and Anthony Warnes. "Gender, Age and Generations: State of the Art." *IMISCOE Working Paper.* Sussex: Centre for Migration and Population Studies, University of Sussex, 2004.

Kobelinsky, Carolina. "Waiting: Asylum Seekers in France." Paper presented at the Ninth EASA Biennial Conference: Migration and Europe Workshop, Bristol, UK, September 18–21, 2006.

Mavroudi, Elizabeth, Ben Page, and Anastasia Christou, eds. *Timespace and International Migration.* London: Edward Elgar, 2017.

Migration Observatory. "Here Today Gone Tomorrow: The Status of EU Citizens Already Living in the UK." *Migration Observatory Commentaries,* 2016. Accessed October 10, 2017. https://www.Migrationobservatory.ox.ac.uk/resources/commentaries/today-gone-tomorrow-status-eu-citizens-already-living-uk/.

Neilson, Brett, and Sandro Mezzadra. *Border as Method, or, The Multiplication of Labor.* Durham, NC: Duke University Press, 2013.

Nowotny, Helga. *Time: The Modern and Postmodern Experience.* Cambridge: Polity, 1994.

Pallitto, Robert, and Josiah Heyman. "Theorizing Cross-Border Mobility: Surveillance, Security and Identity." *Surveillance and Society* 5 (2008): 315–33.

Piore, Michael. *Birds of Passage: Migrant Labor and Industrial Societies.* Cambridge: Cambridge University Press, 1979.

Sandbothe, Mike. "Media Temporalities of the Internet: Philosophies of Time and Media in Derrida and Rorty." *AI and Society* 13 (1999): 421–34.

Simmelink, Jennifer. "Temporary Citizens: U.S. Immigration Law and Liberian Refugees." *Journal of Immigrant and Refugee Studies* 9 (2011): 327–44.

Stendahl, Sara. "To Reside: To Live, Be Present, Belong." *European Journal of Social Security* 18 (2016): 232–45.

Thompson, Edward P. "Time, Work-Discipline, and Industrial Capitalism." *Past and Present* 38 (1967): 56–97.

Ticktin, Miriam. "Invasive Others: Towards a Contaminated World." *Social Research: An International Quarterly* 84 (2016): xxi–xxxiv.

Torpey, John. *The Invention of the Passport: Surveillance, Citizenship and the State.* Cambridge: Cambridge University Press, 1999.

Waldinger, Roger, and Michael Lichter. *How the Other Half Works: Immigration and the Social Organization of Labor.* Berkeley: University of California Press, 2003.

Xiang, Biao. *Global Body Shopping: An Indian Labour System in the Information Technology Industry.* Princeton, NJ: Princeton University Press, 2007.

Yngvesson, Barbara, and Susan Bibler Coutin. "Backed by Papers: Undoing Persons, Histories, and Return." *American Ethnologist* 33 (2006): 177–90.

DORIS MARIE PROVINE AND MONICA W. VARSANYI

3

DOCUMENTING MEMBERSHIP

The Divergent Politics of Migrant Driver's Licenses
in New Mexico and Arizona

The legal status of migrants in the United States is spatially contingent to a degree unacknowledged in federal immigration law, which presumes a uniform standard under federal control. The lived reality of migrants, particularly those without secure legal status, arises out of a patchwork of state and municipal laws. These laws tell a story of differential inclusion based on prevailing local beliefs about membership and its privileges. State governments have no direct power over immigration policy or its enforcement, but they do have law-making powers that can be used to signal inclusion or rejection of noncitizen residents. Those powers include the right to regulate health and safety matters within their jurisdiction, including the issuance of driver's licenses.

As congressional immigration reform has stalled in recent decades, states and cities have become increasingly active in making immigration policy or, more accurately, making policies that impact immigrants living in their jurisdictions. Some states have taken an integrative approach, attempting to protect migrants from deportation by ignoring legal status whenever possible and by declining federal invitations to help enforce immigration law. These state and local legislatures are signaling acceptance of resident migrants and their families as de facto members of their local communities. They are rejecting the federal government's commitment to creating categories of membership and to regulating the right to stay in those terms.

Some states have taken the opposite approach. Among their strategies is the inclusion of proof of legal status among the bureaucratic requirements to receive benefits or to avoid being reported to federal immigration authorities. This is one variety of "immigration policing through the back door."[1] Under the "back door" approach, any reference to migrants or immigration policy is avoided, as states and localities don't have direct power over immigration. Legal status requirements become the watchword for these regulatory initiatives. The goal is clear: to encourage unauthorized migrants to "self-deport."

The issuance of driver's licenses has become a central tool in the effort to encourage unauthorized immigrants to leave. Inability to get a driver's license does more than discourage a sense of civic membership and make getting car insurance more difficult. It also puts immigrants without secure legal status at risk of deportation. Local law enforcement agencies, in their traffic-control work, can easily become the first stage in the deportation process. Federal and state laws passed since the mid-1990s have enabled local police to become involved in immigration enforcement, giving rise to what some authors have called "crimmigration," or the increasing convergence of criminal and immigration law.[2] Within this changing context, routine interactions with police while driving or otherwise navigating through communities without a driver's license can result in deportation and achieve "attrition through enforcement."[3]

As a result, driver's licenses are an obvious choice for our investigation. At a basic level, a driver's license is simply a license to drive a motor vehicle. Having a driver's license certifies that a state resident has learned the rules of the road, passed a driving test, and obtained auto insurance (including liability insurance and uninsured motorist coverage in many states). But in the United States, where driving is ubiquitous and almost a necessity, a license to drive can be considered more akin to a basic right. Driving also signifies power over machine and space and offers pleasure as well as convenience.

In a country without a national identification card, however, driver's licenses offer a workable substitute. They are a near-essential document for many purposes. Residents are asked to present a driver's license or other government-authorized picture identification document when engaging with law enforcement, making purchases with credit cards, accessing government benefits, receiving certified mail, buying alcohol or cigarettes, enrolling children in school, applying for many jobs, renting a house or apartment, boarding an airplane, entering a state or federal facility, buying a cell phone, applying for a marriage license, picking up theater tickets, and much more. They are also a "breeder" document, facilitating the creation of other identifying documents, as discussed in Horton's chapter in this book. As the primary means of accessing and navigating so many services, the driver's license is a powerful symbol of legitimate membership in local, state, and (given some federal requirements) national communities.

For that reason, documentary requirements for driver's licenses are an obvious tool for state legislatures that seek to have an impact on immigrants in their jurisdiction and on immigration policy more generally. By targeting the most commonly relied-upon identification document in the United States, state legislators have incorporated retail outlets, real estate agents, bank tellers, employers, and street-level bureaucrats of every description into the process of immigration control, as Menjívar's chapter in this book shows, thus drastically extending "the disciplinary arm of the state."

What explains whether states accept or resist the federal push to deport all unauthorized residents? A considerable body of scholarship has developed to explain state-by-state differences, mostly using quantitative methods that search for answers in available measures of state-level characteristics like crime rates and percentage of migrants in the local population.[4] Our approach is different. We focus on the most crucial document that states can control to signal their attitude toward immigrants, particularly those residents lacking secure legal status. We argue that analyzing the criteria that states set down through documentary requirements is a more promising, and more direct, approach to understanding "immigration policing through the back door" than attempting to draw conclusions about state attitudes from demographic or other environmental measures.

Comparison across states is an essential aspect of our methodology. We have chosen two neighboring states, Arizona and New Mexico, that have developed vastly different relationships with resident unauthorized migrants. Located in the southwestern desert region of the United States, these states share a common geographical history. They were, to a large extent, part of the same jurisdictional territory in the mid-1800s. They attained statehood the same year (1912), and both states border Mexico as well as each other. Yet New Mexico and Arizona have taken significantly divergent paths in the realm of migrant policy over the past decade, and they differ dramatically in their approaches to driver's licenses for unauthorized migrants. Arizona has espoused a draconian, anti-migrant, enforcement-oriented model and has sought to restrict migrants' access to driver's licenses, whereas New Mexico has followed a pro-migrant incorporation model and has maintained driving access for unauthorized migrants, intense political debate notwithstanding. In our broader research, we explore the historical roots of this divergence arising out of each state's distinct demographic, political, and economic trajectory throughout the twentieth century.[5] In this chapter, however, we highlight the impact of these divergent state trajectories by focusing on access to driver's licenses.

In both Arizona and New Mexico, the policy path is relatively short. Until the 1990s, unauthorized migrants were able to obtain driver's licenses in all states without question; immigration status was not considered to be a legitimate concern for motor vehicle departments, whose primary mission is to protect safety on the roads and to promote safe driving. In 1993, however, California outlawed driver's licenses for unauthorized migrants. Arizona followed suit in 1996, the same year Congress passed major legislation aimed at discouraging illegal immigration. Shortly thereafter, particularly after the 9/11 terrorist attacks, almost all states enacted similar restrictions. By 2002, the only states that still extended driver's licenses to unauthorized migrants were New Mexico and Washington. They were joined by Utah in 2005. The tide began to turn in 2013, and currently twelve states and the District of Columbia have enacted provisions extending driving privileges (but not full-fledged licenses) to their unauthorized residents.[6]

The situation grew more complicated in 2005, with the passage of the federal REAL ID Act, which places restrictions on the state issuance of driver's licenses. Under REAL ID, states are prohibited from providing unauthorized migrants with driver's licenses that can be used as an official form of government-issued identification. With this new law, a complex negotiation began between the state and federal levels, with each level leveraging the tools at its disposal. States seeking to discourage unauthorized immigration have relied upon their non-immigration-related ("back door") policy power to issue driver's licenses, while the federal government has relied on its national security mandate and its plenary power over immigration to enter, for the first time, this previously state-level arena.

The debates that have accompanied this era of shifting policy on driver's licenses neatly illustrate the themes that animate contemporary debates over migrant membership. On one side of the argument, as it often plays out in our current highly polarized political context, are those who see driving privileges as simply *reflecting* the reality that unauthorized migrants are a fixture in American society. Proponents of this view tend to espouse liberal ideals of inclusivity and to readily acknowledge labor-market realities. Their public policy perspective emphasizes the de facto presence of individuals of varying legal statuses, and the need, for the sake of everyone's safety in public, for all drivers to learn the rules of the road and to be insured as they drive to work, school, and the grocery store. In contrast, opponents see the issue from a politically charged perspective in which licensing unauthorized migrants to drive *produces* a claim to membership. Granting a state-controlled privilege to people with no legal right to remain is anathema for those whose ethical framework is more law-and-order, de jure, by-the-book, and sympathetic to the catchphrase "What part of illegal don't you understand?" That lack of a driver's license might result in deportation seems only just from this perspective.

The conflict between these polarized perspectives is evident in a variety of state and local debates: over sanctuary cities, access to public education, and access to other publicly funded programs, such as children's health insurance. In these politically divisive times, therefore, the fundamental issue in each case has tended to boil down to opposing visions of what government bureaucracies do when they extend benefits: Are they accepting the realities of a shared existence? Or are they creating a form of quasi-citizenship that is a magnet for unauthorized immigration?

Racial antipathies complicate this conflict. The face of an unauthorized migrant in the Southwest, for most residents, is Latino, and specifically Mexican. Prevailing assumptions about the class, cultural, and language differences associated with Mexican heritage and lack of legal status help frame ideas about membership. Advocates on either side of the driver's license controversy make differing assumptions about the impact of these differences on their communities, and about what those differences are. The proximity of Mexico and its historic association with the United States and U.S. territory adds another dimension to anxieties about difference that play out in complicated ways in disputes like this one.

In the sections that follow we apply a documentary lens to driver's license controversies, using debates surrounding changes in the law to explore differing ideas about belonging and the role of law in setting boundaries on membership. New Mexico and Arizona offer a convenient point of comparison, but the issues raised in these local disputes have a global dimension in an era of increased human mobility and growing concern about its impact, in accord with Anderson's chapter in this book. Documents are at the center of every state's efforts to maintain boundaries. At the most basic level, they determine who is in the country without authorization, and therefore subject to arrest and possible deportation. This form of government surveillance is growing, as can be seen by the proliferation of documents in migrant lives, the growing number of categories of membership, and the growing number of occasions in which documents, including driver's licenses, must be made available in both public and private sectors.

New Mexico: Public Safety First

The issue of legal status requirements for driver's licenses was a nonissue in New Mexico until 1996, when the federal government adopted the 1996 Illegal Immigration Reform and Immigrant Responsibility Act. This new federal law required applicants for driver's licenses to submit valid social security numbers, with the stated purpose of tracking down "deadbeat dads" who shirked their child-support responsibilities.[7] New Mexico adopted the new requirement without considering the likely impact on the ability to buy auto insurance, which generally requires a driver's license. Soon, the rates of uninsured motorists skyrocketed in New Mexico, reaching one of the highest per capita levels in the nation. By the early 2000s, there was a movement afoot to change the law. In the summer of 2001, at the prompting of the auto insurance industry, the New Mexico Taxation and Revenue Service announced that it would issue driver's licenses to migrants without social security numbers as soon as the state legislature adopted authorizing legislation. Whereas almost all states restricted access to driver's licenses after the attacks of September 11, 2001, New Mexico moved ahead with its plans to extend driver's licenses to legal permanent residents who didn't have social security numbers. The legislature obliged in its next session, and Governor Gary Johnson, a Democrat, signed the law into effect in May 2002. The adoption of this law was noncontroversial in New Mexico.

In early 2003, New Mexico representative Miguel Garcia (D-Albuquerque) moved to extend driver's licenses to all individuals without social security numbers. He sponsored a bill to allow those with individual taxpayer identification numbers (ITINs)—typically unauthorized migrants or workers on a nonmigrant visa—to obtain driver's licenses. Garcia noted, "I had observed that many migrant parents would bring their children to school in a vehicle, yet they were not licensed to drive."[8] Here Garcia introduced the dominant theme that has continued to motivate proponents of migrant driver's licenses into the present: public safety. At the time, New Mexico still had one of the highest rates of uninsured drivers in the United States, approximately 25 percent. Proponents of the law argued that allowing migrants to obtain licenses was common sense, as this would enable them to take the driver's test, to be properly trained in the rules of the road, and, importantly, to purchase car insurance.

In the post-9/11 environment, Garcia's proposal encountered opposition based on national security concerns. Opponents of the measure connected unauthorized immigration to the threat of terrorism, arguing that issuing driver's licenses to unauthorized migrants would "make New Mexico a haven for terrorists."[9] This argument apparently swayed few legislators. Garcia's bill passed without significant controversy and was signed into law in June 2003 by newly elected Democratic governor Bill Richardson. In 2003, therefore, New Mexico became one of two states in the nation to offer driver's licenses to residents without legal status.

The tension between the public safety and national security camps arose again, more vociferously, during the 2005 legislative session. Articulating the dangers of issuing driver's licenses to noncitizens, Representatives Greg Payne (R-Albuquerque) and Keith Gardner (R-Roswell) proposed a plan that would allow unauthorized migrants to be issued a "certificate for driving," as opposed to a full-fledged driver's license. The certificate would serve as a state-sanctioned form of identification. According to Payne and Gardner, creating this two-tier driver's license system was a "key component of protecting the homeland in a post 9-11 world."[10] The bill ended up dying in the House and was not considered by the Senate. It received no support from Governor Richardson, who stated (through a spokesman): "The driver's license program in place is successful and has reduced the number of uninsured drivers in New Mexico."[11]

Congress's adoption of the REAL ID Act in 2005 added a new dimension to the New Mexico political scene. REAL ID prohibits issuing driver's licenses to unauthorized migrants, placing it in direct conflict with New Mexico law. Reaction to the REAL ID Act was particularly swift in the state capital of Santa Fe, a Democratic stronghold. In July 2005, backed by the Santa Fe Police Department and members of Somos un Pueblo Unido, the state's most prominent migrant rights organization, the Santa Fe City Council adopted a resolution declaring its opposition to this new federal law. The resolution asserted that allowing migrants to apply for driver's licenses was a benefit to the state, not a security threat. During a presentation on the resolution before the city council, Santa Fe's police chief, Beverly Lennen, argued that allowing migrants to hold driver's licenses enabled the police to better identify those with whom they come into contact. Only one councilor opposed the measure, arguing that the 9/11 hijackers had driver's licenses that enabled them to board planes, and that New Mexico, in continuing to issue driver's licenses to unauthorized migrants, threatened national security. In response, City Councilor Karen Heldmeyer retorted, "Everyone opposes terrorism. In New Mexico, you are demonstrably at greater risk from unlicensed and unregistered drivers than from terrorists."[12]

By the end of 2005, over 20,000 driver's licenses had been issued to migrants throughout the state, without regard to legal status. Washington State was the only other state extending full-fledged driver's licenses to unauthorized residents. Utah had passed a law that year allowing unauthorized residents to apply for a "driving privilege card" similar to the one proposed by Representatives Payne and Gardner during the 2005 New Mexico legislative session.

Security issues around driver's licenses were not entirely absent in this period. In 2003, Governor Richardson responded to concerns about fraud with an administrative rule that required foreign nationals applying for driver's licenses to present two forms of identification instead of the previous one. Yet this change was conceived and promoted not as an attack on unauthorized migrants, but simply as a security measure. Governor Richardson remained a strong supporter of migrants in his state throughout his administration. For example, during a 2007 televised debate when he was briefly considering a run for the Democratic presidential nomination, he responded to a point about immigration by stating, "You know what? We should stop demonizing migrants."[13]

Richardson's position and the welcoming environment of New Mexico, broadly speaking, stood in stark contrast to the anti-migrant climate simmering in surrounding states. At the same time that New Mexico was licensing migrant drivers regardless of legal status, Arizona, Oklahoma, and Colorado were passing anti-migrant laws seeking "attrition through enforcement." Both Oklahoma and Colorado adopted legislation denying unauthorized migrants driver's licenses and all public benefits, including state-funded welfare payments, health benefits, and unemployment compensation. Colorado and Arizona also passed laws barring unauthorized students from paying in-state tuition at public colleges and universities.[14]

In New Mexico, security issues took on more concrete dimensions in 2008 when local law enforcement unearthed a number of high-profile driver's license fraud rings. These schemes brought foreigners from out of state—and sometimes from countries as far away as China—to fraudulently obtain driver's licenses in New Mexico, typically at a significant price. In one case, Russian migrants brought Brazilian migrants from Newark airport to Albuquerque to obtain licenses. In another, a want ad was discovered in a Chicago-area Polish-language newspaper, stating: "Driver's license in the State of New Mexico. Social Security not necessary. 100% guarantee."[15]

Law enforcement agencies throughout the state took contradictory stances on how to proceed. The Santa Fe Police Department maintained its support for the 2003 law on public safety grounds. The Albuquerque Police Department, in response to a lawsuit filed by the Mexican American Legal Defense and Education Fund (MALDEF), a prominent national Latino-rights organization, issued new procedures in 2007 limiting the power of its officers to inquire about the immigration status of persons in custody or under investigation.[16] In stark contrast, sheriffs in the southern counties of Otero and Doña Ana were forging tighter relationships with the federal government under the auspices of Operation Stonegarden, which funnels federal dollars to counties near the border in the service of national security goals, focusing specifically on anti-narcotics and anti-migrant smuggling efforts. Most often, this involved sheriffs' deputies setting up roadblocks near the U.S.-Mexico border.[17] The 2010 election of Republican Susana Martinez as governor altered this relatively low-key, localized dynamic. The issue was ripe for broader debate. A 2010 *Albuquerque Journal* poll reported that 72 percent of U.S. citizens living in New Mexico were opposed to the 2003 driver's license law. Making the matter more complicated was the fact that by that year 50,000 licenses had been issued to foreign nationals in the state[18] and that the federal REAL ID law would soon be forcing New Mexico to make changes in its law.

Newly elected Governor Martinez made repealing the 2003 law a centerpiece of her legislative agenda for 2011. This precipitated a long-standing battle with the Democratic-controlled state legislature. With that debate, the driver's license issue in New Mexico became deeply polarizing and almost entirely partisan—a matter of politics, not policy.

The first salvo in the battle came during the regular legislative session in January 2011, just after Governor Martinez was sworn in. Members of the House Labor and Human Resources Committee voted along party lines, 5–4, to table a measure that would have required the now 83,000 foreign nationals with licenses to turn them in for a one-year driving permit or face revocation. Later in the session, after a seven-hour debate, the full House voted to overturn the 2003 law. This decision had the support of all House Republicans and seven Democrats. Following the vote, Representative Andy Nuñez (I-Hatch) echoed their sentiments: "We are sitting here aiding and abetting people who are breaking federal law."[19] Almost simultaneously, however, the state Senate passed a bill allowing unauthorized residents to keep their licenses, but beefing up security measures for obtaining them in the future. Ultimately, the bills could not be reconciled, and as the legislative session ended without any progress, Martinez reiterated her position: "I promised the people of New Mexico that I will fight to repeal this law, and that fight will continue."[20] As part of that effort, she called a special legislative session in the fall of 2011.

That summer, another fraud ring came to light, this time involving a group smuggling heroin as well as obtaining fraudulent driver's licenses for foreign nationals. Governor Martinez announced that she would look for ways to tighten administrative requirements for noncitizens applying for driver's licenses if she was unable to force repeal of the 2003 law. Her first action was to announce a new program to verify the residency of 10,000 randomly selected noncitizen recipients of the now 85,000 New Mexico licenses that had been issued. Verification would require an in-person visit to Albuquerque or Santa Fe.

This proposal raised an unusual problem. The governor would have to find a way to accommodate unauthorized migrants living in the border region who could not drive north to Albuquerque or Santa Fe without serious risk of being stopped along the way by the U.S. Border Patrol.[21] Soon after letters announcing the new requirements began to appear, MALDEF filed suit in federal court to stop implementation. On September 1, 2011, a judge halted the program.

During this period, the state's powerful Catholic bishops also entered the debate. Santa Fe Archbishop Michael Sheehan, Las Cruces Bishop Ricardo Ramírez, and Gallup Bishop James Wall signed a statement in favor of keeping the 2003 law, titled: "Licenses for All Drivers: A Matter of Mercy, Fairness and Safety." They argued that providing licenses for all drivers in the state, regardless of legal status, would ensure public safety and provide a means for law enforcement to keep track of individuals. If migrant drivers were denied licenses, they "would not be able to travel to their places of employment, undermining the economic stability of their families as well as the many New Mexico businesses, farms, and ranches that depend on their labor."[22] Bishop Sheehan was later quoted as saying, "Priests do not make laws; we know that. Legislators make laws. But when laws have a moral or ethical dimension, we offer our teachings."[23] Governor Martinez, frustrated by her defeat in the courts, hoped for support from the state legislature in the fall special session she had called. Much to her dismay, however, the session resulted in no new legislation concerning eligibility for driver's licenses.

In the following year, 2012, police discovered three more driver's license fraud rings, and the battle between the governor and the legislature wore on. The issue was becoming entangled with concerns about unauthorized immigration, a new issue in New Mexico politics. Though Governor Martinez's staff continued to maintain that "this has never been an immigration issue. . . . This is simply about public safety and security,"[24] others disagreed, arguing that driver's licenses had become a lightning rod for growing anti-migrant sentiment in the state. According to Allen Sanchez, executive director of the New Mexico Conference of Catholic Bishops: "These efforts are creating anti-migrant sentiments, and it's destructive to us as a community."[25] Santa Fe mayor David Coss echoed Sanchez in discussing one bill supported by the governor: "The bill is divisive. The bill is anti-migrant. And the bill is bad for New Mexico."[26] The 2012 legislative session ended without action. As it had in 2011, the House Labor and Human Resources Committee tabled a measure that would have repealed the 2003 law.

The federal government's deadlines for compliance with REAL ID licensing requirements gave Governor Martinez a new angle to press for change. She announced that starting in 2016, individuals from states that were not REAL ID–compliant would not be able to board airplanes or use their driver's licenses to enter the many federal facilities in the state. She also benefited from support from county sheriffs throughout the state. Sheriffs from all thirty-three counties (all elected officials) joined the effort to repeal the 2003 law. The governor's REAL ID argument, however, drew opposition. Pete Simonson, executive director of the New Mexico ACLU affiliate, argued that the governor's attempts to link noncitizen driver's licenses to REAL ID was a straw man and "a scare tactic meant to advance her agenda of dismantling New Mexico's drivers' license law."[27] He and others argued that the federal law was "practically defunct" because a large number of states had not complied with its requirements.[28] Neither Martinez nor Simonson was entirely correct. New Mexico had filed for a waiver and therefore would not be subject to the early deadlines as Arizona was. But Simonson was overoptimistic about the "defunct" nature of REAL ID, as events in Arizona were to show.

Despite, or perhaps because of REAL ID, the political winds across the United States were starting to shift toward driving privileges for unauthorized migrants. REAL ID allowed states to issue a limited-use driving permit to anyone it deemed qualified, but this document had to clearly state that it could not be used as an identification for federal purposes. This two-tier approach offered a way out for some states attempting to satisfy competing constituencies. At the beginning of the 2013 state legislative season, only three states—Washington, New Mexico, and Utah—were issuing licenses or driving privilege cards to migrants without regard to legal status. But that year seven additional states changed their policies to grant driving privileges to unauthorized migrants: Illinois, Maryland, Oregon, Nevada, Colorado, Vermont, and Connecticut. Bills to expand access were introduced in at least nineteen states that year, as well as the District of Columbia and Puerto Rico. New Mexico was starting to look as if it were in the vanguard, as opposed to hopelessly behind the times.

Positions on whether New Mexico should issue migrants driver's licenses seemed to be frozen in partisan blocs. A poll run in 2012 by the conservative *Albuquerque Journal* reported that 71 percent of the electorate was opposed to the 2003 law,[29] while a poll from America's Voice/Latino Decisions,[30] a research center at the University of New Mexico, reported that 70 percent of Hispanic voters in New Mexico favored driver's licenses for migrants (albeit with some enhanced security provisions). With Democrats in control of both legislative chambers and steadfast in their support of the 2003 law, Governor Martinez could not move forward in attempting to repeal the 2003 law. The situation forced her to shift the way she spoke about the issue. Co-opting the language of her opponents, and perhaps reflecting the declining resonance of national-security arguments, she reframed the repeal argument as a "public safety" issue. So "public safety" now meant two things, depending on the audience: to Republicans, "public safety" referred to fraud prevention and, secondarily, to national security. Governor Martinez reinforced this perspective in responding to the discovery of yet another fraud ring: "New Mexico's driver's license policy has once again attracted criminal elements to our state in pursuit of a government-issued identification card. Our current system jeopardizes the safety and security of all New Mexicans and it is abundantly clear that the only way to solve this problem is to repeal the law that gives driver's licenses to illegal migrants."[31]

For Democrats supporting the 2003 law, "public safety" had always meant safety on the roads and the ability to buy car insurance regardless of legal status. Marcela Díaz, executive director of Somos un Pueblo Unido and a frequent voice in the driver's license debate, framed the issue in these terms: "Many of these folks have U.S. citizen children who depend on their parents' ability to drive them around legally, be insured, register their vehicle, have an identification for purposes of picking up medication for their kids. These driver's licenses are a good thing, not just for our community, but a good thing for the state."[32]

Compromise, however, was in the air in the 2013 session. Reflecting the national shift toward two-tier driver's licensing schemes, state Senator Pete Campos (D-Las Vegas) reintroduced a two-tier driver's license system, and the governor indicated that she might be amenable to this approach. In the past, she had promised to veto any measure that did not involve an outright repeal of the 2003 law. Her willingness to tolerate a two-tier approach did not extend to softening her remarks linking unauthorized immigration to crime and dependency. As Martinez's reelection efforts heated up, she increasingly framed the driver's license debate in immigration terms. As her campaign literature noted, "Governor Martinez has been working extremely hard to end the policy of our state granting driver's licenses to illegal migrants. This is a public safety issue that puts our communities at risk and makes New Mexico a magnet for illegal migrants."[33] She also portrayed her gubernatorial opponent, Democrat Gary King, as pro–illegal immigration and soft on border security: "Gary King's plan for border security: Keep giving illegal migrants driver's licenses. Every day, thousands of illegal migrants cross our borders and we're left holding the bag."[34]

No driver's license legislation passed in the 2013, 2014, or 2015 legislative sessions, but the debates raged on. Representative Bill Rehm (R-Albuquerque), favoring the two-tier approach, claimed support from the New Mexico Sheriffs' Association and the state Fraternal Order of Police.[35] Representative Javier Martinez (D-Albuquerque) maintained his support for the 2003 law as a public safety measure: "When we punish an unauthorized migrant for nothing more than wanting to provide for their children . . . you punish every single one of us. So stop playing politics with our families. Stop playing politics with our kids' lives. Stop punishing us."[36]

The Republicans remained in control of the state House of Representatives during the 2016 legislative session, making resolution of the driver's license debate unlikely. But the federal government brought the matter to a head. After years of accepting waivers from states to avoid conflict over the unpopular law, it set January 10, 2016, as the final deadline for REAL ID compliance. After this date, individuals from states without REAL ID–compliant licenses would not be able to board airplanes or access federal facilities—no small matter in New Mexico, which ranks first in the nation in dependency on federal funding.[37]

This deadline kicked compromise into action. A deal was finally reached that created a two-tier system: New Mexicans would be able to apply for a newly enhanced, REAL ID–compliant license by providing documents that demonstrated their legal status (i.e., birth certificates, documents with social security numbers), and unauthorized migrants or others who did not want a REAL ID–compliant license would now have access to a "driving authorization card." The most controversial aspect of this two-tier system was that individuals applying for the driving authorization card for the first time were required to submit fingerprints and undergo a background check, thus making them increasingly legible to the state. Additionally, advocates expressed concern that the documentation required to obtain the card, such as a birth certificate, might be hard for some to provide[38] and that police may not be properly trained in how to handle driving authorization cards and might treat holders differently than those with REAL ID–compliant licenses.[39] Signing the bill, Governor Martinez brushed aside her anti-migrant rhetoric of prior years: "This has never been an immigration bill—it's always been a public safety bill."[40]

Arizona: Politics Trumps Public Policy

In Arizona, as in New Mexico, legal status requirements for driver's licenses were, for most of the state's history, a nonissue. Public safety was the key criterion for evaluating the administration of the traffic laws and the Motor Vehicle Division (MVD). In the words of a 1988 performance audit: "The driver's license program is responsible for ensuring the safety of the general public on the streets and highways of this state."[41] In pursuit of that goal, the report explained, it is charged with testing applicants, issuing driver's licenses, and removing unsafe drivers from the road. There is no mention of migrants in this exhaustive report.

The hands-off policy toward unauthorized-migrant drivers was reversed in April 1996 when Governor Fife Symington signed HB 2154. The Arizona Revised Statutes were amended to read:

> Notwithstanding any other law, the department shall not issue to or renew a driver license or non-operating identification license for a person who does not submit proof satisfactory to the department that the applicant's presence in the United States is authorized under federal law. The director shall adopt rules necessary to carry out the purposes of this subsection. The rules shall include procedures for:
>
> 1 Verification that the applicant's presence in the United States is authorized under federal law.
> 2 Issuance of a temporary driver permit pursuant to section 28-3157 pending verification of the applicant's status in the United States.[42]

Arizona's new law, it should be noted, was adopted six months before Congress made the first tentative move toward encouraging legal-status restrictions on state driver's licenses in the Illegal Immigration Reform and Immigrant

Responsibility Act of 1996, with its requirement (noted above) that applicants for a driver's license submit a valid social security number. In midsummer 1996, when Arizona's law took effect, the MVD immediately began turning away license applicants who could not prove their legal status.

Reaction to the legislation was swift. By the final months of 1996, the number of driver's license applications had fallen by 160,000, according to a spokesperson for the Arizona Motor Vehicle Division. Insurance became harder to obtain, creating incentives for drivers involved in accidents to flee the scene. Emilia Bañuelos, an immigration attorney, said in a 2000 statement: "It's happening all the time where the crashes involve [unauthorized migrants] with no insurance and they flee the scene." The law also, she explained, created a market for false identification and turned motor vehicle employees into immigration agents: "Applicants of Hispanic origin are consistently being interrogated and questioned about their documentation."[43]

HB 2154 was drafted by the director of the MVD, Russell Pearce, a man who would later become famous in the state and beyond for his harsh attitude toward resident unauthorized migrants. Elected four years later to the Arizona House of Representatives, Pearce quickly became the leading advocate of the policy of "attrition through enforcement." During his first year as a lawmaker, he proposed two anti-migrant bills that failed. His clout grew over time as he continued to revise and reintroduce bills to discourage unauthorized residents from staying in the state. By 2010, he had become president of the state Senate and was widely regarded as one of the state's most powerful political figures. It was at this point that he helped to craft and promote SB 1070, Arizona's now-famous policy of using local policing to push for more aggressive federal enforcement efforts against unauthorized migrants, and to establish the state's policy as "attrition through enforcement." This achievement, however, may have been the key to his eventual downfall. In 2013, he became the first legislator in the state's history to be recalled via a citizen's initiative.

The personal link between HB 2154 in 1996 and SB 1070 in 2010 reinforces the intuition that by 1996 "attrition through enforcement" was already the mind-set of key legislative leaders in the state. Without state-issued identification, non-status migrants were vulnerable to arrest for any traffic infraction. Such arrests involve booking in the local jail to establish identification, potentially precipitating a chain of events that could lead to deportation. As one critic commented: "As with the recent federal legislation denying soc sec [sic] benefits to LEGAL aliens who are required by law to pay into the system and can by law be required to serve in the US armed forces, this appears to my untrained eye to be yet another case of isolationist paranoia. I despair of backwater state legislators, I really do."[44]

The reasoning behind this new law also represented a reweighing of the state's traditional priorities. In place of the old goal of maximizing public safety by effectively regulating driver's licenses, the new goal was to increase the vulnerability of one element of the population, even at some cost to overall public safety. No state legislator could have believed that all unauthorized migrants would cease driving when their existing driver's licenses expired. Obviously, the number of hit-and-run accidents would rise and cooperation with local police would decline. Some drivers would be less familiar with the rules of the road. These apparently were perceived as costs worth bearing in the name of reducing the tendency of unauthorized migrants to settle in the state.

Senator Joe Eddie Lopez, a Democrat from Arizona's heavily Democratic and Latino House District 22, responded in the next legislative session with a bill, SB 1382, which simply canceled the new language. There were no other sponsors, and the bill died without a hearing before the Senate's Transportation Committee. Lopez was at the time an experienced legislator with a long history of activism on behalf of Latino and Chicano causes, beginning while he was in high school when he took part in a student walkout.[45] A consistent advocate for better educational opportunities for Spanish-speaking students, he pushed with equal enthusiasm for recognition of Latino achievements. He sponsored a bill to recognize Cesar Chávez Day, for example, and cofounded Chicanos Por La Causa, a group initially dedicated to addressing the problems of the barrios of south-central Phoenix and continuing to serve the Latino community more broadly.

Senator Lopez persisted in sponsoring bills to reverse the 1996 law. While his efforts in the legislature failed, his activism helped to maintain support for changing the law. In the 2000 legislative session, he offered SB 1241 to return to the prior norm and allow driver's licenses regardless of legal status. More than 16,000 people signed petitions in support of the change. A group claiming to represent them held a three-day vigil to draw the legislature's attention to the victims of accidents caused by unlicensed unauthorized migrant drivers. Despite overwhelming support from the Transportation Committee, however, SB 1241 died.

In 2000, Arizona was one of only three states that proactively required that driver's license applicants prove that they are in the United States legally. Bills to reverse that distinction were introduced and failed in 2001 and 2002, despite support from the Senate Transportation Committee. As

Ricardo Pimentel noted in a 2002 article, "Arizona has toyed with the idea of driver's licenses for unauthorized migrants. Each time, however, false piety has won over pragmatism. Bills have been introduced this year in both the state House and Senate. Defeating previous efforts has been hypocritical piety that says, 'We can't reward lawbreakers by validating their existence. But isn't it grand that I pay significantly less for groceries, housing, lawn care and a cheeseburger at my local diner because they're here.'"[46]

Advocates of granting driver's licenses without regard to legal status became hopeful in 2003 when California made driver's licenses available to all residents without proof of legal status. Arizona governor Janet Napolitano, a moderate Democrat, announced her support: "I have the same position I do now that I had last year. Driver's licenses are not immigration documents."[47] Democratic lawmakers, however, were not optimistic about the prospects for a reversal of state policy. As the minority party in both legislative chambers, Democratic bills were often ignored and seldom adopted. In the words of state Senator Pete Rios: "It ain't going to make a hill of beans. We are going to keep pushing for it, but I'm telling people: Don't get your hopes too high regardless of what New Mexico and California have done."[48]

Rios was right to be pessimistic. Freshman Senate Republican Jack Harper was vehement in denouncing Napolitano for her support: "It is time to comment on Gov. Janet Napolitano's latest political pandering disgrace. . . . This would be a complete surrender of our immigration laws. . . . The Department of Motor Vehicles would have its offices flooded with illegal aliens."[49] That prediction was probably incorrect. At the time, according to a report from the federal General Accounting Office, getting a fake driver's license in Arizona was easy. For as little as twenty dollars, these counterfeit documents could be obtained on a corner of downtown Phoenix from men known as *miqueros*. One miquero reported that he had been in operation since 1996.[50]

And so the matter rested, with arguments on both sides of the controversy following a well-worn script, but featuring uniquely Arizona preoccupations. As in New Mexico, opponents ignored safety issues, but in Arizona the principal reasons for opposing an open-door policy toward driver's licenses involved the perceived cost of public support for low-wage migrants and fear that their numbers in the state would grow. A driver's license, from this perspective, represented a kind of invitation to live in Arizona. In the words of one advocate, a driver's license "will only make it easier for them to get jobs or qualify for public services."[51] Those favoring licenses without regard to legal status tended to reject the assumption that migrants represent a social cost; their focus remained on the benefits to public safety when licenses are available to all drivers. From this perspective, licensing simply reflected the already-existing reality of large numbers of settled migrants with families and jobs and a need to drive.

State Sovereignty versus the REAL ID Law in Arizona

When Congress passed the REAL ID Act in 2005, its requirements were deeply resented in Arizona, as in nearly every state. Driver's licenses had always been a matter under state, not federal, jurisdiction, so the REAL ID Act was viewed as a major shift toward federal control. The new federal law, in short, represented a scalar change in the documentation process required for licensing drivers. Passive resistance to the new requirements was common across the United States. Most states simply asked for extra time to comply, pushing the limit on compliance as far as it would go. Arizona, with its long tradition of opposing any expansion of federal authority, took a more aggressive course, adopting a law *forbidding* the state MVD from cooperating in any way with REAL ID. The state also refused to ask for a waiver from the federal requirements, which were (at first) scheduled to take effect in 2014 and 2015. These actions were widely regarded by Arizona's political leaders as an appropriate way to push back against federal overreach and the new costs REAL ID imposed on the states.

Arizona believed that it had satisfactorily resolved any security issues associated with state driver's licenses on its own initiative, with an earlier authorization for the MVD to design a security-enhanced license. The new, Arizona-designed licenses were to become available in March 2015. They would feature a larger photo, a laser perforation shaped like Arizona, and an embossed date of birth that would be difficult to alter. Holders of the previous version of the license would still be able to use them, but renewals and new licenses would have a new look. Unauthorized migrants would continue to be prohibited from obtaining a driver's license.

This celebratory moment was short-lived, however. Arizona successfully escaped federal sanctions for noncompliance with the REAL ID law for over a decade, despite its open refusal to cooperate in any way with the federal law's requirements. As the January 2016 deadline for compliance neared, however, a few members of the legislature began to grow uneasy. Arizona's failure to cooperate with REAL ID was going to have consequences. The new reality first took shape in Nevada, another state that had failed to apply for a waiver promising progress toward implementation of REAL ID. In January, as they had warned, federal officials began to refuse Nevada's noncompliant driver's licenses as identification at some secure federal facilities in the state.

The long-hoped-for demise of REAL ID through massive state resistance was not to be; most states had quietly requested waivers and begun the implementation process.

Representative Bob Worsley (R-Mesa), a conservative, led a lonely fight to persuade his colleagues to change the law prohibiting cooperation with REAL ID requirements. The idea of standing on the principle of state sovereignty in the face of federal threats appealed to many of the state's conservative, libertarian-leaning Republican legislators. Many of them assumed that Arizonans would blame the federal government, not the members of the state legislature, if noncompliant driver's licenses were judged to be insufficient identification to access federal facilities. But the specter of massive numbers of Arizona citizens being turned back by Transportation Security Administration (TSA) agents at the airport finally persuaded most of them that citizens were likely to direct at least some of their ire at the legislature for its high-handed attitude toward REAL ID. Practical concerns finally won out against the principle of state sovereignty. The solution to this political dilemma emerged through a small change in documentary requirements. On the last day of the legislative session, without any public input, the legislature amended the law prohibiting cooperation with REAL ID to make it possible for the MVD to issue compliant licenses to anyone who requested a compliant license and was willing to pay an additional fee. The issue of national security against terrorism, the rationale behind the REAL ID law, was never part of this saga. Nor was Arizona, in this instance, drawing upon the persistent racism and xenophobia that underlay Arizona's own earlier legal status requirement. The paper trails in this case told a story of federal intervention, state resistance on libertarian grounds, and eventual reluctant, partial capitulation.

Arizona's Stance on DACA Recipients

Another conflict with federal requirements was brewing during the final years of the REAL ID debate. The stage for this battle had been set on June 15, 2012, when President Obama announced a two-year reprieve from deportation for qualifying young migrants lacking legal status, the so-called Dreamers. Under a directive from the Department of Homeland Security, these young people would be granted temporary permission to stay, or "deferred action." For conservative Arizonan political leaders and many citizens, Deferred Action for Childhood Arrivals (DACA) was yet another example of the federal government acting beyond its constitutional powers. There was also resistance because Obama's action was at odds with Arizona's policy of attrition through aggressive enforcement of state and federal immigration laws. The state had staked its reputation on a different approach in 2010 when it adopted SB 1070, with its goal of pushing the federal government to deport unauthorized migrants. DACA's reprieve from enforcement went in the opposite direction, toward acceptance and integration of these young residents.

One element of the DACA program created a political opportunity for then-Arizona governor Jan Brewer and Republican legislators who backed her restrictionist approach. DACA recipients were entitled to work permits and employment authorization documents (generally known as EADS) from the U.S. Citizenship and Immigration Services. These documents were identical to others the state had recognized as making recipients eligible for driver's licenses without proof of permanent legal status, including asylum seekers and victims of domestic violence.[52] Arizona, the governor decided, would no longer honor these federal authorization documents as sufficient to obtain an Arizona driver's license. The idea, clearly, was to provoke a showdown over the power of the federal government to force states to accept these young residents as legitimate members of local communities.

Every other state except Nebraska chose the uncontroversial route of making DACA recipients eligible for driver's licenses. But in the mind of Governor Brewer, an arch opponent of unauthorized migrants and ardent supporter of SB 1070, resistance was imperative. Driving privileges, despite REAL ID, had always been a state preserve, and Arizona did not want to back down on its opposition to granting driving privileges to migrants without secure (read permanent) legal status. The ensuing legal battle was predictable. It began in the legislature, where Democratic senator Steve Gallardo, an activist on behalf of migrants, introduced a bill to allow licenses for DACA recipients. Gallardo was unable to get a hearing for his bill, signaling the Republican majority's decision to back up the governor's defiant stand.

Meanwhile, a coalition of civil rights organizations had organized to challenge Arizona's and Nebraska's denial of driving privileges for DACA recipients. Supporters of the Dreamers filed a class action suit in federal court, and on May 16, 2013, district Judge David Campbell issued a preliminary finding that Arizona's policy violated the Equal Protection Clause of the federal Constitution. He was, however, unwilling to block Arizona from implementing its no-license policy, so the case went up on appeal. Sensing that a court might rule against Arizona's policy of singling out DACA recipients from other noncitizen recipients of work permits and deferred action, Governor Brewer expanded the no-license policy to include everyone in this category, thereby denying driver's licenses to asylum seekers and victims of domestic violence, human trafficking, and other human rights violations.

On July 7, 2014, the Ninth Circuit Court of Appeals ruled that the policy was presumptively unconstitutional and granted a preliminary injunction. Arizona lost an appeal from that decision and took the case to the U.S. Supreme Court, which denied review on December 17, 2014. Within a week, Arizona began issuing driver's licenses to DACA recipients for the first time. A few days later a federal district court permanently enjoined Arizona from blocking driver's licenses under Governor Brewer's policy.

Hundreds of young people lined up for licenses at Arizona's Department of Motor Vehicles offices after the Supreme Court declined to intervene. The decision made approximately 22,000 DACA recipients eligible to apply for driver's licenses. By this time, Governor Brewer had left office, and the state had a new governor, Douglas Ducey. The changing of the guard made it relatively easy to take the matter under advisement and defer further action, but Governor Ducey chose not to rescind the original order denying driver's licenses to DACA recipients. For a time, nothing happened, but after the election of immigration hardliner Donald Trump to the presidency and the appointment of conservative Justice Neil Gorsuch to the Supreme Court, Arizona's attorney general, Mark Brnovich, opted to renew the fight. On March 29, 2017, he filed papers in the U.S. Supreme Court to overturn earlier court decisions and reinstate the ban on licenses for Dreamers. In doing so, he reignited a fire set earlier—Brnovich had issued a statement justifying further litigation when he filed notice of appeal two years earlier: "Driving is a privilege and not a right. Attorney General Brnovich believes it is up to each state, not the president, to determine who is eligible to receive a driver's license."[53] The Supreme Court turned down Arizona's appeal in March 2018, leaving the district court's 2012 ruling favoring licenses for DACA recipients in place. Arizona finally recognized the necessity of complying with the 2012 decision in January 2019, when Governor Ducey ordered an end to further appeals.

As the situation now stands in Arizona, DACA recipients are treated like other individuals with Temporary Protected Status—they are entitled to work permits and equal treatment regarding eligibility for driver's licenses. Citizens and legal permanent residents can obtain an enhanced, REAL ID–compliant driver's license for a fee of twenty-five dollars. The Arizona Voluntary Travel ID is not yet required, thanks to the Arizona legislature's decision to promise compliance instead of continuing its claims of immunity from REAL ID's requirements. Residents must obtain one of these new licenses by October 2020, however, if they want to pass through airport security or to gain access to restricted areas in federal facilities. Migrants who lack legal status are not eligible to drive in Arizona. Many do, which makes them vulnerable to arrest and possible deportation, with uncertain consequences for the safety of drivers throughout the state.

Conclusion

A state's decision to add legal status to requirements for driving privileges is a body blow for residents who lack that status, and it is understood as such by everyone concerned. Car insurance immediately becomes more difficult to secure. Identification for daily activities becomes more difficult. Most ominously, the possibility of deportation arising from a routine traffic stop becomes a possibility. The state's message of hostility and indifference to the fate of residents lacking secure legal status is unmistakable. That this rejection is set forth in a bland document outlining licensing requirements is no comfort, but rather faintly ironic from the affected immigrant's perspective.

Our comparative analysis reveals the significance of deeply held images and stereotypes about race, class, religion, and productivity in determining who will have the right to drive. In Arizona, for example, the idea that unauthorized migrants are mainly a burden is taken for granted by large proportions of the population, including some migrants, despite much evidence to the contrary. Convictions about the dangers to one's preferred community can be powerful enough, the Arizona experience suggests, to overcome any argument for safety on the state's highways. In New Mexico, the dominant understanding of migrants is much more positive and accepting, which tends to neutralize hardline arguments like those favored by Governor Martinez and some Republican legislators. The power of New Mexico's culture of acceptance was strong enough to preserve driver's licenses, even in the face of repeated evidence of scandals associated with fraudulent licensing. Interestingly, in neither New Mexico nor Arizona did the federal imagining of a terrorist threat carry any weight locally, perhaps because the image of an unauthorized migrant in the Southwest is Mexican, Catholic, working class, and not associated with Islamic extremism.

While the REAL ID Act ultimately forced both states to act on the driver's license issue, the federal presence in this debate, we found, was somewhat marginal to local concerns, mostly providing a backdrop for the local debate about who belongs and who does not. It also seems clear that each state considers immigration-related issues strictly on their own terms, with little regard for what other places do. A quick survey of driver's license rules currently in effect supports this assertion. There is a lot of variety in the restrictions that states impose on licenses for drivers who cannot demonstrate legal status. Nevada, for example, offers one-year driver's authorization cards. Maryland prohibits use of the license to make firearm purchases. Illinois requires that the card state, in large capital letters, that it may not be used for identification purposes. The District of Columbia requires this information as well, but specifies that the information be in the smallest font size otherwise on the card.

Journalist Julia Preston uses the term *immigration geography* to describe the propensity she has observed for states to think about immigration policy with their own interests at the forefront. In Preston's view, states reveal a consistent stance on unauthorized immigration, whether they are making policy on mundane issues like driver's licenses and in-state tuition for unauthorized migrants, or engaging in high-profile actions like challenging the president in court over his executive actions to protect migrants.[54] We agree, and would add that in this discussion there is a large potential role for individual political entrepreneurs like Russell Pearce and Susana Martinez. These issue entrepreneurs know how to deploy stereotypes about race and difference, tapping into deep wells of sentiment about newcomers and the treatment they deserve.

Though cast into the shadows of the driver's license drama by each of these states, the federal government's decision to become involved is an important marker in the consolidation of mobility regulation at the national level. REAL ID's passage and eventual acceptance exemplifies the power of the national government to rewrite the traditional boundaries of federalism. This rescripting is an artifact of the times in which we live. A century ago, Congress could hardly have considered federalizing driver's license requirements because it did not have the capacity to make such policies effective. The states had almost free rein in setting standards for the residence of immigrants within their jurisdictions until well into the twentieth century. The same was true for citizens, as the regime of Jim Crow legislation in the southern states reminds us.

The patchwork of driver's license policies that remains even after the imposition of federal requirements is more than a marker of continuing debate in the United States over immigration and its proper relation to the American polity. It is also a reminder of the dispersal of immigration policy across a disaggregated national landscape, with the policy instability that entails.

Subnational governments are determined to play a role in this drama, and documents are the means to this political end. The driver's license, we have argued, is a state government's most powerful tool in expressing its views about migrants. The federal government's entrance into this field hardly disturbs this discretion. What it does, however, is to assert an apparently federal interest in securitizing the personal information of residents. As with any identification document, bureaucratic inscription makes both citizens and immigrants more visible and easier to surveil. The government makes no promises as to what it will do with this information.

From the perspective of lived experience, however, battles over the contours of federal power are not immediately relevant. Living in a state where one can acquire a right to drive is a key practical benefit. A driver's license, even with the limitations states are imposing, offers unauthorized immigrants a kind of quasi-inclusion that provides mobility, opportunity, and the ability to identify oneself easily in transactions of all sorts. But the larger context in which this privilege is exercised remains unsettled, creating an existential threat that cannot be escaped by anyone whose documentary existence is deemed insufficient.

Notes

We thank our fellow contributors for their feedback on earlier drafts of this chapter, and our research assistants, Alexandra Smith and Rachel Corey, for their helpful work on the references and final formatting of the manuscript.

1 Monica W. Varsanyi, "Immigration Policing through the Backdoor: City Ordinances, the 'Right to the City' and the Exclusion of Unauthorized Day Laborers," *Urban Geography* 29 (2008): 29–52.

2 Juliet Stumpf, "The Crimmigration Crisis: Immigrants, Crime, and Sovereign Power," *American University Law Review* 56 (2006): 367–419; Maria João Guia, Maartje van der Woude, and Joanne van der Leun, eds., *Social Control and Justice: Crimmigration in the Age of Fear* (The Hague: Eleven International Publishing, 2012).

3 Angela Stuesse and Mathew Coleman, "Automobility, Immobility, Altermobility: Surviving and Resisting the Intensification of Immigrant Policing," *City and Society* 26 (2014): 51–72, accessed May 21, 2019, https://doi.org/10.1111/ciso.12034; Marie Provine et al., *Policing Immigrants: Local Law Enforcement on the Front Lines* (Chicago: University of Chicago Press, 2016); Amada Armenta, *Protect, Serve, and Deport: The Rise of Policing as Immigration Enforcement* (Berkeley: University of California Press, 2017); Nolan Kline, *Pathogenic Policing: Immigration Enforcement and Health in the U.S. South* (New Brunswick, NJ: Rutgers University Press, 2019).

4 Pratheepan Gulasekaram and S. Karthick Ramakrishnan, *The New Immigration Federalism* (New York: Cambridge University Press, 2015); Tom Wong, *The Politics of Immigration: Partisanship, Demographic Change, and American National Identity* (New York: Oxford University Press, 2016); Daniel J. Hopkins, "Politicized Places: Explaining Where and When Immigrants Provoke Local Opposition," *American Political Science Review* 104 (2010): 40–60; Jorge M. Chavez and Doris Marie Provine, "Race and the Response of State Legislatures to Unauthorized Immigrants," *Annals of the American Academy of Political and Social Sciences* 623 (2009): 78–92.

5 For more on the distinct ethnic and political trajectories of each state, taken individually, please see Katherine Benton-Cohen, *Borderline Americans: Racial Division and Labor War in the Arizona Borderlands* (Cambridge, MA: Harvard University Press, 2009); Laura E. Gómez, *Manifest Destinies: The Making of the Mexican American Race* (New York: New York University Press, 2007); Phillip B. Gonzales, *Política: Nuevomexicanos and American Political Incorporation, 1821–1910* (Lincoln: University of Nebraska Press, 2016); Charles Montgomery, *The Spanish Redemption: Heritage, Power, and Loss on New Mexico's Upper Rio Grande* (Berkeley: University of California Press, 2002); John M. Nieto-Phillips, *The Language of Blood: The Making of Spanish-American Identity in New Mexico, 1880s–1930s* (Albuquerque: University of New Mexico Press, 2004); Thomas Sheridan, *Los Tucsonenses: The Mexican Community of Tucson, 1854–1941* (Tucson: University of Arizona Press, 1986). Please also see Monica W. Varsanyi and Doris Marie Provine, "Understanding Contemporary Immigration Politics in New Mexico and Arizona: The Chicano Movement (1962–1975) as Critical Juncture" (paper presented at the Social Science History Association Annual Meeting, Phoenix, Arizona, November 9, 2018); Doris Marie Provine and Monica W. Varsanyi, "Borders and Bridges: Explaining Immigrant Policy Divergence in Arizona and New Mexico" (paper presented at the Law and Society Association Annual Meeting, Mexico City, June 20–23, 2017); Monica W. Varsanyi and Doris Marie Provine, "Comparing Immigration Policy and Enforcement in Two Neighboring States" (paper presented at the Annual Conference of the American Political Science Association, San Francisco, California, September 3–6, 2015); Monica W. Varsanyi and Doris Marie Provine, "Immigration Federalism in the Shifting Political Sands of Two Desert States, Arizona and New Mexico" (paper presented at the Annual Meeting of the Law and Society Association, Seattle, Washington, May 28–31, 2015).

6 The twelve states, in addition to the District of Columbia, include California, Colorado, Connecticut, Delaware, Hawaii, Illinois, Maryland, Nevada, New Mexico, Utah, Vermont, and Washington. Pew Charitable Trusts, "Driver's Licenses for Unauthorized Immigrants: Highlights: An Update on States' Latest Policies and Implementation Efforts," last modified November 22, 2016, http://www.pewtrusts.org/en/research-and-analysis/analysis/2016/11/22/drivers-licenses-for-unauthorized-immigrants-2016-highlights; Pew Charitable Trusts, "Deciding Who Drives: State Choice Surrounding Unauthorized Immigrants and Driver's Licenses," last modified

September 3, 2015, http://www.pewtrusts.org/~/media/assets/2015/08/deciding
-who-drives.pdf.

7 Jonathan McDonald, "Study Says S.F. Treats Immigrants Poorly," *Santa Fe New Mexican*, May 9, 2000.

8 Debra Dominguez, "Immigrants Line Up for Licenses," *Albuquerque Journal*, July 16, 2003, B2.

9 Deborah Baker, "Senate Passes License Change," *Albuquerque Journal*, March 11, 2003, A6.

10 Kate Nash, "Driving Rules May Shift for Illegal Immigrants," *Albuquerque Journal*, January 29, 2005, A6.

11 Nash, "Driving Rules May Shift for Illegal Immigrants."

12 Laura Banish, "Council Sides against Federal REAL ID Act," *Albuquerque Journal*, July 14, 2005, 3.

13 Leslie Linthicum, "Others' Message to Illegal Immigrants: Leave! N.M. Surrounded by States with New, Tougher Laws," *Albuquerque Journal*, November 18, 2007.

14 Linthicum, "Others' Message to Illegal Immigrants."

15 Editorial Board, "Driver's License Policy Odd Tourist Attraction," *Albuquerque Journal*, August 4, 2010.

16 Rene Romo, "Operation Using Deputies Creates Mistrust in Border Town," *Albuquerque Journal*, September 18, 2007.

17 Romo, "Operation Using Deputies Creates Mistrust."

18 Sean Olson, "Voters Support Strong Policy on Immigrants," *Albuquerque Journal*, September 5, 2010, A1.

19 Dan Boyd, "House Rejects Illegals' Licenses: 8 Dems Join GOP in Bid to Overturn 2003 Law," *Albuquerque Journal*, March 5, 2011.

20 Dan Boyd, "Ban on Illegal Licenses Falters: Gov. Vows to Continue Fight, but Chances in Legislature Appear Slim," *Albuquerque Journal*, March 11, 2011.

21 Deborah Baker, "Border Patrol a Challenge for License Reviews. Some Drivers Could Have Trouble Clearing Checkpoints," *Albuquerque Journal*, July 28, 2011.

22 ABQnews Staff, "Bishops Back Extending Driver's License Law for Immigrants," *Albuquerque Journal*, August 16, 2011.

23 Dan Boyd, "Gov., Bishops Still Split over Driver's Licenses. Abortion Bill Has Martinez Backing," *Albuquerque Journal*, January 19, 2012.

24 Deborah Baker, "Driver's License Bill Hits Roadblocks. House Panel Rejects Governor's Proposal," *Albuquerque Journal*, January 27, 2012.

25 Baker, "Driver's License Bill Hits Roadblocks."

26 Baker, "Driver's License Bill Hits Roadblocks."

27 Barry Massey, "Gov. Vows to Meet Federal License Requirements," *Albuquerque Journal*, October 11, 2012.

28 Massey, "Gov. Vows to Meet Federal License Requirements."

29 James Monteleone, "Opposition Still Strong to License Law," *Albuquerque Journal*, September 12, 2012.

30 Gabriel Sánchez, "The Context of Immigration Policy in New Mexico Reflects National Trends," *America's Voice*, October 31, 2012, accessed May 21, 2019, https://

americasvoice.org/blog/the-context-of-immigration-policy-in-new-mexico
-reflects-national-trends/.

31 Russell Contreras, "Another License Fraud Ring Busted. 5 Albuquerque Residents
Named in Federal Indictment," *Albuquerque Journal*, June 21, 2012.

32 Thomas J. Cole, "Election Timing May Explain Governor's Shift on Licenses,"
Albuquerque Journal, January 26, 2012.

33 James Monteleone, "Martinez Drives Licenses into Race with King. Gov. Ties Immigration Debate to Long-Running NM Issue," *Albuquerque Journal*, July 26, 2014.

34 Monteleone, "Martinez Drives Licenses into Race with King."

35 Deborah Baker, "House OKs Bill to Repeal Driver's License Law," *Albuquerque
Journal*, February 13, 2015.

36 Baker, "House OKs Bill to Repeal Driver's License Law."

37 Richard Metcalf, "NM No. 1 in Dependency on Federal Funds," *Albuquerque Journal*, March 30, 2015.

38 Justin Horwath, "Rules for New State IDs Draw Criticism," *Santa Fe New Mexican*,
October 19, 2016; Steve Terrell, "Padilla Defends Rollout of Real ID System amid
Broad Criticism," *Taos News*, December 10, 2016.

39 Somos un Pueblo Unido, "Somos un Pueblo Unido: Call to Action," last modified
2017, https://retakeourdemocracy.org/somos-un-pueblo-unido-call-to-action/.

40 Maggie Shepard and Deborah Baker, "Governor Signs REAL ID Measure into Law:
Fight Settled over Legally Allowing Unauthorized Immigrants to Drive," *Albuquerque Journal*, March 9, 2016.

41 Auditor General of Arizona, "Performance Audit: Department of Transportation,
Motor Vehicle Division—Driver's Licensing and Title/Registration Programs," October 1988, last modified September 10, 2008, http://azmemory.azlibrary.gov/cdm
/singleitem/collection/statepubs/id/6735/rec/1.

42 Section 5(C) of Section 28-413 of Arizona Revised Statutes (Chapter 230).

43 Daniel Gonzalez, "Driver's License Bill Focus of Vigil Law Called Biased against
Illegals," *Arizona Republic*, March 8, 2000.

44 Stephen Cobb, "Re: AZ DMV: Citizenship to Drive (fwd)," response to a post by
George Diaz Jr., August 20, 1996, http://cypherpunks.venona.com/date/1996/08
/msg01656.html.

45 Lopez was elected to the Maricopa County Board of Supervisors in 1972. In 1990
he became the first Mexican American elected to the Phoenix Union High School
District Board of Education. In 1991 he was elected to the Arizona House of
Representatives, a post he held until 1996, when he was elected to the Arizona state
Senate, where he continued to serve until 2010.

46 Ricardo Pimentel, "Local Police Shouldn't Be Doing INS' Work," *Arizona Republic*,
April 9, 2002.

47 Daniel Gonzalez, "Immigrant Licenses Face Ariz. Test: Napolitano Would Support
Driving Privileges," *Arizona Republic*, September 10, 2003.

48 Gonzalez, "Immigrant Licenses Face Ariz. Test."

49 Jack W. Harper, "Licenses for Illegals Would Hamper State," letter to the editor,
Arizona Republic, September 24, 2003.

50 Daniel Gonzalez, "Fake-ID Market Flourishing on Valley's Streets," *Arizona Republic*, December 11, 2003.

51 Gonzalez, "Driver's License Bill Focus of Vigil Law," 21.

52 Arizona Revised Statutes, Section 28-3153(D).

53 Ray Stern, "Mark Brnovich Says 'No' to Arizona Dreamers, Launches Appeal of License Ruling," *Phoenix New Times*, February 20, 2015, accessed May 21, 2019, http://www.phoenixnewtimes.com/news/mark-brnovich-says-no-to-arizona -dreamers-launches-appeal-of-license-ruling-6660676.

54 Julia Preston, "States Are Divided by the Lines They Draw on Immigration," *New York Times*, March 29, 2015.

Bibliography

Armenta, Amada. *Protect, Serve, and Deport: The Rise of Policing as Immigration Enforcement*. Berkeley: University of California Press, 2017.

Auditor General of Arizona. "Performance Audit: Department of Transportation, Motor Vehicle Division—Driver's Licensing and Title/Registration Programs." October 1988. Last modified September 10, 2008. http://azmemory.azlibrary.gov/cdm /singleitem/collection/statepubs/id/6735/rec/1.

Benton-Cohen, Katherine. *Borderline Americans: Racial Division and Labor War in the Arizona Borderlands*. Cambridge, MA: Harvard University Press, 2009.

Chavez, Jorge M., and Doris Marie Provine. "Race and the Response of State Legislatures to Unauthorized Immigrants." *Annals of the American Academy of Political and Social Sciences* 623 (2009): 78–92.

Cobb, Stephen. "Re: AZ DMV: Citizenship to Drive (fwd)," response to a post by George Diaz Jr., August 20, 1996. http://cypherpunks.venona.com/date/1996/08 /msg01656.html.

Gómez, Laura E. *Manifest Destinies: The Making of the Mexican American Race*. New York: New York University Press, 2007.

Gonzales, Phillip B. *Política: Nuevomexicanos and American Political Incorporation, 1821–1910*. Lincoln: University of Nebraska Press, 2016.

Guia, Maria João, Maartje van der Woude, and Joanne van der Leun, eds. *Social Control and Justice: Crimmigration in the Age of Fear*. The Hague: Eleven International, 2012.

Gulasekaram, Pratheepan, and S. Karthick Ramakrishnan. *The New Immigration Federalism*. New York: Cambridge University Press, 2015.

Hopkins, Daniel J. "Politicized Places: Explaining Where and When Immigrants Provoke Local Opposition." *American Political Science Review* 104 (2010): 40–60.

Kline, Nolan. *Pathogenic Policing: Immigration Enforcement and Health in the U.S. South*. New Brunswick, NJ: Rutgers University Press, 2019.

Montgomery, Charles. *The Spanish Redemption: Heritage, Power, and Loss on New Mexico's Upper Rio Grande*. Berkeley: University of California Press, 2002.

Nieto-Phillips, John M. *The Language of Blood: The Making of Spanish-American Identity in New Mexico, 1880s–1930s*. Albuquerque: University of New Mexico Press, 2004.

Pew Charitable Trusts. "Deciding Who Drives: State Choice Surrounding Unauthorized Immigrants and Driver's Licenses." Last modified September 3, 2015. http://www.pewtrusts.org/~/media/assets/2015/08/deciding-who-drives.pdf.

Pew Charitable Trusts. "Driver's Licenses for Unauthorized Immigrants: 2016 Highlights: An Update on States' Latest Policies and Implementation Efforts." Last modified November 22, 2016. http://www.pewtrusts.org/en/research-and-analysis/analysis/2016/11/22/drivers-licenses-for-unauthorized-immigrants-2016-highlights.

Provine, Doris Marie, and Monica W. Varsanyi. "Borders and Bridges: Explaining Immigrant Policy Divergence in Arizona and New Mexico." Paper presented at the Law and Society Association Annual Meeting, Mexico City, June 20–23, 2017.

Provine, Marie, Monica Varsanyi, Paul Lewis, and Scott Decker. *Policing Immigrants: Local Law Enforcement on the Front Lines.* Chicago: University of Chicago Press, 2016.

Sánchez, Gabriel. "The Context of Immigration Policy in New Mexico Reflects National Trends." *America's Voice*, October 31, 2012. Accessed May 21, 2019. https://americasvoice.org/blog/the-context-of-immigration-policy-in-new-mexico-reflects-national-trends/.

Sheridan, Thomas. *Los Tucsonenses: The Mexican Community of Tucson, 1854–1941.* Tucson: University of Arizona Press, 1986.

Somos un Pueblo Unido. "Somos un Pueblo Unido: Call to Action." Last modified 2017. https://retakeourdemocracy.org/somos-un-pueblo-unido-call-to-action/.

Stuesse, Angela, and Mathew Coleman. "Automobility, Immobility, Altermobility: Surviving and Resisting the Intensification of Immigrant Policing." *City and Society* 26 (2014): 51–72. Accessed May 21, 2019. https://doi.org/10.1111/ciso.12034.

Stumpf, Juliet. "The Crimmigration Crisis: Immigrants, Crime, and Sovereign Power." *American University Law Review* 56 (2006): 367–419.

Varsanyi, Monica W. "Immigration Policing through the Backdoor: City Ordinances, the 'Right to the City' and the Exclusion of Unauthorized Day Laborers." *Urban Geography* 29 (2008): 29–52.

Varsanyi, Monica W., and Doris Marie Provine. "Comparing Immigration Policy and Enforcement in Two Neighboring States." Paper presented at the Annual Conference of the American Political Science Association. San Francisco, California, September 3–6, 2015.

Varsanyi, Monica W., and Doris Marie Provine. "Immigration Federalism in the Shifting Political Sands of Two Desert States, Arizona and New Mexico." Paper presented at the Annual Meeting of the Law and Society Association, Seattle, Washington, May 28–31, 2015.

Varsanyi, Monica W., and Doris Marie Provine. "Understanding Contemporary Immigration Politics in New Mexico and Arizona: The Chicano Movement (1962–1975) as Critical Juncture." Paper presented at the Social Science History Association Annual Meeting, Phoenix, Arizona, November 9, 2018.

Wong, Tom. *The Politics of Immigration: Partisanship, Demographic Change, and American National Identity.* New York: Oxford University Press, 2016.

PART II

DOCUMENTS AS SECURITY, DOCUMENTS AS VISIBILITY

As vehicles through which the state controls mobility and creates distinctions between categories of people, documents shape migrants' experiences of space and time. While part I of this volume laid out this general framework, part II provides grounded ethnographic analyses of the multiple and unpredictable spaces in which migrants encounter the power of the state. The first two chapters show us the stakes involved for migrants in submitting applications for regularization, as doing so exposes migrants to the unpredictability of state power. They show that although migrants and their advocates attempt to maneuver as much as possible—exploiting new opportunities for status adjustment and strategically repurposing old documents to new ends—they are ultimately beholden to the rules and logics of state bureaucracies. While Boehm and Coutin document how migrants voluntarily and involuntarily engage with state bureaucracies, Menjívar shows us that migrants unexpectedly encounter the power of the state even in private spaces as they go about their daily lives. Indeed, because state-issued identification documents have become so fundamental to modern life, migrants face repeat demands for "their documents" when merely attempting to buy furniture, open a bank account, or rent a video.

Boehm's and Coutin's chapters address a central theme of the volume by illustrating the double-edged nature of official documentation for migrants. Even as submitting an application for regularization promises the possibility of security and legitimacy, it simultaneously comes at the price of visibility to an arbitrary sovereign power.[1] This central paradox posed by migrants' entry into state processes of bureaucratic inscription is all the more salient in this particular political moment. In her timely discussion of the Deferred Action for Childhood Arrivals program, for example, Boehm shows that youths must confront the risks of identifying themselves to the state as they dutifully assemble their dossiers. Taking as her case studies three different forms unauthorized status may take—DACAmented status, detained migrants, and deportees—Boehm insightfully shows that each group occupies a distinct subject position vis-à-vis the state because of different modes of bureaucratic entry. Documents (and legal status) may be voluntarily *achieved*—as in the case of DACA recipients who submit dossiers to achieve DACA status—or legal status may be involuntarily *ascribed*, as in the case of deportees or those apprehended by immigration authorities. Due to changes in immigration policy in the United States since the 1990s, those undocumented immigrants who remain entirely outside state bureaucratic systems may ironically feel more safe than even legal immigrants who are deeply embedded within bureaucratic systems.[2] Thus documents not only confer the status that migrants seek but also create "paper trails": they potentially ensnare and entrap migrants during a moment of heightened criminalization and enforcement.

As Boehm and Coutin illustrate, navigating state bureaucracies can be a confusing, time-consuming, and unpredictable process—one in which migrants find themselves at a significant disadvantage. If there is an error in the official bureaucratic record, a missing file, or a discrepancy with a migrant's own records, the state retains unilateral authority to establish the "official facts." Moreover, state bureaucratic records are, so to speak, protected by a one-way mirror. Migrants can never know the entirety of the paper trails attached to their identifiers in the state's records, making their entry into state bureaucratic systems a gamble. As Susan Coutin shows, because of the arbitrariness of state bureaucracies as well as the specialized knowledge they require, migrants must depend on the expertise of legal service providers. Coutin's chapter takes us inside the walls of a legal advocacy clinic, illustrating the important role of advocates' "technocratic expertise" in assisting migrants in assembling and submitting their files. Thus, Coutin underscores the way such legal technicians help translate the logics of the state for migrants and defuse the threat entailed by their legibility.

The chapters by Boehm and Coutin illustrate that the opacity of state bureaucracies to migrants is a principal technique of state power. The state's very "illegibility" to migrants helps ensure its control; even as states strive to render their populations "legible," they have no reciprocal obligation of transparency.[3] Indeed, as Boehm shows, this power asymmetry is particularly obvious in the case of the lack of accessible records regarding migrant detention. Family members are often unable to locate detainees, and detainees may be arbitrarily transferred to another state without explanation or notification to families. State detention practices are shielded from public view, making it difficult to obtain accurate statistics on the number of such transfers, or for advocates to hold the state accountable. Indeed, the inscrutability of state bureaucracies makes the technocratic expertise of legal advocates all the more vital. Susan Coutin shows that making state bureaucracies less opaque to individuals is not only a technical endeavor but also an art; moreover, it is a key means through which legal service providers loosen the grip of state control.

Coutin explores the ways that legal service providers creatively use the logics of the state to open up opportunities for regularization. On the one hand, these "legal technicians" must stay abreast of new legal developments. On the other hand, being an effective legal advocate depends not only on one's mastery of the law but also on the idiosyncracies of state bureaucracies. Finally, Coutin shows us that regularization is not only a legal and bureaucratic but also a profoundly human process. Legal technicians must appease the state bureaucrats who read clients' files, learning how to present a client's case like a narrative, and understanding the value of a well-placed sticky note. Thus, the first two chapters in this section illustrate the unpredictable and almost whimsical nature of sovereign power because it is fundamentally enacted by individuals—whether at ports of entry, in detention centers, or in immigration offices. For this reason, a valid visitor's visa can unexpectedly lead to a legal bar to reentry, and the careful narrative packaging of a client's case can facilitate approval.

If Boehm and Coutin provide a window onto the contradictory and often subjective processes through which state power is reproduced, Menjívar's provocative chapter takes us outside the halls of the state. She shows that even as migrants—and Latinos in general—pursue their everyday lives, their routine interactions are marked by constant requests for "papers." A wealth of literature has examined the way that "street-level bureaucrats" in public institutions—social workers, eligibility workers, clinic staff, teachers, police, and even zoning officers—extend the role of the state in instructing immigrants about their place in the nation. Menjívar's contribution is to show that private-sector actors—real estate agents, bank tellers, and even store clerks—also figure prominently in the state's disciplinary project. Because these private individuals depend on the official identity documents provided by the state in their ordinary business transactions, migrants—and anyone who has the misfortune to "look Latino"—encounter repeated demands for "their documents" every day. As a result, in Arizona, even naturalized citizens continue to carry their documents with them, bracing for the possibility of being asked to produce proof of status. Menjívar's chapter thus illustrates the extensive reach of the state in migrants' lives, as well as its enduring imprint.

Finally, by focusing on documents and the bureaucratic processes associated with them, these chapters illustrate that official immigration statuses do not map neatly onto experiences of the state and of the law. In her discussion of the different relationships that those often glossed as "unauthorized migrants" have with the state, Boehm shows that an unauthorized individual's sense of security and future prospects may vary depending on their mode of entry into bureaucratic systems. That is, in terms of the paper trails attached to them, there are profound differences between these groups and those who have never entered state systems. Meanwhile, in her analysis of the constant demands for "papers" faced by Latinos in Arizona—whether those with TPS, legal permanent residents, or even naturalized citizens—Menjívar shows how racialized identities supersede immigration status in shaping Latinos' unequal incorporation. Menjívar reminds us that the meaning of documents—and of being suspected of *not possessing* the requested documents—is context-dependent. Moreover, everyday requests for documents play a key role in reinforcing racialized groups' sense of social illegitimacy. As state systems for identification and verification have become hegemonic, such people are reminded of their second-class citizenship in myriad ordinary interactions.

In short, these grounded analyses highlight both the arbitrariness of state power as well as its enduring effects. Through documents, and requests for documents, the state follows migrants into unanticipated spaces. Moreover, the specter of state power looms over migrants even once they adjust their legal status.

Notes

1 Gray Abarca and Susan Coutin, "Sovereign Intimacies: The Lives of Documents within US State-Noncitizen Relationships," *American Ethnologist* 45 (2018): 7–19.

2 Asad L. Asad, "On the Radar: System Embeddedness and Latin American Immigrants' Perceived Risk of Deportation," preprint draft (Ithaca, NY: Center for the Study of Inequality, Cornell University, 2017).

3 Ruth Gomberg-Muñoz, *Becoming Legal: Immigration Law and Mixed-Status Families* (Oxford: Oxford University Press, 2016); Miriam Ticktin, "Where Ethics and Politics Meet: The Violence of Humanitarianism in France," *American Ethnologist* 33 (2006): 33–49.

Bibliography

Abarca, Gray, and Susan Coutin. "Sovereign Intimacies: The Lives of Documents within US State-Noncitizen Relationships." *American Ethnologist* 45 (2018): 7–19.

Asad, Asad L. "On the Radar: System Embeddedness and Latin American Immigrants' Perceived Risk of Deportation." Preprint Draft. Ithaca, NY: Center for the Study of Inequality, Cornell University, 2017.

Asad, Asad L. "Reconsidering Immigrant Illegality: How Immigrants Perceive the Risk of Immigration Law and Enforcement." Ph.D. dissertation, Harvard University, 2017.

Gomberg-Muñoz, Ruth. *Becoming Legal: Immigration Law and Mixed-Status Families.* Oxford: Oxford University Press, 2016.

Ticktin, Miriam. "Where Ethics and Politics Meet: The Violence of Humanitarianism in France." *American Ethnologist* 33 (2006): 33–49.

DEBORAH A. BOEHM

4

DOCUMENTED AS UNAUTHORIZED

Look at all these documents!
—Sofía, DACA recipient

Your search has returned zero (0) matching records.
—Online Detainee Locator System, U.S. Immigration
and Customs Enforcement

Can you explain what all these papers mean?
—Rodrigo, deported while attempting to enter the United States
with a valid tourist visa

Migrants who are deported, those who are detained, and those who are recipients of DACA (Deferred Action for Childhood Arrivals) are all unauthorized in the sense that they do not (or do not yet) have state permission to reside permanently in the United States. However, in contrast to unauthorized
migrants who have never entered within the state's bureaucratic ambit, they
have markedly different relationships to, and exchanges with, the U.S. government. DACA recipients, or DACAmented migrants, have been granted
work authorization; they are able to travel domestically and in some cases
internationally, and most importantly, they receive relief from deportation:
the possibility of formal expulsion is—at least temporarily—"deferred." In
contrast, those who are deported are legally and physically banished from

the nation. Deportees have little, if any, recourse once deported; for most, the reality is that they will likely never be able to enter the United States with government authorization in the future. And for people held in immigration detention, outcomes and future trajectories are unknown—depending on the specifics of the case and a number of other factors, those in detention might be released or deported, they may acquire or be denied a change in status that permits them to stay in the United States, or they may be admitted to or permanently expelled from the country. Still, despite these differences in status, DACAmented migrants and those who have been detained and deported also share certain elements of their position vis-à-vis the U.S. state— namely, through each process, undocumented status becomes documented as such.

This chapter draws on research from three separate ethnographic research projects on the relationship between unauthorized migrants and the state: (1) research with DACA applicants and recipients and their allies; (2) a multisited study (Mexico and the United States) of deportation and its effects on families;[1] and (3) a current project about immigration detention in the United States. The research about DACA began in the summer of 2012 when President Obama announced the start of the program. For this project, I have interviewed DACA applicants and recipients, volunteered at information sessions put on by community organizations in Nevada, assisted applicants as they completed and compiled required forms and documents, and interviewed service providers about their work with DACA applicants. And, in the fall of 2014, I joined a group of Mexican nationals with DACA status who were guests of the Mexican government, conducting participant observation and interviews with those invited to a gathering in Mexico City.

Deportation and its effects on family life were the focus of binational research I conducted from 2008 through 2014. In 2008, I met a number of individuals in the Mexican states of Zacatecas and San Luis Potosí who had been deported from the United States. I then embarked on multisited research in the United States and Mexico, including a year of fieldwork based in Mexico in 2010. Research included interviews, participant observation, and collaborative and visual methodologies with people who had been deported and their family members. Finally, a current and ongoing study of the unseen spaces of U.S. immigration detention began in 2015, with fieldwork based in communities in Arizona, California, Nevada, Oregon, and Washington. The project has included collaborative and participatory research with community organizations and interviews with formerly detained migrants, family members of migrants who are currently in detention, attorneys and other legal service providers, and volunteers who visit people in detention.

While these research projects have been focused on particular—and seemingly disparate—aspects of immigration policy and enforcement, ethnographic research across contexts has also underscored the ways that individuals from these three groups share a similar experience within the United States: in each of these studies, research collaborators have repeatedly expressed and shown how documents matter. People have often talked about paperwork, forms, and the challenges of the bureaucratic systems they have had to navigate. Others have lamented that they might not have the necessary documents to adjust their status or to ensure protection from deportation. Nearly all migrants have described the confusion, stress, or insecurity that comes from being *"sin papeles"* (without papers, or undocumented). These conversations have led me to think about how these diverse circumstances are, at least in part, shaped by common threads: the character of government bureaucracies, the processes through which the state categorizes foreign nationals, and the paperwork required by or generated through immigration policies and procedures.

These three projects have revealed the profoundly distinct challenges that state power—wielded through deportation and the prospect of deportation—poses to different groups of migrants. And yet this research has also illuminated the way that, paradoxically, documentation is often a process of *unauthorization*—the very steps that concretize one's unlawful status. I argue that it is precisely through the state's documentation of foreign nationals—whether applications for DACA, the bureaucratic processes of immigration detention, or paperwork filed during deportation proceedings—that the government records, formally recognizes, and in the end *produces* one's unauthorized status. Here I follow the often confusing and contradictory "paper trails"[2] generated by the state to trace how being "unauthorized" is officially marked by the government.

Above all, as unauthorized status is concretized by governments, migrants move from spheres of illegibility to legibility, and invisibility to visibility. As migrants are documented as unauthorized, individuals who were once living in the shadows—and whose presence was previously unrecorded—become visible to the state as paper trails develop and as the state amasses documents. When unauthorized statuses are recorded, migrants become known to the state and identified as foreign nationals living in the country without the government's permission. The making of unauthorized subjects is shaped by a pronounced asymmetry between states and migrants in terms of the accessibility of documents and the knowledge of state recordkeeping (see also Coutin, this volume). Even as the process of unauthorization makes migrants more legible to the state, the state does not become similarly legible to transnational subjects.

Migrants may "choose" to engage with the state—like those who apply for DACA or those who arrive at the nation's border seeking asylum—or they may be forced to do so, such as those held in detention after being apprehended or those who are deported. Nevertheless, these three distinct experiences—applying for DACA, being held in U.S. immigration detention facilities, and being deported by the state—share certain elements in common, namely, the contradictory characteristics that frame this process of unauthorization. For DACAmented migrants, the documentation required for deferred action can result in increased flexibility, activism, and forms of community; at the same time, because DACA recipients are now on record as being in the country without authorization, they also experience new state controls. For migrants in detention, the documents generated (or not) while being held by the U.S. government or in contracted public and private prisons can impact unknown future trajectories by, for example, facilitating release or resulting in deportation. And for deportees, the forced documentation of deportation nearly always creates visibility that is highly restrictive and likely to block any future "documented" or authorized return migration, even as many of those deported continue to be de facto members of the nation that formally expels them.

Undocumented to DACAmented

Sitting in a hallway outside a classroom, Sofía shuffled through a stack of papers. "I know I have it somewhere," she explained. "Maybe I left it at home, or it could be here." She reached for a book bag full of more papers and started to go through those. "I'm undocumented, but look at all these documents!" she said wryly. "These are the papers that I have, papers that were meaningful to someone in our family." And, indeed, Sofía had a lot of documents with her—her birth certificate, report cards, bank statements, college transcripts, certificates of achievement, and letters from previous teachers, neighbors, and family friends. She was organizing the papers in preparation for a workshop put on by a local immigrant advocacy organization to assist with applications for deferred action. Later that day, Sofía moved through the different stations designed to guide youth through the DACA application process and all the paperwork it entails.

As those who have gone through the process describe, applications for DACA have required the management of a large—if not overwhelming—number of documents. Based on conversations with DACA applicants and recipients, and observations during this workshop and in other settings, it is clear that DACA has depended on these paper trails.[3] Sofía told me that there are indeed "quite a few things you need to prove" through papers, including a list of "every single address you have ever lived at in the United States" and notarized affidavits that demonstrate your presence in the country. Sofía aimed to thoroughly document her life in the United States. As she explained: "I was told, 'the more you have, the better.'"

This point was reiterated at the workshop Sofía attended later that day. The setup involved stations in several classrooms at a local school, with volunteers at each stop ready to verify some aspect of eligibility ranging from age (documented by a birth certificate or passport) to continuous presence (demonstrated through, for example, bank statements, school records, and/or rental contracts). The workshop was designed to streamline the daunting task of compiling necessary papers, an attempt to make the process as transparent and accessible as possible for those who were eligible. And, as additional evidence of the complexity of the application process: shortly after the announcement of DACA, the U.S. Citizenship and Immigration Services (USCIS) created its own materials to guide applicants through this murky process, including a flyer with a game board–like labyrinth of application requirements and procedures.

When applying for DACA—as when applying for other temporary (and thus liminal) immigration statuses[4]—individuals go from being undocumented to documented (or partially documented) and from having an unrecognized presence within the nation to establishing a presence that must be thoroughly detailed. The documentation process of DACA can be followed through the submission of the initial application and renewals, as well as through applications for advance parole (permission required prior to international travel) if requested. The steps of such documentation can be confusing, frustrating, anxiety-inducing, and, inevitably, enmeshed in bureaucracy. DACA applicants and recipients describe the application process as a perplexing and convoluted one, a process that paradoxically requires filing multiple documents to prove one's long-term presence in a place where residence is not officially permissible.

Thus, for DACA recipients, bureaucratic inscription has led to some security: work authorization, the possibility of domestic travel, and the potential to travel internationally (even if "risky," as advance parole has been described by the Immigrant Legal Resource Center).[5] Most significantly, DACA (if approved) has provided temporary relief from the threat of deportation. But this has been a threat *deferred*: recipients may not qualify for renewal, or, as many DACAmented people have experienced, they may face a kind of "deferral of renewal," because processing times for renewal applications can be lengthy and unpredictable. And, of course, "all these documents" are submitted to USCIS, an arm of the U.S. Department of Homeland Security—the very agency that monitors and arbitrates authorized and unauthorized status, a contradiction that follows migrants long after their DACAmented status has been approved.

In 2013, a few months after the workshop was held, Sofía contacted me to let me know that she had heard from USCIS about her appointment to gather *biometrics*, the term the agency uses for photographing and fingerprinting applicants. When I later saw Sofía in person, she described the anxiety of such an event: "I was apprehensive, scared, unsure. There were metal detectors, and I had to go in alone." She talked about how strange it was to spend much of her life avoiding immigration officials, but then one day to go to the immigration office and walk through the front door. "It is unlikely that they would take you away if you are there for an appointment," she said. "But still. . . ." Her voice trailed off, her silence underscoring the contradictions of DACA.

And, in fact, Sofía's concerns foreshadowed shifts in immigration enforcement that have taken place under the Trump administration. Since President Trump took office in 2017, a number of apprehensions have occurred during migrants' scheduled check-ins with U.S. Immigration and Customs Enforcement (ICE) officials. In one high-profile case shortly after Trump's inauguration, Guadalupe García de Rayos was detained during a routine meeting with ICE agents in Phoenix, Arizona; she had been in the United States for twenty-one years and had, without fail, attended required annual ICE appointments for eight years when she was deported to Mexico.[6] Since García de Rayos was targeted during her check-in appointment, fear has grown among immigrant communities as "what was routine is now roulette."[7] Such apprehensions underscore how the state's role as administrator, arbiter, monitor, and enforcer of immigration status overlaps. Especially troubling to DACA recipients and others with temporary statuses is that migrants risk apprehension and deportation through the very processes that are required by, and meant to demonstrate migrants' compliance with, the federal government's system of documentation.

Ultimately, Sofía received a letter confirming that her application for DACA had been approved. After hearing this news, Sofía was relieved, but she also wondered aloud if DACA, and the process of documenting her life in the United States, would fully eliminate her struggles. "It is hard to say if I'll ever have all that heaviness lifted." Her tone shifted, highlighting the importance of living in the moment, "but I don't get too caught up with the future. . . . I always say, 'where are the opportunities right now?'" Still, she was hesitant to assume that DACA, or any change of status, would ever be complete: "I wonder, even if I ever go through the ceremony and become a citizen, if I'll still have this heaviness."

On September 5, 2017, U.S. attorney general Jeff Sessions announced that President Trump would end the DACA program, placing Sofía and fellow DACA recipients in a position that is in some ways even more precarious than their status before applying for a deferral of removal through DACA. Now, after complying with the state's requirements and closely following the state's direction, nearly 800,000 young people are on record as having migrated to the United States without state authorization. In a disturbing example of how the government documents—and produces—unauthorized migrants, those who have received or even applied for temporary security under DACA now find themselves facing new and perhaps greater risks of apprehension by the state. Furthermore, although DACA applicants embarked on the application process voluntarily, the possibility of deportation facilitated by the very information the state collected to provide protection from deportation underscores the ways that even applying for a stay of removal can—quite literally against their will—place individuals in an insecure relationship with the state.

"Detainee Not Found"

When searching for someone being held in U.S. immigration detention, the primary portal is an ICE website, titled the Online Detainee Locator System. The database can be searched using an A-Number (short for "Alien Number") and nationality of the individual being held or by "biographical information" including name, country, and date of birth. While the system initially seems straightforward, those who use it—family members, advocates, attorneys—describe it as anything but. "Be patient," one volunteer from a visitation program warned me, "it can be very challenging." She explained that in order to find a record, all information—the nine-digit A-Number, the precise spelling of all names, an accurate date of birth—is required. "You will often receive the message, 'Detainee Not Found,' but keep trying." She described how a search can be very troubling, especially given that some people are, in fact, impossible to locate: an *s* instead of a *z* in a name, two digits reversed, or an error during data entry can render migrants in detention invisible to those who are looking for them.

So, while documents circulate, proliferate, or are imbued with value when one applies for DACA, the documentation of detention tends to be scant. One of the many contradictions of immigration detention is that even as individuals are held in secure facilities and closely followed and documented by government agents, the people connected to those in detention, including family members and even the attorneys representing them, may be unable to find them at all. In fact, the "records" of detention—and, most significantly, the people connected to them—can easily go missing or be entirely out of view. The documentation of detention is often obscured by the state, making opaque the ways that migrants move through a complex detention labyrinth.

The bureaucratic process of detention, like that of DACA and deportation, is arguably a way for the state to formally mark those held as "unauthorized." As with other immigration processes, the government assigns an "Alien Number" to each migrant in detention, including infants and toddlers, thus also assigning them the label of "alien." And, in some detention centers, such as the Eloy Detention Center in Arizona (run by CCA, formerly the Corrections Corporation of America, now "rebranded" as CoreCivic),[8] all people in detention are assigned a "deportation officer" regardless of the circumstances that led to detention. Thus, not only are those in detention processed as "aliens," but assigning them a deportation officer leads to the (incorrect) notion that everyone in detention will ultimately be deported.

When I asked one attorney why, for example, an individual who had gone to a port of entry requesting asylum would immediately be assigned a deportation officer, she paused: "Good question—I haven't thought about it that way. I think I've been working in detention centers for so long that much of it has become normalized." And, indeed, the process of creating records for those in detention assumes (or even constructs) a particular status—a status that endures during one's time in detention and potentially beyond. Through the documentation of detention, "deportable aliens" proliferate, further underscoring the state's reduction of people to this homogenizing category despite the specifics of each migrant's individual case.

There is also a disconnect between the family or public records regarding an individual, and especially their location in detention, and those of the state. Just as those in detention may not be "found," the state's detailed documentation of detention is rarely transparent. The (lack of) documentation of one man, Diego, underscores this point. After a traffic stop, Diego was apprehended. When he did not return home for dinner, his family feared the worst but was unsure how to find him. His wife, also an unauthorized migrant, enlisted the help of a local nonprofit in hopes of locating him. After extensive searching, volunteers discovered that he was being held in a private detention center several hours from his home.

Diego was in detention for nearly a year, during which time he received regular visits from advocates in the area and from his U.S.-citizen children. Other family members were unable to see Diego because of their unauthorized status. But then, after a hearing resulted in a deportation order, the family and friends who had been visiting were again unable to locate Diego, much like when he had been initially apprehended. After weeks without contact with his family, Diego was finally able to make a collect call. He had been transferred to a facility in another state, where he was told he would likely remain until he was deported. Although no one explained to Diego or his family members the reason for his transfer, advocates and attorneys speculate that transfers are a way for ICE to fill bed quotas at facilities around the country.[9] Human Rights Watch estimates that some 2 million transfers occurred among different detention facilities between 1998 and 2010; the fact that current numbers of transfers have been difficult for research organizations to obtain[10] reflects a lack of accountability on the part of the state. Here, the official record, including accurate documentation of individual transfers and data on the total number of transfers of those held by ICE, is notably opaque.

Thus, for those in detention, official bureaucratic records can be inscrutable to family and friends, pointing to the illegibility of the state to migrants and the invisibility of migrants to their loved ones. Visitation programs are one effort to counter this state-created obscurity. Through visitation, there is the possibility of seeing, "finding," or following those who are often out of view. But visitation in detention centers requires its own systems of documentation, including the use of U.S. government–issued IDs and, for certain facilities, government-approved clearance prior to entering a facility for any reason. Certain documents, or insufficient paperwork, can lead to denied, limited, or even revoked access to detention facilities, as the state tracks the documentation of migrants but also of those who try to visit them, including attorneys who represent people in detention, family members and friends hoping to see loved ones, and volunteers and advocates who enter facilities to visit and support migrants. For unauthorized migrant family members, a lack of particular papers—namely, evidence of authorized presence in the United States—typically makes entry into detention facilities impossible.

In the absence of face-to-face visits, letters are alternative "documents" that can serve as a lifeline. Several community groups make letter writing a central part of their efforts to support migrants in detention, and in many cases visitation requires that a migrant first connect with advocates in writing—either by writing a letter to a community organization or by filling out a form that volunteers ask to be distributed within detention facilities. Still, these documents—despite being created or written by advocates and loved ones—are managed and overseen by detention center staff. As I learned from volunteers who visit people in detention, because letters are opened and read before delivery, many family members are reluctant to write, or document, any communication with loved ones being held. In interviews, advocates also reported that guards and other officials often did not return completed intake forms with A-Numbers needed to visit individual migrants; these volunteers suspected that staff at the detention centers were probably not distributing materials about the visitation program in the first place, thereby undermining community efforts to connect with people in detention. Here, as migrants "go missing," so too can the documents that are intended to reach them.

Finally, it can be difficult—or even prohibited—for migrants to have documents in their possession while in detention. Although some asylum seekers come to the United States with papers they hope might prove their "credible fear," these documents are also easily lost—misplaced during the journey, washed away while crossing the Rio Grande/Río Bravo, or even taken from individuals when they are apprehended. As one woman told me, when she was transferred to a detention center, government officials confiscated the only copies she had of the "evidence" that she thought might bolster her claims to asylum: news articles, her husband's death certificate recording the death as a homicide, their marriage license. Similarly, an American Immigration Council report found that among those traveling with Mexican identification cards, one in four migrants had their card taken by U.S. Border Patrol agents and never returned.[11] And inside detention, documents can circulate almost like contraband. For example, while I was visiting one woman, she asked how to spell my name, reaching into her bra and producing a small scrap of paper with names and phone numbers of family members in the United States. She pointed to a small white space, and after I wrote down my name, she swiftly refolded the paper and again placed it inside her shirt. We laughed as she did so, but the exchange highlighted the limited documents in (and of) detention.

While these alternative forms of recordkeeping—the creation or tracing of paperwork on the margins, or outside, of the official record—can perhaps be read as resistance to the state's monopoly over documentation, such actions are very limited in the context of detention. In this case, the state holds migrants captive—physically, of course, but also through the very system of constructing restrictive categories. Even if one's status changes at some point in the future, time in detention marks migrants and places them on the record as "unauthorized." Although it can be challenging (if not impossible) to do, following the documents of individuals who are removed from communities and isolated in secure facilities around the country can reveal state strategies of unauthorization.

Expulsion, Documented

While I was conducting research with individuals and families affected by deportation, "papers" and their whereabouts were a frequent topic of conversation. Research participants often mentioned, referenced, and/or showed me the documents linked to their deportation, or—in cases when those who had been deported or "voluntarily returned" had no physical record of the process—people were frustrated that they had lost their only copy of the paperwork or, in some cases, had never been given documents in the first place (also see Gomberg-Muñoz, this volume). Documents that record the state's "removal" of a noncitizen from the United States are closely tied to the process, even if they are no longer (or never were) in one's possession. Even if not visible or accessible, documents and documentation follow those who are deported.

When Rodrigo was deported, the process generated a series of government documents that outlined, formalized, and, ultimately, concretized his expulsion.[12] Prior to the deportation, Rodrigo had traveled twice to the United States with a valid visitor visa, each time careful to return to Mexico within the six-month period stipulated by the stamp placed in his passport upon entering the United States. On his third trip north, however, when Rodrigo arrived at the bridge in El Paso, Texas, and presented his passport and visa, he was taken aside and questioned for several hours. As outlined in the documents he was later given—including a form titled "Notice to Alien Ordered Removed/Departure Verification"—Rodrigo was deported because he was "suspected of being an intended immigrant." Curiously, this was before he had actually entered the country and despite the fact that he had previously traveled on the visa and returned to Mexico both times. Rodrigo's

Mexican passport, with the valid U.S. visa inside, was confiscated, and he was formally "removed."

Just prior to being deported, Rodrigo was given a packet of paperwork that included a transcript of his exchange with U.S. Border Patrol agents. Several of the questions in the transcript of Rodrigo's removal documents aim to verify the clarity of the proceedings and his understanding of the events; the transcript ends on a definitive note, with Rodrigo's signature at the bottom of the document indicating that the information was correct and that he understood the ramifications. However, while these documents represent the proceedings as clear and straightforward, they were, for Rodrigo, a source of great confusion: "I didn't understand it . . . honestly, I'm still not sure what happened. It was all very confusing." He showed me the forms, spreading them out on his dining room table, and asked if there was anything that could be done. "Can you," he asked, "explain what all these papers mean?"

The process that converted Rodrigo from his status as a "nonimmigrant" with a valid visitor visa to "deportee" can be traced over a period of years. Rodrigo's path to deportation was documented at different stages, beginning more than a decade earlier when he first filed for a Mexican passport and then when he applied for and—despite very low rates of tourist visa approval in the region—received a U.S. visitor visa from the U.S. consulate in Guadalajara. Finally, on that fateful day at the border, Rodrigo was deported through expedited removal, a process that bypasses immigration court proceedings but that nevertheless produces documents with the same ramifications as any other deportation. Here, documentation of Rodrigo's status also included the taking away of valid documents he once possessed: the U.S.-approved visa stamped within a passport issued by the Mexican state. Now, in the eyes of the law, Rodrigo was a "documented deportee."

While I was conducting fieldwork, several people showed me the documents that outlined their deportation, just as Rodrigo had. During one interview, a woman took out a chair, moved it across the room, and used it to access a cupboard high above her bed. She carefully reached for a box of paperwork and placed a pile of documents in front of us—a record of a life-altering event and a government-generated archive of information. She too asked if I could make sense of the materials and especially what they meant for a possible return to the United States, mentioning that she had read and reread the documents several times, hoping to discover an opportunity that she had perhaps previously overlooked.

And, as in the case of detention, even when there are no documents, papers still hold value or can present challenges—perhaps even more so in their absence. A young man told me that he remained angry that ICE agents had not given him any documents when he was deported. He wondered if the documents might have helped his case in the future and explained that, in the chaos of the bus ride to the border the day of his deportation, he and several of the other men deported had lost the few objects they could presumably take with them to Mexico.[13] Another man I interviewed, Tito, said that he did not have the "right" documents at the border to ensure that the Mexican government would pay for return travel to his hometown in the state of Zacatecas; he recounted how Mexican officials had turned him away after reading over the paperwork. When I asked if perhaps he was "voluntarily returned" rather than formally deported—and therefore not eligible for funds for a return ticket—he said that he had "no idea." (On Mexican government programs to assist deportees—which require formal deportation orders—see Gomberg-Muñoz, this volume.) He recounted how, shortly after embarking on his return trip, he had lost the papers he had received during the process. "*Ni modo* [Oh well]," he said—because he had never learned to read, the papers were, in any event, illegible to him.

Thus, a migrant's own records may be absent, incomplete, and/or distinct from those compiled by the state. As these cases show, some who are deported have no record of their deportation while others do receive paperwork and guard the documents as significant, even if such documentation concretizes their exclusion from the United States. After deportation, migrants become legible to the state in a new way, and—even if not fully transparent or understood by migrants themselves, such as Tito's experience of not being able to read the documents he did receive—state actions are clearly "seen" and known by those who are deported. Finally, in nearly every case of deportation, the state's record does not match the individual experience of a life lived in the United States. Just as migrants describe having their lives abruptly halted—as they "disappear" or "vanish" from the United States after deportation[14]—they also say there are rarely documents that can accurately account for their previous residence and sense of belonging.

Detention and deportation underscore the disjuncture between "official" records compiled by the state and the documents that individual migrants receive or are able to preserve. As the state enacts a "removal," it thoroughly documents the process and generates a series of records. Yet, although these are records that can and do alter migration trajectories, the personal archives of deportation are unlikely to match those of the state. There are nearly always discrepancies between state records and the collection of documents that individual migrants may be able (or unable) to gather, have in their possession, lose, or preserve. As with detention, these inconsistencies reflect the power imbalances that shape the relationship between governments and migrants, as well as the ways that migrants must maneuver bureaucracies from a disadvantaged position. The bureaucracies that record presence, authorization (or lack of authorization), immigration status, and—in the case of deportation—removal are imbued with inequalities and a profound imbalance of power.

Like migrants with DACA status and those held in detention facilities, deportees go on record as unauthorized, but this documentation has a very different effect. Unlike those who apply for DACA, individuals who are deported are forced to move through processes of documentation. And unlike the unknown outcomes after spending time in detention—which could result in deportation, but might result in one's release from a detention facility and/or a change in immigration status—the result of formal deportation, at least in legal terms, is systematically limited and predictable. Rodrigo and the millions of others who have been deported are now officially unauthorized to be present in the United States—on the record as expelled and outside the nation, geographically and in terms of membership. For those who are "removed" by the state, documents are most likely to lead to a dead end, leaving many to reflect on the ways that an undocumented life in the United States that is not documented as such—that is, an existence that continues under the radar—might have provided security despite the many risks and uncertainty of living in the shadows. Instead, deportees are officially labeled as outcasts and legally banished from the country, often indefinitely.

Documenting Unauthorization

In each of these cases—DACA, detention, and deportation—*unauthorization* manifests in degrees and shifts as it comes to define one's relationship with the U.S. state. Thus, the state's efforts to document, and officially "unauthorize," migrant trajectories can be plotted along scales of time (for a discussion of documentation and temporality, see Anderson, this volume). After a DACA approval, a migrant's status changes, but remains uncertain: DACA recipients are underdocumented in the sense that they continue to live in the United States, now with government permission, but for an unknown length of time and still without permanent legal status or any possible path to U.S. citizenship. Thus, DACA recipients continue to be, in many ways, defined by the state as "unauthorized," with the future effects of such status uncertain. In the case of immigration detention, systems of recordkeeping assign an

A-Number, effectively defining individuals as "alien" despite a range of possible outcomes in their individual cases. And, for those who have been deported, documentation multiplies risk, as they are now registered as without a claim to belonging in the nation; this kind of documentation carries more certainty, as those who are deported lose most opportunities for a status change.

So, despite obvious differences in the position of DACA recipients, those in detention, and people who are deported, they also share their (now formalized) unauthorized status. As I have argued, following these diverse paper trails can reveal the very process of unauthorization itself. Tracing the government's documentation of migrants is one way to record how unauthorized status is made material by the state and becomes recorded as fact.[15] The legal and procedural processes of documentation formalize one's unauthorized status and—in some ways for those with DACA status and those who are detained, but nearly always for those who have been deported— make more vulnerable the already precarious status of those living in the United States without the "right" documents. Documents proliferate even as people go on record as having insufficient documents, incorrect documents, or a complete absence of any documents that would make their presence in the United States "legal."

DACAmented migrants, people in detention, and those who have been deported find themselves in a common space of liminality and contradiction as the state's "de facto authorization" of unauthorized presence—what Luis Plascencia calls "informally authorized" migration[16]—can swiftly become its inverse. Now unauthorized migrants are recorded by the government as having a kind of "formally unauthorized" status, one defined by and documented as the absence of U.S. citizenship. For those with DACA, their liminal status carries some protections, and yet the risk of deportation is present. Detention and deportation, too, are processes of documentation— albeit systems that are involuntary and that record migrants as outside the nation. The unauthorization of detention may or may not be temporary, but deportation, by definition, results in the formal (and physical) exclusion of migrants. Through recorded "removals," the state attempts to concretize expulsion. Still, many of those who are deported continue to reside in a liminal space as their concrete ties to the nation continue and may even be reconstituted through a return to the United States.

Scholars have identified similarly contradictory immigration statuses, including the "spaces of nonexistence" described by Susan Bibler Coutin among Salvadorans in the United States,[17] the "vulnerable stability" of those with Temporary Protected Status as outlined by Leisy Abrego,[18] and the "liminal legality" described by Cecilia Menjívar[19] that blur the supposed binary of documented versus undocumented status. Even if not fully actualized, the state attempts, through its recordkeeping bureaucracies, to resolve such liminality and to place migrants in a more definitive category. Indeed, "measurement technologies can produce certainties out of ambiguous and contested situations."[20] A future change in status may be feasible for DACA recipients—as a member of one NGO's legal team told me, once temporary status is conferred on a particular group, it is unlikely to be taken away, although this is precisely what the Trump administration announced will take place. All who are detained, regardless of their status prior to detention or the outcome of their individual cases, go on record as "aliens." And, for those deported, the chance of relief or a pardon is unattainable in any practical sense, rendering unauthorized presence a probable status for life.

By following the process of unauthorization and deauthorization, the contradictions of visibility and invisibility are thrown into relief. Although official paper trails might make the state more legible to some migrants—for example, DACA recipients may see state bureaucracies in a new way as they are required to maneuver through them—for the most part, processes of documentation only add to the state's illegibility, underscored by the opacity (and often, impenetrability) of state systems that direct and implement apprehensions, deportations, and an expansive immigration detention regime. In other words, although government-generated documentation makes migrants legible to the state—and serves as a method of exerting control over migrants more broadly (see Coutin, this volume)[21]—such processes of documentation rarely result in any increased transparency of state action. Instead, state bureaucracies, and ultimately state accountability, are rendered opaque and even more difficult to track.

Such analysis points to what may be a fourth case for consideration: unauthorized migrants who are and who continue to be, in fact, undocumented. Migrants who have not directly interacted with the state due to detention or deportation, and those who have not submitted an application for DACA or another temporary status, are not formally on record (or, specifically, on state records) as unauthorized. By remaining undocumented, some unauthorized migrants evade being recorded as such. In these cases, official state records have not—or have not yet—amassed in a way that might mark, and thus specifically target,[22] migrants. For people living in the United States without documents and who have not directly interacted with the state, willingly or through force, security might paradoxically come from invisibility.[23]

Although living in the shadows comes with great risk,[24] in the current moment, being unauthorized but undocumented as such might lead to some (albeit limited) security and protections. Given how anti-immigrant sentiment and discourse undergirds nearly every action of the Trump administration, this seems more true than ever today in the United States.

In addition, tracing the paperwork that leads to unauthorization is a way to question the extent to which such engagement with the state is voluntary. Whether or not migrants elect to interact with government institutions, as is the case with DACA applicants, or are forced to, such as when migrants are detained or deported, unauthorization is arguably thrust on individuals as migrants who are already unauthorized become formally so. Unauthorization results in a form of what Sarah B. Horton calls "phantom citizenship"[25] or the inverse of what Hiroshi Motomura identifies as "territorial personhood"[26]—that is, a kind of "territorial nonpersonhood."[27] Once documented by the state as unauthorized, an absence of membership becomes precisely that. The process of unauthorization, particularly when recorded explicitly as such, underscores the ways that state bureaucracies—whether calculated or incompetent, legible or illegible, accessible or out of reach, comprehensible or not—follow migrants at different moments and in diverse circumstances.

Thus, whether or not statuses are liminal and temporary such as with DACA, uncertain as in the case of immigration detention, or presumably final as when one is deported, the effects can be surprisingly consistent and durable. Unauthorized migrants—and their loved ones—live with a constant, chronic fear of being forced into (or of being again forced into) the state's system of unauthorization, whether they are DACA recipients, those in detention, those living in the shadows, those who have been deported and have returned to the United States, or the loved ones of unauthorized migrants. And, given the current climate in the United States, even immigrants living in the country with authorization, such as legal permanent residents, are likely to question the actual permanency of their authorized status. Indeed, as is evident in the cases I have described, state bureaucracies and systems of documentation can be used to reach a number of ends, including expulsion, even when migrants have gone through processes meant to "legalize" their status.

Regardless of the path that leads there or the immigration status that the state does or does not assign, the stakes of government documentation—and the risk of being documented as unauthorized—are very high: at best, those cast as noncitizens hope for an outcome or change in status that provides some security, and at worst, documentation regimes concretize unauthorized status, at times indefinitely. Here the state authorizes, partially authorizes, or unauthorizes presence in the nation, making real and concrete the absence of citizenship but also of possibility for millions of the nation's residents.

Notes

1 Deborah A. Boehm, *Returned: Going and Coming in an Age of Deportation* (Berkeley: University of California Press, 2016).

2 Barbara Yngvesson and Susan Bibler Coutin, "Backed by Papers: Undoing Persons, Histories, and Return," *American Ethnologist* 33, no. 2 (2006): 184.

3 See discussion in Sally Engle Merry and Susan Bibler Coutin, "Technologies of Truth in the Anthropology of Conflict," *American Ethnologist* 41, no. 1 (2014): 1–16.

4 See, for example, Leisy J. Abrego, *Sacrificing Families: Navigating Laws, Labor, and Love across Borders* (Stanford, CA: Stanford University Press, 2014); Susan Bibler Coutin, *Legalizing Moves: Salvadoran Immigrants' Struggle for U.S. Residency* (Ann Arbor: University of Michigan Press, 2000); Susan Bibler Coutin, *Exiled Home: Salvadoran Transnational Youth in the Aftermath of Violence* (Durham, NC: Duke University Press, 2016); Cecilia Menjívar, "Liminal Legality: Salvadoran and Guatemalan Immigrants' Lives in the United States," *American Journal of Sociology* 111, no. 4 (2006): 999–1037.

5 Immigrant Legal Resource Center, "Travel for DACA Applicants (Advance Parole)," Immigrant Legal Resource Center, 2015, accessed September 8, 2015, http://www .ilrc.org/files/documents/advance_parole_guide.pdf.

6 Fernanda Santos, "She Showed Up Yearly to Meet Immigration Agents. Now They've Deported Her," *New York Times*, February 8, 2017, accessed January 5, 2018, https://www.nytimes.com/2017/02/08/us/phoenix-guadalupe-garcia-de-rayos.html.

7 Liz Robbins, "Once Routine, Immigration Check-Ins Are Now High Stakes," *New York Times*, April 11, 2017, accessed January 5, 2018, https://www.nytimes.com/2017 /04/11/nyregion/ice-immigration-check-in-deportation.html.

8 Bethany Davis, "Corrections Corporation of America Rebrands as CoreCivic," *Inside CCA*, accessed May 24, 2019, http://staging.cca.com/insidecca/corrections -corporation-of-America-rebrands-as-corecivic.

9 For example, Detention Watch Network, "Banking on Detention: Local Lockup Quotas and the Immigrant Dragnet," Detention Watch Network, 2015, accessed January 5, 2018, https://www.detentionwatchnetwork.org/sites/default/files/reports /DWN%20CCR%20Banking%20on%20Detention%20Report.pdf; Libby Rainey, "ICE Transfers Immigrants Held in Detention around the Country to Keep Beds Filled. Then It Releases Them, with No Help Getting Home," *Denver Post*, September 17, 2017, accessed January 5, 2018, https://www.denverpost.com/2017/09/17/ice -detention-transfers-immigrants/.

10 See discussions in, for example, Human Rights Watch, "Locked Up Far Away: The Transfer of Immigrants to Remote Detention Centers in the United States," Human

Rights Watch, 2009, accessed January 5, 2018, https://www.hrw.org/report/2009/12/02/locked-far-away/transfer-immigrants-remote-detention-centers-united-states; Human Rights Watch, "A Costly Move: Far and Frequent Transfers Impede Hearings for Immigrant Detainees in the United States," Human Rights Watch, 2011, accessed January 5, 2018, https://www.hrw.org/report/2011/06/14/costly-move/far-and-frequent-transfers-impede-hearings-immigrant-detainees-united; Rainey, "ICE Transfers Immigrants Held in Detention"; TRAC Immigration, "Huge Increase in Transfers of ICE Detainees," TRAC Immigration, 2009, accessed January 5, 2018, http://trac.syr.edu/immigration/reports/220/.

11 Daniel E. Martínez, Jeremy Slack, and Josiah Heyman, "Bordering on Criminal: The Routine Abuse of Migrants in the Removal System," Immigration Policy Center, American Immigration Council, 2013, accessed January 5, 2018, https://www.americanimmigrationcouncil.org/sites/default/files/research/bordering_on_criminal.pdf.

12 See Boehm, *Returned*, 13–14, for this vignette about Rodrigo's experiences.

13 Also see Martínez, Slack, and Heyman, "Bordering on Criminal."

14 Boehm, *Returned*.

15 Merry and Coutin, "Technologies of Truth in the Anthropology of Conflict."

16 Luis F. B. Plascencia, "The 'Undocumented' Mexican Migrant Question: Re-Examining the Framing of Law and Illegalization in the United States," *Urban Anthropology and Studies of Cultural Systems and World Economic Development* 38, nos. 2–4 (2009): 410.

17 Coutin, *Legalizing Moves*, 27.

18 Abrego, *Sacrificing Families*, 91.

19 Menjívar, "Liminal Legality."

20 Merry and Coutin, "Technologies of Truth in the Anthropology of Conflict," 1–2.

21 Also see Matthew S. Hull, "Documents and Bureaucracy," *Annual Review of Anthropology* 41 (2012): 251–67; Miriam Ticktin, "Where Ethics and Politics Meet: The Violence of Humanitarianism in France," *American Ethnologist* 33, no. 1 (2006): 33–49; Miriam Ticktin, *Casualties of Care: Immigration and the Politics of Humanitarianism in France* (Berkeley: University of California Press, 2011).

22 Jonathan Xavier Inda, *Targeting Immigrants: Government, Technology, and Ethics* (Malden, MA: Blackwell, 2006).

23 See also Asad L. Asad, "Reconsidering Immigrant Illegality: How Immigrants Perceive the Risk of Immigration Law and Enforcement" (Ph.D. diss., Harvard University, 2017).

24 For example, Leo Chavez, *Shadowed Lives: Undocumented Immigrants in American Society*, 2nd ed. (Belmont, CA: Wadsworth, 1997).

25 Sarah B. Horton, "Phantom Citizenship: The Retirement Dilemmas of Legally Anomalous Migrants" (paper presented at the Annual Meeting of the American Anthropological Association, Minneapolis, Minnesota, November 16–20, 2016).

26 Hiroshi Motomura, *Americans in Waiting: The Lost Story of Immigration and Citizenship in the United States* (Oxford: Oxford University Press, 2006), 10.

27 I am grateful to Susan Coutin for suggesting this at a Wenner-Gren Workshop, "Paper Trails," at the University of Colorado, Denver, in August 2017.

Bibliography

Abrego, Leisy J. *Sacrificing Families: Navigating Laws, Labor, and Love across Borders*. Stanford, CA: Stanford University Press, 2014.

Asad, Asad L. "Reconsidering Immigrant Illegality: How Immigrants Perceive the Risk of Immigration Law and Enforcement." Ph.D. dissertation, Harvard University, 2017.

Boehm, Deborah A. *Returned: Going and Coming in an Age of Deportation*. Berkeley: University of California Press, 2016.

Chavez, Leo. *Shadowed Lives: Undocumented Immigrants in American Society*, 2nd ed. Belmont, CA: Wadsworth, 1997.

Coutin, Susan Bibler. *Exiled Home: Salvadoran Transnational Youth in the Aftermath of Violence*. Durham, NC: Duke University Press, 2016.

Coutin, Susan Bibler. *Legalizing Moves: Salvadoran Immigrants' Struggle for U.S. Residency*. Ann Arbor: University of Michigan Press, 2000.

Davis, Bethany. "Corrections Corporation of America Rebrands as CoreCivic." *Inside CCA*. Accessed May 24, 2019. http://staging.cca.com/insidecca/corrections-corporation-of-America-rebrands-as-corecivic.

Detention Watch Network. "Banking on Detention: Local Lockup Quotas and the Immigrant Dragnet." Detention Watch Network, 2015. Accessed January 5, 2018. https://www.detentionwatchnetwork.org/sites/default/files/reports/DWN%20CCR%20Banking%20on%20Detention%20Report.pdf.

Horton, Sarah B. "Phantom Citizenship: The Retirement Dilemmas of Legally Anomalous Migrants." Paper presented at the Annual Meeting of the American Anthropological Association, Minneapolis, Minnesota, November 16–20, 2016.

Hull, Matthew S. "Documents and Bureaucracy." *Annual Review of Anthropology* 41 (2012): 251–67.

Human Rights Watch. "A Costly Move: Far and Frequent Transfers Impede Hearings for Immigrant Detainees in the United States." Human Rights Watch, 2011. Accessed January 5, 2018. https://www.hrw.org/report/2011/06/14/costly-move/far-and-frequent-transfers-impede-hearings-immigrant-detainees-united.

Human Rights Watch. "Locked Up Far Away: The Transfer of Immigrants to Remote Detention Centers in the United States." Human Rights Watch, 2009. Accessed January 5, 2018. https://www.hrw.org/report/2009/12/02/locked-far-away/transfer-immigrants-remote-detention-centers-united-states.

Immigrant Legal Resource Center. "Travel for DACA Applicants (Advance Parole)." Immigrant Legal Resource Center, 2015. Accessed September 8, 2015. https://www.ilrc.org/sites/default/files/documents/advance_parole_guide.pdf.

Inda, Jonathan Xavier. *Targeting Immigrants: Government, Technology, and Ethics*. Malden, MA: Blackwell, 2006.

Martínez, Daniel E., Jeremy Slack, and Josiah Heyman. "Bordering on Criminal: The Routine Abuse of Migrants in the Removal System." Immigration Policy

Center, American Immigration Council, 2013. Accessed January 5, 2018. https:// www.americanimmigrationcouncil.org/sites/default/files/research/bordering_on _criminal.pdf.

Menjívar, Cecilia. "Liminal Legality: Salvadoran and Guatemalan Immigrants' Lives in the United States." *American Journal of Sociology* 111, no. 4 (2006): 999–1037.

Merry, Sally Engle, and Susan Bibler Coutin. "Technologies of Truth in the Anthropology of Conflict." *American Ethnologist* 41, no. 1 (2014): 1–16.

Motomura, Hiroshi. *Americans in Waiting: The Lost Story of Immigration and Citizenship in the United States.* Oxford: Oxford University Press, 2006.

Plascencia, Luis F. B. "The 'Undocumented' Mexican Migrant Question: Re-Examining the Framing of Law and Illegalization in the United States." *Urban Anthropology and Studies of Cultural Systems and World Economic Development* 38, nos. 2–4 (2009): 375–434.

Ticktin, Miriam. *Casualties of Care: Immigration and the Politics of Humanitarianism in France.* Berkeley: University of California Press, 2011.

Ticktin, Miriam. "Where Ethics and Politics Meet: The Violence of Humanitarianism in France." *American Ethnologist* 33, no. 1 (2006): 33–49.

TRAC Immigration. "Huge Increase in Transfers of ICE Detainees." TRAC Immigration, 2009. Accessed January 5, 2018. http://trac.syr.edu/immigration/reports/220/.

Yngvesson, Barbara, and Susan Bibler Coutin. "Backed by Papers: Undoing Persons, Histories, and Return." *American Ethnologist* 33, no. 2 (2006): 177–90.

5

OPPORTUNITIES AND DOUBLE BINDS

Legal Craft in an Era of Uncertainty

In 2011, Tina, a U.S. citizen, and Jaime, her undocumented husband, met with a Board of Immigration Appeals–accredited paralegal at a Los Angeles nonprofit to determine whether Tina could petition for Jaime to obtain lawful permanent residency in the United States.[1] With the permission of all present, I observed the meeting as a researcher and volunteer. Tina and Jaime took their seats with hopeful expressions on their faces. The paralegal asked them a series of questions about when Jaime had entered the country, whether he ever had left, what statuses he had had since entering, whether he had been the victim of any crimes, and whether anyone had petitioned for him previously. It turned out that Jaime had entered the United States in the 1990s, and had left and reentered the country once during the 2000s.[2] He had no criminal convictions, had not been a victim of a crime, and no one had petitioned for him.

The paralegal then delivered some devastating news. He explained that family visa petitions have multiple steps. The first step is that the U.S. citizen or legal permanent resident applies for their relative. He told Tina that she had every right to apply for her husband and that this part of the application would probably be easily approved.

The second step, he said, is to apply for legal permanent residency when the petition becomes current. But, because no one had petitioned for Jaime while "245(i)"—a provision of immigration law that, prior to April 30, 2001, enabled individuals who had entered the country without inspection to adjust their status in the United States—was in effect, Jaime would be unable to obtain residency in the United States. Instead, he would have to go to Mexico, his country of origin. Unfortunately for Jaime, individuals who have accrued one year of unlawful presence in the United States trigger a ten-year bar on lawful reentry when they leave the country, and those who reenter the United States unlawfully after triggering this bar are subject to a permanent bar. Unknowingly, Jaime triggered the ten-year bar when he first left the country in the 2000s and the permanent bar when he reentered. So, the paralegal explained, Jaime was now permanently barred from becoming a legal resident in the United States. However, if he remained outside the United States for ten years, he could apply for a waiver of the permanent bar. Also, if he fell victim to a crime, he could apply for a U-visa, which is for individuals who suffer substantial harm from a crime and who collaborate with the police in an investigation.[3]

As the paralegal finished delivering his analysis of Jaime and Tina's circumstances, Tina began to cry. The couple quickly left. The paralegal told me sadly that the scenario that Tina and Jaime faced is so common that he has created text to simply cut-and-paste into his notes after such consultations.

Later the same day, Jasmina, a lawful permanent resident who would be naturalizing at a ceremony in a few weeks, met with the same paralegal to learn whether, as a U.S. citizen, she could petition for her sisters who were in the United States, her nephews who were in El Salvador, or her husband, who was in the United States. Again, the paralegal asked her about entry dates, departures, statuses held, parents' statuses, criminal convictions, and whether anyone was a victim of a crime. Based on Jasmina's answers, the paralegal explained that her sisters would face ten-year bars on reentry, and her nephews would likely be over twenty-one and therefore ineligible by the time any petition for her sisters was approved. However, her husband, the paralegal continued, was another matter. Because Jasmina had qualified for U.S. residency through the Nicaraguan Adjustment and Central American Relief Act (NACARA) and because she was married to her husband at the time, her husband was already eligible for residency, without Jasmina filing a petition.

Jasmina was surprised by this news. She related that the person who had prepared her NACARA application (which had not been submitted through the nonprofit where the paralegal worked) had said that it was risky to include her husband's information in her NACARA application, but she had done so anyway.

The paralegal advised her to have her husband come in for his own consultation, and he gave her a form for her husband to complete, along with a list of the documents that her husband should bring to prove seven years of continuous presence and good moral character, two of the requirements for NACARA. These documents included a copy of Jasmina's NACARA application, receipts or other records for every couple of months for the last seven years, birth certificates, marriage certificates, bank account information, educational certificates and awards, and school records, if any.

Jasmina took this information and left happily, planning to return with her husband as soon as possible.

The disparate prognoses in these two consultations demonstrate the legal craft involved in deciphering the ways that records foreclose and create regularization opportunities for undocumented individuals living in the United States. Tina and Jasmina were similarly situated. Both married undocumented men, gained legal status, and sought to petition for their spouses. Nonetheless, seemingly arbitrary differences in the ways that time, presence, securitization, and documentation figured within these couples' legal histories resulted in strikingly different outcomes. Jaime's year of unlawful presence subjected him to a ten-year bar on reentry,[4] and his departure and reentry made him be legally treated as something like a "flagrant offender," whereas Jasmina's husband's seven years of continuous presence fulfilled one of the requirements for NACARA.[5] Jasmina's husband benefited from the fact that special programs and provisions, such as 245(i), NACARA, and U-visas, privilege humanitarian concerns, creating limited oases within the criminalization of immigration. Jasmina's husband's legal history could aid him in qualifying for residency, whereas Jaime's record of entries and exits could subject him to a permanent bar.

The expertise to develop and evaluate legal strategies is formulated in a context of legal uncertainty. One of the ways that state bureaucracies exert control, whether deliberately or not, is through their opacity and arbitrariness,[6] qualities that are exacerbated in the case of the U.S. Citizenship and Immigration Service (USCIS). According to the "plenary powers" doctrine, Congress and the executive branch of government have extensive and largely unreviewable discretion to establish policies regarding foreign nationals who are present within U.S. borders or who seek entry.[7] As a result, rules can change, groups that have been permitted to settle in the country can suddenly be uprooted, and barriers to regularization can be established.[8] Examples of such changes include the revocation of reentry documents issued to Chinese residents in the late 1800s,[9] the removal of individuals (including U.S. citizens) of Mexican descent through Operation Wetback during the 1950s,[10] and the creation of presence bars through the 1996 Illegal

Immigration Reform and Immigrant Responsibility Act (IIRIRA).[11] The U.S. immigration system is made more opaque by the fact that many legalization applications are processed through the mail, without a face-to-face meeting between the applicant and the officer who evaluates applications. Service providers have knowledge of both state actors and migration realities and therefore serve as intermediaries within regularization processes.[12] Yet, even they face uncertainty about whether and how law and policy may change in the future.

Examining the legal craft practiced by migrants and advocates highlights the quasi-magical power of papers and records[13] to transform persons by regularizing or criminalizing their presence.[14] This power derives from demands for documentation that migrants may or may not have. Documents therefore create opportunities and double binds: they are key to obtaining legal status, but they also can make legalization impossible.[15] Deciphering these opportunities and double binds involves a sort of technocratic expertise in mundane but nonetheless crucial facets of immigration law—how to fill out a form, how long it takes for applications to be processed, the amount and type of evidence that officials generally require. Exploring the nature of such expertise sheds light not only on the work of low-level service providers but also on migrants' own agency. Recent work on migrant subjectivity has emphasized the liminality produced by enforcement practices that treat long-term noncitizen residents as outsiders.[16] Uncertainty shapes migrants' engagement with legal opportunities, creating a mixture of hope and cynicism that leads to creative redefinitions of immigration law and policy.

My analysis of service providers' and migrants' legal craft is based on fieldwork and volunteer work at a Los Angeles nonprofit that provides legal services to Spanish-speaking migrants. From 2011 to 2015, I spent one day per week at this organization, for six months in 2011 and approximately eight months each year thereafter. I shadowed service providers during consultations, case review meetings, public presentations on immigration law, and appointments at which applications for family petitions, naturalization, green card renewals, work authorization, U-visas, Temporary Protected Status (TPS), NACARA, and Deferred Action for Childhood Arrivals (DACA) were prepared.[17] As a volunteer, I translated documents such as birth and marriage certificates, letters of support, and declarations. I was also trained to prepare applications and renewals for TPS, work authorizations, and DACA, and to take declarations for U-visa applications. All volunteer tasks were performed under the supervision of attorneys and Board of Immigration Appeals–accredited paralegals. I had countless informal conversations with legal staff and other volunteers, and I conducted formal interviews with forty-two of the nonprofit's clients. Two doctoral students, Gray Abarca and Véronique Fortin, also assisted with fieldwork. Here, I draw particularly on observations and volunteer experiences from June to December 2011, a period when the Obama administration pursued contradictory policies, prioritizing deportation and immigration enforcement while also calling for immigration reform and developing limited measures to provide relief on a humanitarian basis. Revisiting immigrant advocacy at this moment, when enforcement had intensified and pressures for reform were strong, sheds light on legal craft in a context of considerable uncertainty.

Legal Uncertainty and the Power of Papers

In the United States, intensified immigration enforcement coupled with efforts to create regularization opportunities have made documentation necessary, scarce, and overabundant. Documents are necessary in that social security numbers, green cards, proof of work authorization, and other forms of identification are increasingly required in order to work, drive, travel, study, and engage in myriad everyday transactions. They are scarce in that legalization opportunities have been curtailed, making such documents hard to obtain. And they are overabundant in that for many, daily life in the United States leaves a paper trail consisting of receipts, notifications, statements, and records, some of which (such as criminal records) are the result of state surveillance and therefore outside the control of the individuals to whom documents refer. Furthermore, certain key identity documents, such as birth certificates and passports, are issued by migrants' countries of origin, therefore requiring would-be applicants to access multiple national and local record systems.[18] Noncitizens do not know whether they will be apprehended by immigration officials, what records exist about them, when a legalization opportunity may arise, or how their histories and future potential would be evaluated if it did. In this context, documentary processes have the potential to prove key claims but also to fall short.

Over the past few decades, exclusionary and inclusionary pressures have intensified. These competing trends were evident in the 1986 Immigration Reform and Control Act (IRCA), which authorized regularization of undocumented individuals who had been in the United States continuously since January 1, 1982, as well as certain agricultural workers, but which also sanctioned employers who hired undocumented workers.[19] During the 1990s, IIRIRA in combination with the Anti-Terrorism and Effective Death Penalty

Act restricted regularization; subjected adults who accrued six months or one year of unlawful presence to three- and ten-year bars on lawful reentry, respectively; expanded the range of criminal convictions that made individuals ineligible for lawful permanent residency; made detention mandatory for a broad range of individuals in removal proceedings; and increased funding for border and interior enforcement.[20] These trends continued during the 2000s, as federal officials enlisted local police in immigration enforcement.[21] As a result, contact with criminal justice officials increasingly puts noncitizens, including lawful permanent residents, at risk of deportation,[22] and the criminal penalties associated with immigration violations have escalated.[23] Meanwhile, as regularization opportunities dwindled, the size of the undocumented population in the United States increased from 3.5 million in 1990 to 11 million in 2015.[24]

Migrants and advocates have pushed back against these enforcement trends by attempting to establish regularization opportunities. During the 1980s, faith-based communities declared themselves sanctuaries for Salvadoran and Guatemalan refugees in an effort to secure asylum for migrants fleeing wars in Central America.[25] This advocacy work led to the passage of NACARA, which enabled certain Salvadorans, Guatemalans, and Nicaraguans to apply for U.S. residency. Trafficking and crime victims have secured the opportunity to apply for T- and U-visas on humanitarian grounds,[26] while domestic violence victims are able to petition for themselves (instead of relying on abusive spouses) through the Violence against Women Act (VAWA).[27] Students and migrant youth successfully pressured the Obama administration to create the DACA program in 2012.[28] And in 2006, millions of migrants marched publicly to oppose making it a felony to be undocumented, and to advocate for comprehensive immigration reform.[29] In 2011, when I began the research for this project, the Obama administration had prioritized deportation and border enforcement (reasoning that securing the borders would create bipartisan political support for immigration reform) while also deprioritizing the removal of certain longtime residents on humanitarian grounds. In June 2011, ICE director John Morton issued a memo (which came to be known as the "Morton Memo") articulating grounds on which officials should decline to pursue the removal of particular individuals. Groups such as longtime lawful permanent residents, the elderly, or those who had lived in the United States since childhood were considered to "warrant particular care."[30] Despite this memo, ICE continued "removing record numbers of ordinary status violators."[31]

These enforcement and advocacy trends played out within Los Angeles, impacting the work of the nonprofit with which I collaborated. The Los Angeles metropolitan area has long been a site of migrant settlement and in 2014 had an estimated 1 million undocumented migrants, the second largest concentration in the country.[32] Los Angeles also has a thriving nonprofit sector that attempts to serve migrant communities.[33] Founded during the 1980s to meet the needs of Central American asylum seekers, the nonprofit where I carried out observations and volunteer work had expanded its services to include U-visas, VAWA cases, status adjustment, and naturalization on a fee-for-service basis at a fraction of the cost charged by private attorneys. The organization primarily served Spanish-speaking migrant groups and offered consultations, public presentations on immigration law, and appointments to review documents, complete forms, and prepare declarations. Fees were sometimes waived for volunteers or the lowest-income clients, and the organization also funded some of its services through grants and donations. In addition to providing direct services, the organization engaged in outreach and advocacy.

This nonprofit's work takes place in a legal context in which low-cost representation is scarce and fraud is rampant. Because immigration hearings are administrative procedures, respondents have a right to an attorney, but only at their own expense. In migrant communities, public notaries take advantage of Spanish speakers who think that a "notary" in the United States has the extensive legal training and authority of a *notario* in many Latin American countries.[34] It is not uncommon for notaries to charge migrants thousands of dollars to prepare applications that result in deportation.[35] Chinese-speaking migrants often rely on travel agents who lack legal training to assist with immigration cases. The lack of affordable, competent legal representation adversely impacts migrants' ability to regularize. A 2016 study found that detained migrants who had counsel were twice as likely to prevail in court as were those without counsel, while undetained migrants were five times more likely to win court cases than those without attorneys.[36] Yet the same study found that only 37 percent of migrants nationally had legal representation. This legal context contributes to the uncertainty that shapes migrants' legal strategies.

Deciphering Documentary Histories

The challenges and opportunities created by legal records do not exist independently of the analysis that allows them to be identified and made part of a legal strategy. The service providers who perform these analyses are "legal technicians" who do "back office work" involving document preparation and form filing.[37] Examining their work makes it possible to "truly study legalism as a cultural phenomenon in its own right."[38] A conversation that I had early on with the lead attorney at the nonprofit is instructive in this regard. When I remarked that in the absence of major revisions to U.S. immigration law, only a dwindling population would be eligible to regularize, he responded that although from the outside it probably appears that the last major revision to immigration law was in the mid-1990s, in fact, interpretations of the law are changing all of the time. In other words, from the "inside"—that is, through work that engages the law's own logics—law "on the books" is quite active. Moreover, written law inheres in the documents that migrants gather, the declarations that service providers type up, the forms that paralegals complete, the files that advocates assemble, and the notices and documents that officials send to migrants. This material quite literally moves, between institutions, homes, offices, and agencies. Thus, service providers keep law on the books alive and in force by attempting to anticipate and influence the actions of state bureaucrats.

A key aspect of the way that service providers keep law alive is by examining the past with an eye to the future. The service providers I shadowed had developed the ability to decipher individuals' legal and immigration histories based on their clients' verbal accounts, any documentation that they provided, additional information that could be gleaned from external resources, and providers' understandings of the paths that legal cases can take. Knowing the sort of file needed to qualify for a particular benefit as well as the records that existed or could be gathered about an individual enabled them to evaluate the viability of regularization strategies. For example, a U.S. citizen who was in her mid-fifties met with a paralegal for a consultation regarding a petition that she had submitted for her brother in Mexico in the mid-1990s. The paralegal examined the woman's paperwork, which she had brought in a blue American Automobile Association tote bag. After questioning the woman about her and her brother's criminal records (they had none), her brother's relationships (to learn whether he would be able to include his spouse and children), and the woman's income (to understand whether she qualified to sponsor him without securing an additional sponsor), the paralegal determined that there were not likely to be any problems with the case. Service providers thus exercised a kind of double vision in which they "saw like a state," to paraphrase James Scott,[39] but also like the migrants they represented.

Form completion, which one might imagine to be somewhat routine, is also something of an art. The craft involved in filling out forms was made evident in a training session that I attended on TPS renewal. Attendees learned that an addendum must be used to explain individuals' prior interaction with criminal justice officials; that a question about applicants' "country of residence" refers to their country of citizenship, not where they live; that if an individual's Alien Number does not begin with "094" then they might have an old case of some sort, and therefore one must call the immigration court hotline to check; and that signatures must fit completely within a box on the form or else the application might be rejected. Those sorts of understandings are not obvious and come from working closely with forms over time. Service providers also seemingly memorized the forms that they worked with. For instance, during one consultation that I observed, a woman who was considering applying for naturalization was worried about a discrepancy regarding her reported date of entry into the United States. Without even pulling up the twenty-one-page naturalization application form, the paralegal with whom she was consulting was able to tell her that there was no question about her entry date on the form.

Much like completing application forms, assembling application packets was part of service providers' craft. My notes from one observation of preparing an application for a family visa read as follows:

> As I watched [name deleted] assemble all of the forms, I realized there is an art to this. She had to get the primary forms and supporting documentation in the right order, two-hole-punched, attached with a metal bracket, and including the two photos for the green card as well as a note on the front which she highlighted using a yellow highlighter. She gave all of this back to [her client] in two envelopes addressed to two different offices at the same address, to make sure that the forms went to the correct people. She also explained to [her client] that she had included copies of her original documents (the originals also had to be included) so that hopefully, the consular official will give her back her original documents (birth certificate, passport, etc.) and keep the copy for their records, instead of keeping the originals for their records and requiring [her client] to have all of her original documents reissued.

The documentation had to be assembled in a way that anticipated the subsequent review; and indeed, the order of documentation suggested a kind of logic or narrative. Usually application forms came first, followed by identity documents, declarations (if applicable), and supporting documentation, which was also ordered according to the elements that needed to be proven (for example, years of continuous presence). Providers generally disliked submitting forms online instead of in hard copy because it disabled strategies that they relied on to ensure accuracy and strengthen applications. For example, when they submitted hard copies, they could add a Post-it note, highlight text, and double check the entirety of the printed application form before submitting it.

Because convictions could make individuals ineligible for immigration benefits, understanding service providers' clients' criminal histories was key.[40] For example, I observed one consultation in which a Salvadoran man who had been convicted of drunk driving and leaving the scene of an accident sought to learn whether he could appeal a denial of TPS. He was informed that a single felony or two misdemeanor convictions made an individual ineligible for TPS. According to a service provider, his only hope was to reopen his felony case, obtain a new trial, and achieve a different outcome, a process known as "post-conviction relief." Obtaining an expungement would be insufficient, the paralegal who conducted the consultation explained, because expungements do not count for immigration purposes. This case was enveloped in legal uncertainty.

While a history of criminal convictions posed challenges, other sorts of records could unexpectedly make individuals eligible for status. One Salvadoran woman, Mireya, who lacked work authorization, sought to learn whether she could apply for a work permit. She informed a service provider that she had applied for asylum in the 1990s, obtained TPS, and had work permits in the past. Her last work permit had been renewed fifteen years earlier, in 1995 or 1996. She had brought her expired work permits, which she handed to the service provider for inspection. The service provider informed Mireya that it was likely that she actually was eligible for lawful permanent residency (which grants more rights than mere work authorization) through NACARA. With the service provider's help, she prepared a Freedom of Information Act request to obtain a copy of her immigration file and agreed to return for a follow-up appointment after it arrived. As Mireya left, the service provider told her to take good care of her expired work permits: "They are very strong evidence that you may be eligible for NACARA." Interestingly, in this case, the force of these documents came not from their validity—they were expired and could not be used to prove work authorization—but rather from the history that they documented. Documentation that on its face might appear to be worthless in fact was seemingly key to this individual's legal future.

Of course, service providers are not the only ones who practice legal craft. In addition, migrants themselves are key agents within regularization processes. The forms of agency that they practice are also shaped by their relationship to documents.

Devising Regularization Strategies

Migrants' legal craft has been shaped by their experiences living in the United States without documents. A key facet of this experience has been the securitization of immigration, that is, treating migrants as a national security risk rather than, for instance, a source of labor.[41] Securitization treats migrants with suspicion, subjects them to surveillance through checkpoints and demands for proof of residency, makes criminal issues of paramount importance within individuals' cases, exaggerates the importance of any discrepancies or temporal gaps in their records, increases the documentary burden to which migrants are subjected,[42] and makes it critical for migrants to know the content of any files that the state holds about them. These challenges are intensified by the fact that immigration is a bureaucracy—files can be lost, and the officials to whose discretion migrants appeal are often distant, given that applications are frequently submitted by mail. Migrants, rather than officials, are often held accountable for documentary deficiencies. So if officials—whether in the United States or in migrants' countries of origin—insert errors in the record, migrants have to explain, correct, or overcome these.

The degree to which securitization pervades immigration processes can be seen by the many security-related questions that appear on immigration forms. For example, pages 6–9 of the June 17, 2011, version of the N-400 "Application for Naturalization" form feature questions covering applicants' affiliations, moral character, and criminal histories. Examples include: "Since becoming a lawful permanent resident, have you ever failed to file a required Federal, State, or local tax return?" (6); "Between March 23, 1933, and May 8, 1945, did you work for or associate in any way (*either directly or indirectly*) with ... the Nazi government of Germany?" (7); "Have you ever been a member of or in any way associated (*either directly or indirectly*) with ... The Communist Party?" (7); "Have you ever committed a crime or offense for which you were not arrested?" (8); and "Have you ever ... [b]een a prostitute or procured anyone for prostitution" (8; emphases in the original). In my experience, individuals were sometimes baffled, startled, or a bit offended by such questions. Applicants typically responded "no" to the vast majority but sometimes had to report traffic violations, arrests, criminal charges, convictions, or having assisted others in entering the United States without authorization.

In response to securitization, migrants resorted to hyperdocumentation.[43] Even though the term *undocumented* is commonly used for those who lack legal status, such individuals actually have access to a multiplicity of documents—transcripts, report cards, receipts, church attendance records, rental agreements, letters—all of which have differing legal significance depending on when they were created and the sort of case an individual is pursuing. Saving such records was a way to prepare for future legalization opportunities.[44] As one nonprofit client who was pursuing naturalization recalled, "Everything is useful. And so they even asked me for checks from my job when I began to get my residency, checks from work, all that. And I save them, my check stubs, everything. The taxes, that too. One saves everything, because they ask one for *everything*. Even when you shop. . . . I have them in a box . . . because there I just go and look for what I need" (emphasis in the original). Hope leads migrants to save receipts, tax returns, and check stubs; stay abreast of news about legalization opportunities; and come into offices such as the nonprofit to explore options and file paperwork.

Applying for legal status can also be a form of resistance to securitization, particularly given that not everyone who is eligible actually applies.[45] Scholars have noted the ways that, increasingly, a status granted to immigrants may be liminal, "characterized by its ambiguity, as it is neither an undocumented status nor a documented one, but may have the characteristics of both."[46] Thus, TPS recipients have the ability to remain in the United States with work authorization for specified periods of time but are not on a pathway to citizenship. The undocumented experience liminality by virtue of living in many ways as if they were lawfully present even though they may lack legal status.[47] When migrants apply for legal status, they redefine liminality as belonging, for example, by providing evidence of the years they have lived in the United States, their family relationships, and their work histories. There is some potential for individuals to choose among, amend, or create new records in ways that promote the version of reality that is of greatest utility, given their legal goal.[48] Indeed, doing so is, in essence, assembling a file, and is much of what legal work consists of. Of course, not applying was also a form of legal craft, and was appropriate for those, such as Jaime, who had little hope of prevailing.

To apply for status, migrants had to overcome challenges created by the application process itself. For U-visa and VAWA applicants, case preparation entailed recounting the details of a traumatic experience, something that many found painful. It was also common for migrants to experience difficulty obtaining the required information and documentation, especially given deadlines. One U-visa applicant was attempting to include her children in her application but had to rely on her relatives in Mexico to get their original birth certificates. Because her oldest daughter would turn twenty-one in one month and "age out" of eligibility, she needed to gather these documents quickly. She described repeated efforts to mobilize her relatives to obtain these documents. In some cases, individuals had to fax or email documents to their countries of origin so that relatives could sign them and mail them back, all under time constraints. Gustavo, who was gathering documentation to include his nephew in a petition he had filed for his sister, complained to a service provider that his nephew's town is not like Los Angeles, where there are internet cafés on every corner. His nephew would have to travel thirty to sixty minutes to access a computer. Moreover, the application fees that individuals paid did not guarantee the outcome of their cases. Such expenses were significant, especially for low-income individuals, and gathering documents could mean missing days of work. Nonetheless, applicants had to accept these conditions.

While seeking to regularize, migrants also maintained understandings of their lives that differed from the officially constructed versions. For example, a man who had not been able to prove that being deported would create an extreme and unusual hardship commented bitterly, "Yes, they said that my son could do without me because he lives with his mother." "Hardship" was a legal construct that did not include the actual hardship that his son was likely to experience. In another case, after a legal worker asked whether a woman's children had a disease or special needs that would create exceptional hardship if she were deported, the woman started to reply, "Unfortunately not," then corrected herself, saying, "No, *gracias a dios*, they are all very well!" This woman had started to allow the legal construct of hardship to dominate her thinking about her children. The legal definitions of family relations also sometimes differed from those of individual applicants. For instance, one woman referred to her partner as "*mi marido*" (my spouse) throughout the narrative that formed the basis of her U-visa application, then, when asked for the date of her marriage, reported, "We never married." Upon being informed that if she had not legally married, then she had to use another term, such as boyfriend, she commented, "In Honduras, as soon as you have a child with someone they regard him as your marido." Migrants' understandings of their legal situations also sometimes differed from those of service providers. For example, even though many individuals saved documents, they did not always understand which ones would be useful, informing providers that a key document that providers said they needed was at home. Individuals who were eligible to naturalize often seemed to think that they could "test the waters" by simply renewing their green cards, even though service providers argued that a successful green card renewal did not mean that naturalization would be approved.

Despite anxiety, fear, and cynicism, migrants also approached the nonprofit with hope, reasoning that the years that they had lived in the United States, the fact that an acquaintance was able to acquire status, or a change in their own status or that of a relative might open new opportunities.[49] Recall the case of Jasmina, who, knowing that she was about to naturalize, approached the nonprofit to learn whether she could help relatives qualify. Optimism was tempered by frustration over the obstacles that individuals encountered. One woman, who was renewing her TPS after having held this status for twelve years, described the United States as a "*jaula de oro*" (golden cage) because she could not travel internationally without advance parole, which was only granted in emergencies. Still, the optimism that led individuals to save documents, attend presentations on immigration law, schedule consultations, and submit paperwork often paid off. As a woman who had herself gained residency through IRCA and who was now petitioning for her brother remarked, "It is good to have open paths in front of you."

Conclusion: Documentary Paths

In 2011, uncertainty created by intensified enforcement coupled with unfulfilled promises for immigration reform made documents key to migrants' lives. Everyday documents could allow migrants to authenticate their relationships, continuous presence, income, community ties, and other legally significant factors, even as state scrutiny led discrepancies or gaps to potentially be interpreted as evidence of fraud. Most damaging were the reentry bars that individuals encountered. For example, one woman who came in for a consultation had lived in the United States for thirty-two years, had applied for asylum and NACARA, was the beneficiary of a family visa petition, and had TPS. In order to qualify for 245(i), she had obtained advance parole, left the country, and reentered legally. Though it might appear that she had many options, in fact, a service provider informed her that all she could do was to renew her TPS. Both her asylum and NACARA claims were denied (she was not eligible for NACARA due to the date of her asylum application), and, because she had worked in the United States without work authorization and then left the country, she had triggered a ten-year bar. This example illustrates the optimism that would lead an individual to apply for four different regularization opportunities (asylum, NACARA, TPS, and a family visa) as well as the oversecuritization that would attach a ten-year reentry penalty to something as minor as briefly working without authorization. It is striking that living thirty-two years in the United States was insufficient grounds to secure permanent status in the country.

Given current policy trends, the mixture of hope and anxiety that characterizes noncitizens' relationship with documents is likely to continue. This emotional duality is not unlike the temporal duality identified by Melanie Griffiths's research among asylum seekers in the UK: "People wait for what might be long periods of time, longing for an end to the waiting, but with little idea when it might happen and fearful of the change it might bring."[50] Since 2011, enforcement efforts have further intensified, particularly under the Trump administration, which has replaced Obama's efforts to distinguish between high- and low-priority deportees with the policy that removal proceedings can be initiated against any undocumented individual who comes into contact with immigration officials. Such initiatives strengthen noncitizens' need for papers. At the same time, as regularization opportunities at the federal level appear increasingly remote, undocumented individuals who live in localities with migrant-friendly policies have come to focus on securing other types of "papers." For instance, in California, individuals are eligible for driver's licenses regardless of immigration status, and some migrants have developed labor strategies, such as launching their own businesses, obtaining licenses as florists or cosmetologists, or becoming independent contractors, that enable them to work without needing employment authorization (because of not being employees). It remains to be seen how such contests between federal and local policy making will impact the opportunities and double binds experienced by unauthorized migrants.

Notes

1 All names referring to those encountered during fieldwork and volunteer work are pseudonyms.

2 In this and other accounts, some details—such as year of entry—have been omitted or changed in order to preserve confidentiality.

3 Leisy J. Abrego and Sarah M. Lakhani, "Incomplete Inclusion: Legal Violence and Immigrants in Liminal Legal Statuses," *Law and Policy* 37, no. 4 (2015): 271.

4 Ruth Gomberg-Muñoz, "The Punishment/El Castigo: Undocumented Latinos and US Immigration Processing," *Journal of Ethnic and Migration Studies* 41, no. 14 (2015): 2236.

5 Eli Coffino, "A Long Road to Residency: The Legal History of Salvadoran and Guatemalan Immigration to the United States with a Focus on NACARA," *Cardozo Journal of International and Comparative Law* 14 (2006): 195.

6 Matthew S. Hull, "Documents and Bureaucracy," *Annual Review of Anthropology* 41 (2012): 258; Miriam Ticktin, "Where Ethics and Politics Meet: The Violence of Humanitarianism in France," *American Ethnologist* 33, no. 1 (2006): 36.

7 Hiroshi Motomura, "Immigration Law after a Century of Plenary Power: Phantom Constitutional Norms and Statutory Interpretation," *Yale Law Journal* 100, no. 3 (1990): 547.

8 See generally Mae M. Ngai, *Impossible Subjects: Illegal Aliens and the Making of Modern America* (Princeton, NJ: Princeton University Press, 2004).

9 See generally Lucy E. Salyer, *Laws Harsh as Tigers: Chinese Immigrants and the Shaping of Modern Immigration Law* (Chapel Hill: University of North Carolina Press, 1995).

10 See generally Kelly Lytle Hernández, "The Crimes and Consequences of Illegal Immigration: A Cross-Border Examination of Operation Wetback, 1943 to 1954," *Western Historical Quarterly* 37, no. 4 (2006): 421–44.

11 Gomberg-Muñoz, "The Punishment/El Castigo," 2240.

12 See generally Els De Graauw, *Making Immigrant Rights Real: Nonprofits and the Politics of Integration in San Francisco* (Ithaca, NY: Cornell University Press, 2016).

13 Sarah Horton, "Identity Loan: The Moral Economy of Migrant Document Exchange in California's Central Valley," *American Ethnologist* 42, no. 1 (2015): 56–57.

14 Jennifer M. Chacón, "Overcriminalizing Immigration," *Journal of Criminal Law and Criminology* 102 (2012): 613–14; Nicholas P. De Genova, "Migrant 'Illegality' and Deportability in Everyday Life," *Annual Review of Anthropology* 31, no. 1 (2002): 422–23.

15 See also Boehm, this volume.

16 See generally Joanna Dreby, *Everyday Illegal: When Policies Undermine Immigrant Families* (Berkeley: University of California Press, 2015); Tanya M. Golash-Boza, *Deported: Immigrant Policing, Disposable Labor and Global Capitalism* (New York: NYU Press, 2015); Roberto G. Gonzales and Leo R. Chavez, "Awakening to a Nightmare: Abjectivity and Illegality in the Lives of Undocumented 1.5-Generation Latino Immigrants in the United States," *Current Anthropology* 53, no. 3 (2012): 255–81; Cecilia Menjívar, "Liminal Legality: Salvadoran and Guatemalan Immigrants' Lives in the United States," *American Journal of Sociology* 111, no. 4 (2006): 999–1037.

17 TPS is available to nationals of certain countries, such as El Salvador and Honduras, that have suffered natural disasters or political turmoil. TPS is granted for a limited period of time and grants work authorization and relief from deportation, but does not permit recipients to travel internationally without advance parole or to adjust their status to that of a lawful permanent resident. It can

Opportunities and Double Binds 145

be renewed at the discretion of U.S. authorities. The Trump administration terminated TPS for Haiti, Nepal, Sudan, Nicaragua, El Salvador, and Honduras, actions that have been enjoined by the courts (see https://www.uscis.gov /humanitarian/temporary-protected-status). As of this writing, the outcome of these legal cases is uncertain. DACA was created by President Obama in 2012 and is available to individuals who immigrated to the United States before turning sixteen, were under age thirty-one in June 2012, have attended or graduated from a U.S. high school or been honorably discharged from the military, have a clean criminal record, and can prove that they have been continuously present in the United States from June 2007 until the present. Much like TPS, DACA confers work authorization and temporary relief from deportation, but does not place recipients on a path to citizenship. The Trump administration also rescinded DACA, but that rescission was enjoined. A case regarding DACA's legality is now before the U.S. Supreme Court. Oral arguments were heard in November 2019, and a decision has not yet been announced.

18 Julie Mitchell and Susan Bibler Coutin, "Living Documents in Transnational Spaces of Migration between El Salvador and the United States," *Law and Social Inquiry* (2019): 1–28.

19 For an overview of IRCA, see Frank D. Bean, Barry Edmonston, and Jeffrey S. Passel, eds., *Undocumented Migration to the United States: IRCA and the Experience of the 1980s* (Washington, DC: Urban Institute, 1990).

20 See generally Nancy Morawetz, "Understanding the Impact of the 1996 Deportation Laws and the Limited Scope of Proposed Reforms," *Harvard Law Review* 113, no. 8 (2000): 1936–62.

21 For an account of police collaboration with federal immigration enforcement, see Monica W. Varsanyi, Paul G. Lewis, Doris Marie Provine, and Scott Decker, "A Multilayered Jurisdictional Patchwork: Immigration Federalism in the United States," *Law and Policy* 34, no. 2 (2012), 138–58.

22 Chacón, "Overcriminalizing Immigration," 640–47.

23 Jennifer M. Chacón, "Managing Migration through Crime," *Columbia Law Review Sidebar* 109 (2012): 137–38.

24 Jens Manuel Krogstad, Jeffrey S. Passel, and D'Vera Cohn, "5 Facts about Illegal Immigration in the U.S.," Pew Research Center, April 27, 2017, accessed July 11, 2017, http://www.pewresearch.org/fact-tank/2017/04/27/5-facts-about-illegal -immigration-in-the-u-s/.

25 For an account of this movement, see generally Susan Bibler Coutin, *The Culture of Protest: Religious Activism and the U.S. Sanctuary Movement* (Boulder, CO: Westview, 1993).

26 For an account of U-visa applications, see generally Sarah M. Lakhani, "Producing Immigrant Victims' 'Right' to Legal Status and the Management of Legal Uncertainty," *Law and Social Inquiry* 38, no. 2 (2013): 442–73; and for an account of T-visa applications, see generally Jennifer M. Wetmore, "The New T Visa: Is the Higher Extreme Headship Standard Too High for Bona Fide Trafficking Victims?," *New England Journal of International and Comparative Law* 9 (2003): 159–78.

27 Abrego and Lakhani, "Incomplete Inclusion," 270–71.

28 For accounts of the immigrant youth movement, see generally Walter Nicholls, *The DREAMers: How the Undocumented Youth Movement Transformed the Immigrant Rights Debate* (Palo Alto, CA: Stanford University Press, 2013); Marjorie S. Zatz and Nancy Rodriguez, *Dreams and Nightmares: Immigration Policy, Youth, and Families* (Berkeley: University of California Press, 2015).

29 For an analysis of these marches, see generally Adrian D. Pantoja, Cecilia Menjívar, and Lisa Magaña, "The Spring Marches of 2006: Latinos, Immigration, and Political Mobilization in the 21st Century," *American Behavioral Scientist* 52, no. 4 (2008): 499–506.

30 "Exercising Prosecutorial Discretion Consistent with the Civil Immigration Enforcement Priorities of the Agency for the Apprehension, Detention, and Removal of Aliens," memo from John Morton, Director, U.S. Immigration and Customs Enforcement, June 17, 2011, accessed May 24, 2019, https://www.ice.gov/doclib/secure -communities/pdf/prosecutorial-discretion-memo.pdf, 5.

31 Michael J. Sullivan and Roger Enriquez, "The Impact of Interior Immigration Enforcement on Mixed-Citizenship Families," *Boston College Journal of Law and Social Justice* 36 (2016): 43.

32 Jeffrey S. Passel and D'Vera Cohn, "Twenty Metro Areas Are Home to Six-in-Ten Unauthorized Immigrants in U.S.," Pew Research Center, February 9, 2017, accessed July 16, 2017, http://www.pewresearch.org/fact-tank/2017/02/09/us-metro -areas-unauthorized-immigrants/.

33 Geoffrey DeVerteuil, "From E1 to 90057: The Immigrant-Serving Nonprofit Sector among London Bangladeshis and Los Angeles Central Americans," *Urban Geography* 32, no. 8 (2011): 1132–34.

34 Anne E. Langford, "What's in a Name? Notarios in the United States and the Exploitation of a Vulnerable Latino Immigrant Population," *Harvard Latino Law Review* 7 (2004): 116–17.

35 On the general problem of inadequate legal representation in immigration contexts, see Careen Shannon, "Regulating Immigration Legal Service Providers: Inadequate Legal Service Providers: Inadequate Representation and Notario Fraud," *Fordham Law Review* 78 (2009): 577–622; Juan Manuel Pedroza, "Making Noncitizens' Rights Real: Evidence from Legal Services Fraud Complaints," Social Science Research Network, September 7, 2017, accessed May 24, 2019, https:// papers.ssrn.com/sol3/papers.cfm?abstract_id=3032217.

36 Ingrid Eagly and Steven Shafer, "Access to Counsel in Immigration Court," American Immigration Council, September 2016, accessed October 26, 2017, https://www .americanimmigrationcouncil.org/sites/default/files/research/access_to_counsel _in_immigration_court.pdf, 3.

37 Annelise Riles, *Collateral Knowledge: Legal Reasoning in the Global Financial Markets* (Chicago: University of Chicago Press, 2011), 36.

38 Riles, *Collateral Knowledge*, 18. Following in the steps of the sociological jurisprudence and legal realists of the 1920s and 1930s, early sociolegal scholars hoped that by documenting the gap between law-on-the-books and law-in-action, legal

reformers would revise codes and practices in ways that achieved legal ideals. See generally Bryant Garth and Joyce Sterling, "From Legal Realism to Law and Society: Reshaping Law for the Last Stages of the Social Activist State," *Law and Society Review* 32, no. 2 (1998): 409–72; David M. Trubek, "Back to the Future: The Short, Happy Life of the Law and Society Movement," *Florida State University Law Review* 18 (1990): 1–56. Though what came to be known as "gap studies" successfully documented flaws in legal practices, such studies also assumed that written law (the books) is inert and that legal practices are not rule-bound. See June Starr and Jane F. Collier, eds., "Introduction," in *History and Power in the Study of Law: New Directions in Legal Anthropology* (Ithaca, NY: Cornell University Press, 1989).

39 James C. Scott, *Seeing like a State: How Certain Schemes to Improve the Human Condition Have Failed* (New Haven, CT: Yale University Press, 1998).

40 The sorts of double binds created by criminal record checks were explained to me by an attorney, who related that if police who were collaborating with federal officials checked someone's fingerprints and found a record, the person would be in trouble, but that if there was no record whatsoever, then that could be taken as evidence of alienage, because someone from the United States would be presumed to have at least some record.

41 See generally William Walters, "Deportation, Expulsion, and the International Police of Aliens," *Citizenship Studies* 6, no. 3 (2002): 265–92.

42 Didier Fassin and Estelle D'Halluin, "The Truth from the Body: Medical Certificates as Ultimate Evidence for Asylum Seekers," *American Anthropologist* 107, no. 4 (2005): 597–608.

43 Aurora Chang, "Undocumented to Hyperdocumented: A Jornada of Protection, Papers, and PhD Status," *Harvard Educational Review* 81, no. 3 (2011): 508–20; Juan Thomas Ordóñez, "Documents and Shifting Labor Environments among Undocumented Migrant Workers in Northern California," *Anthropology of Work Review* 37, no. 1 (2016): 24–33.

44 Gray Abarca and Susan Bibler Coutin, "Sovereign Intimacies: The Lives of Documents within U.S. State-Noncitizen Relationships," *American Ethnologist* 45, no. 1 (2018): 8–9.

45 Robert Warren and Donald Kerwin, "The U.S. Eligible-to-Naturalize Population: Detailed Social and Economic Characteristics," *Journal on Migration and Human Security* 3, no. 4 (2015): 307.

46 Menjívar, "Liminal Legality," 1008.

47 Angela S. García, "Hidden in Plain Sight: How Unauthorised Migrants Strategically Assimilate in Restrictive Localities in California," *Journal of Ethnic and Migration Studies* 40, no. 12 (2014): 1895–914.

48 Jaeeun Kim, *Contested Embrace: Transborder Membership Politics in Twentieth-Century Korea* (Palo Alto, CA: Stanford University Press, 2016).

49 On the immigrant knowledge economy, compare to Maybritt Jill Alpes, "Bushfalling at All Cost: The Economy of Migratory Knowledge in Anglophone Cameroon," *African Diaspora* 5 (2015): 90–115.

50 Melanie B. E. Griffiths, "Out of Time: The Temporal Uncertainties of Refused Asylum Seekers and Immigrant Detainees," *Journal of Ethnic and Migration Studies* 40, no. 12 (2014): 2005.

Bibliography

Abarca, Gray, and Susan Bibler Coutin. "Sovereign Intimacies: The Lives of Documents within U.S. State-Noncitizen Relationships." *American Ethnologist* 45, no. 1 (2018): 7–19.

Abrego, Leisy J., and Sarah M. Lakhani. "Incomplete Inclusion: Legal Violence and Immigrants in Liminal Legal Statuses." *Law and Policy* 37, no. 4 (2015): 265–93.

Alpes, Maybritt Jill. "Bushfalling at All Cost: The Economy of Migratory Knowledge in Anglophone Cameroon." *African Diaspora* 5 (2015): 90–115.

Bean, Frank D., Barry Edmonston, and Jeffrey S. Passel, eds. *Undocumented Migration to the United States: IRCA and the Experience of the 1980s.* Washington, DC: Urban Institute, 1990.

Chacón, Jennifer M. "Managing Migration through Crime." *Columbia Law Review Sidebar* 109 (2009): 135–48.

Chacón, Jennifer M. "Overcriminalizing Immigration." *Journal of Criminal Law and Criminology* 102 (2012): 613–52.

Chang, Aurora. "Undocumented to Hyperdocumented: A Jornada of Protection, Papers, and PhD Status." *Harvard Educational Review* 81, no. 3 (2011): 508–20.

Coffino, Eli. "A Long Road to Residency: The Legal History of Salvadoran and Guatemalan Immigration to the United States with a Focus on NACARA." *Cardozo Journal of International and Comparative Law* 14 (2006): 177–208.

Coutin, Susan Bibler. *The Culture of Protest: Religious Activism and the U.S. Sanctuary Movement.* Boulder, CO: Westview, 1993.

De Genova, N. P. "Migrant 'Illegality' and Deportability in Everyday Life." *Annual Review of Anthropology* 31, no. 1 (2002): 419–47.

De Graauw, Els. *Making Immigrant Rights Real: Nonprofits and the Politics of Integration in San Francisco.* Ithaca, NY: Cornell University Press, 2016.

DeVerteuil, Geoffrey. "From E1 to 90057: The Immigrant-Serving Nonprofit Sector among London Bangladeshis and Los Angeles Central Americans." *Urban Geography* 32, no. 8 (2011): 1129–47.

Dreby, Joanna. *Everyday Illegal: When Policies Undermine Immigrant Families.* Berkeley: University of California Press, 2015.

Eagly, Ingrid, and Steven Shafer. "Access to Counsel in Immigration Court." American Immigration Council, September 2016. Accessed October 26, 2017. https://www .americanimmigrationcouncil.org/sites/default/files/research/access_to_counsel_in _immigration_court.pdf.

Fassin, Didier, and Estelle D'Halluin. "The Truth from the Body: Medical Certificates as Ultimate Evidence for Asylum Seekers." *American Anthropologist* 107, no. 4 (2005): 597–608.

García, Angela S. "Hidden in Plain Sight: How Unauthorised Migrants Strategically Assimilate in Restrictive Localities in California." *Journal of Ethnic and Migration Studies* 40, no. 12 (2014): 1895–914.

Garth, Bryant, and Joyce Sterling. "From Legal Realism to Law and Society: Reshaping Law for the Last Stages of the Social Activist State." *Law and Society Review* 32, no. 2 (1998): 409–72.

Golash-Boza, Tanya M. *Deported: Immigrant Policing, Disposable Labor and Global Capitalism.* New York: NYU Press, 2015.

Gomberg-Muñoz, Ruth. "The Punishment/El Castigo: Undocumented Latinos and US Immigration Processing." *Journal of Ethnic and Migration Studies* 41, no. 14 (2015): 2235–52.

Gonzales, Roberto G., and Leo R. Chavez. "Awakening to a Nightmare: Abjectivity and Illegality in the Lives of Undocumented 1.5-Generation Latino Immigrants in the United States." *Current Anthropology* 53, no. 3 (2012): 255–81.

Griffiths, Melanie B. E. "Out of Time: The Temporal Uncertainties of Refused Asylum Seekers and Immigrant Detainees." *Journal of Ethnic and Migration Studies* 40, no. 12 (2014): 1991–2009.

Horton, Sarah. "Identity Loan: The Moral Economy of Migrant Document Exchange in California's Central Valley." *American Ethnologist* 42, no. 1 (2015): 55–67.

Hull, Matthew S. "Documents and Bureaucracy." *Annual Review of Anthropology* 41 (2012): 251–67.

Kim, Jaeeun. *Contested Embrace: Transborder Membership Politics in Twentieth-Century Korea.* Palo Alto, CA: Stanford University Press, 2016.

Krogstad, Jens Manuel, Jeffrey S. Passel, and D'Vera Cohn. "5 Facts about Illegal Immigration in the U.S." Pew Research Center, April 27, 2017. Accessed July 11, 2017. http://www.pewresearch.org/fact-tank/2017/04/27/5-facts-about-illegal -immigration-in-the-u-s/.

Lakhani, Sarah M. "Producing Immigrant Victims' 'Right' to Legal Status and the Management of Legal Uncertainty." *Law and Social Inquiry* 38, no. 2 (2013): 442–73.

Langford, Anne E. "What's in a Name? Notarios in the United States and the Exploitation of a Vulnerable Latino Immigrant Population." *Harvard Latino Law Review* 7 (2004): 115–36.

Lytle Hernández, Kelly. "The Crimes and Consequences of Illegal Immigration: A Cross-Border Examination of Operation Wetback, 1943 to 1954." *Western Historical Quarterly* 37, no. 4 (2006): 421–44.

Menjívar, Cecilia. "Liminal Legality: Salvadoran and Guatemalan Immigrants' Lives in the United States." *American Journal of Sociology* 111, no. 4 (2006): 999–1037.

Mitchell, Julie, and Susan Bibler Coutin. "Living Documents in Transnational Spaces of Migration between El Salvador and the United States." *Law and Social Inquiry* (2019): 1–28.

Morawetz, Nancy. "Understanding the Impact of the 1996 Deportation Laws and the Limited Scope of Proposed Reforms." *Harvard Law Review* 113, no. 8 (2000): 1936–62.

Morton, John. "Exercising Prosecutorial Discretion Consistent with the Civil Immigration Enforcement Priorities of the Agency for the Apprehension, Detention, and Removal of Aliens." U.S. Immigration and Customs Enforcement, June 17, 2011. Accessed July 16, 2017. https://www.ice.gov/doclib/secure-communities/pdf /prosecutorial-discretion-memo.pdf.

Motomura, Hiroshi. "Immigration Law after a Century of Plenary Power: Phantom Constitutional Norms and Statutory Interpretation." *Yale Law Journal* 100, no. 3 (1990): 545–613.

Ngai, Mae M. *Impossible Subjects: Illegal Aliens and the Making of Modern America.* Princeton, NJ: Princeton University Press, 2004.

Nicholls, Walter. *The DREAMers: How the Undocumented Youth Movement Transformed the Immigrant Rights Debate.* Stanford, CA: Stanford University Press, 2013.

Ordóñez, Juan Thomas. "Documents and Shifting Labor Environments among Undocumented Migrant Workers in Northern California." *Anthropology of Work Review* 37, no. 1 (2016): 24–33.

Pantoja, Adrian D., Cecilia Menjívar, and Lisa Magaña. "The Spring Marches of 2006: Latinos, Immigration, and Political Mobilization in the 21st Century." *American Behavioral Scientist* 52, no. 4 (2008): 499–506.

Passel, Jeffrey S., and D'Vera Cohn. "Twenty Metro Areas Are Home to Six-in-Ten Unauthorized Immigrants in U.S." Pew Research Center, February 9, 2017. Accessed July 16, 2017. http://www.pewresearch.org/fact-tank/2017/02/09/us-metro-areas -unauthorized-immigrants/.

Pedroza, Juan Manuel. "Making Noncitizens' Rights Real: Evidence from Legal Services Fraud Complaints." Social Science Research Network, September 7, 2017. Accessed May 24, 2019. https://papers.ssrn.com/sol3/papers.cfm?abstract_id=3032217.

Riles, Annelise. *Collateral Knowledge: Legal Reasoning in the Global Financial Markets.* Chicago: University of Chicago Press, 2011.

Salyer, Lucy E. *Laws Harsh as Tigers: Chinese Immigrants and the Shaping of Modern Immigration Law.* Chapel Hill: University of North Carolina Press, 1995.

Scott, James C. *Seeing like a State: How Certain Schemes to Improve the Human Condition Have Failed.* New Haven, CT: Yale University Press, 1998.

Shannon, Careen. "Regulating Immigration Legal Service Providers: Inadequate Legal Service Providers: Inadequate Representation and Notario Fraud." *Fordham Law Review* 78 (2009): 577–622.

Starr, June, and Jane F. Collier, eds. *History and Power in the Study of Law: New Directions in Legal Anthropology.* Ithaca, NY: Cornell University Press, 1989.

Sullivan, Michael J., and Roger Enriquez. "The Impact of Interior Immigration Enforcement on Mixed-Citizenship Families." *Boston College Journal of Law and Social Justice* 36 (2016): 33–57.

Ticktin, Miriam. "Where Ethics and Politics Meet: The Violence of Humanitarianism in France." *American Ethnologist* 33, no. 1 (2006): 33–49.

Trubek, David M. "Back to the Future: The Short, Happy Life of the Law and Society Movement." *Florida State University Law Review* 18 (1990): 1–56.

Varsanyi, Monica W., Paul G. Lewis, Doris Marie Provine, and Scott Decker. "A Multilayered Jurisdictional Patchwork: Immigration Federalism in the United States." *Law and Policy* 34, no. 2 (2012): 138–58.

Walters, William. "Deportation, Expulsion, and the International Police of Aliens." *Citizenship Studies* 6, no. 3 (2002): 265–92.

Warren, Robert, and Donald Kerwin. "The U.S. Eligible-to-Naturalize Population: Detailed Social and Economic Characteristics." *Journal on Migration and Human Security* 3, no. 4 (2015): 306–29.

Wetmore, Jennifer M. "The New T Visa: Is the Higher Extreme Headship Standard Too High for Bona Fide Trafficking Victims?" *New England Journal of International and Comparative Law* 9 (2003): 159–78.

Zatz, Marjorie S., and Nancy Rodriguez. *Dreams and Nightmares: Immigration Policy, Youth, and Families.* Berkeley: University of California Press, 2015.

6

DOCUMENT OVERSEERS, ENHANCED ENFORCEMENT, AND RACIALIZED LOCAL CONTEXTS

Experiences of Latino/a Immigrants in Phoenix, Arizona

U.S. immigration law has been altered significantly in the past two decades to include a panoply of provisions that criminalize an increasing number of immigrants holding various legal statuses,[1] while at the same time narrowing paths to permanent status. In addition to restrictions now inscribed in federal law, since the mid-2000s states and municipalities around the country have introduced thousands of bills and laws designed to block immigrants' access to locally funded social and public services, among other sanctions.[2] And even though legislative activity at the state and local levels often follows party lines, with Democrats supporting immigrant-friendly laws,[3] this is not the case at the federal level. Regardless of the party in power in Washington, the trend toward restrictive legislation and an expanded punitive approach to immigration has continued unabated in the past two decades, culminating in the various proposals, enforcement policies, and executive orders put in place by the administration in power as of this writing. But whereas the intensity and degree of enforcement may vary by level of government, the different levels of government share an unprecedented legislative activity in recent history. Thus, in parallel to the administration's executive orders on immigration signed since January 2017, immigration-related legislation at the state level also has increased; it went up by 90 percent during the same period, from seventy laws passed in 2016 to 133 enacted in 2017.[4]

Ostensibly, states endorse immigration-related legislation in order to "take matters into their own hands" due to alleged inaction on the part of the federal government to address the "problem" of unauthorized immigration. However, it is unclear exactly how state-level laws can fix what the federal government supposedly cannot. Furthermore, it seems that all levels of government engage almost simultaneously in legislative activity, in contagion mode, rather than states first waiting for the federal government to act, to then determine if the federal government is indeed "not doing enough." And, as Møller[5] notes, such explanations for increased legislative activity at municipal and state levels seem inadequate, as the federal government is already "doing enough" as it has expanded immigration enforcement to unprecedented levels.[6] Thus, Møller[7] points to the racism embedded in such state- and municipal-level legislative activities, which are responses to a presumed loss of culture, fears of crime, unease about national security, and an overall decline in standards of living, wages, and property values.

Unsurprisingly, such legislative activity breeds hostility and anti-immigrant sentiment, as media images disseminate public officials' narratives criminalizing immigrants and blaming them for a host of troubles, promoting anxieties that then justify restrictive actions. Such media images prime an already anxious public; politicians then respond with additional legislation to exclude and expel immigrants as the public demands that something be done to "stop the flow."[8] Indeed, in media analyses we have found[9] that the terminology used in media reports may not matter (e.g., undocumented vs. "illegal") in priming the public to see immigrants as a problem when the context is saturated with immigration-related media, as has been the case in Arizona. Importantly, although criminalized immigrants still hold certain rights,[10] a paradigm of enforcing immigration laws through crime[11] undermines the conferring of such rights on immigrants, and soon immigrants themselves start to believe that they have no rights.[12]

Following one of this volume's themes on "decentralized membership policy," which focuses on how subnational policies regarding "papers" structure life for immigrants[13] living in different states across the country, I examine the experiences of "quasi-legal" immigrants (those who hold temporary statuses and those who wait in line for applications to be approved, among others), unauthorized immigrants, as well as individuals who have moved to more permanent statuses such as lawful permanent residence or even citizenship through naturalization, who live in the Phoenix, Arizona, metropolitan area. I focus on these immigrants' interactions with individuals who in practice implement immigration policies: employers, workers in government offices, or clerks in private businesses. For the most part, immigrants in my study do not have direct contact with immigration officials or enforcement agents, but it is in encounters with a variety of "gatekeepers" where the significance of papers emerges and where it can shape immigrants' lives in consequential ways, including their sense of self, their rights, and their sense of belonging. Thus, my examination focuses on an expanded field of actors, beyond the government workers who deal on a daily basis with the gap between policy intentions and street-level discretion,[14] that is, "street-level workers."[15] Instead, I focus on private-sector individuals who act prominently as "overseers of documents" beyond the formal milieu of agencies and bureaucracies. Caplan and Torpey note the presence of these actors who ultimately contribute to sustaining bureaucracies—"and not only the state: private economic and commercial activities would also grind to a halt unless companies had the ability to identify and track individuals as property owners, employees, business partners, and customers."[16]

Document Overseers, Street-Level Workers, and State Power

In the course of conducting routine business, employers, bank tellers, store owners who sell on credit, and real estate agents, among others, request documentation from the immigrants with whom they deal, which buttresses the larger state project of placing immigrants in dominant classifications.[17] As such, this expanded cast of private-sector actors contributes to reproduce the actions of street-level workers in reifying the state's presence in immigrants' everyday lives through making documentation critical to their dealings with immigrants and for the immigrants' livelihood.[18] These actors are largely unfamiliar with the intricacies of immigration law, and especially with the complex set of documents conferred on people in "in-between" statuses and, depending on the context in which they conduct their business, could be more or less strict regarding which documents they accept as legitimate for business purposes. It is likely that they are less familiar with the intricacies of immigration statuses than street-level workers. And even though ostensibly they may not have as much to lose as those government workers who mistakenly accept the wrong documents and can be penalized for it, these actors live in a context where identity and documents are tightly related, and where a lack of documents signals "illegality" and therefore, in the eyes of these actors, crime. To avoid the risk of conducting business with criminals, these actors must exercise caution and even err on the safe side, but, as government workers do, they also apply discretion. Thus, in the course of routine business, this cast of actors contributes to "state making"[19] as they establish norms, practices, and precedents in requesting and verifying documents involving documentary evidence beyond the "identity tags" legible to bureaucrats.[20] In this way, these actors also contribute to the production of a modern sense of self by linking identity and identification[21] and making documents integral to an individual's life and identity, as they also rely on documentary identification produced by the state and public institutions to identify the uniqueness of the individuals with whom they do business.

Following Heyman,[22] I distinguish between people's identifications and their identities: "the former authorized by the power of the U.S. state and the latter complexly developed among various webs of people, in garbled communication with the official letter of the law."[23] Thus, I differentiate the expanded cast of actors on whom I focus from state actors who formally classify immigrants. I argue that the actions of these two groups are distinct, given their different positions vis-à-vis state power and state bureaucracy. However, their actions are related and intertwined, given the close link between identifications and identities, and thus, rather than juxtaposing their actions, they should be seen as a continuum. State actors and the non-state actors on whom I focus inflect documents with meaning, enhance state power by relying on state classifications of immigrants, and contribute to disciplinary projects and to the (re)production of the modern self. Documents have no value independent of what state workers and the expanded cast of actors do, as both impart meaning to documents based on the power of the state to demarcate who belongs and deserves and who does not. Thus, non-state actors also become part of the expanded system of social control and surveillance of immigrants, as the expanded cast of actors also operates under similar principles and deploys tactics similar to those found in "people-processing" institutions.[24]

A second, related point I make deals with the context in which demands for "papers" and the meaning attached to them take place. Asking for and showing papers does not occur in a sociopolitical vacuum; such interactions are informed by the expanded enforcement regime that criminalizes immigrants, which becomes racialized in its implementation. Such racialized enforcement practices target Latinos/as with particular acuteness, and more so in certain contexts (such as Arizona). As such, it is imperative to examine the experiences of unauthorized immigrants, but also of those Latino/a immigrants in other legal and citizenship statuses; the inclusion of this variation reveals the racialized enforcement of immigration law.

Furthermore, racialized enforcement becomes more injurious for certain groups, such as Latinos/as, when legislative obstacles keep these immigrants from moving to more permanent legal statuses, such as the backlogged system under which immigrants wait for years to obtain family-based visas, as well as the increasing uncertainty that now threatens lawful permanent residents. This system affects all immigrants, but given the structure of family reunification visas, it affects certain groups in particular, especially Mexicans, who have more demand for such visas.[25]

Asking for and producing immigration papers takes on context-specific meanings, as documents mean more than government-issued papers. For targeted immigrants who also face long waits for legalization and who live in contexts of heightened racial profiling and acute enforcement, interactions around documents can be anxiety provoking, even for the U.S.-born members of the targeted group. This can even be the case when Latinos/as make up a substantial share of the population, as in the Phoenix metro area, where approximately 40 percent of the residents are Latinos/as (they constitute 30 percent of the population in Maricopa County).[26] In such contexts, Latino/a immigrants in various legal and citizenship statuses[27] live "hyperaware" of the law,[28] a condition concretized in demands to show papers and in the possibility that they will come to the attention of authorities if they find themselves in the wrong place at the wrong time and their documents are deemed questionable.

And third, the effects of living hyperaware of the law, reinforced and reproduced by demands for documentary evidence, are long-lasting.[29] Individuals who for years live with reminders that they must prove their presence (and deservingness) through documents do not stop experiencing these effects when they receive documents that guarantee permanence of residence or even citizenship through naturalization. Their insecurity and anxiety persist well beyond attaining such documents. In other work I have documented the transformative effects of the regularization process itself on immigrants.[30] Similarly, the importance of carrying documentation and being ready to show documents at any moment does not end with the conferral of permanent legal status or naturalization.[31]

Contextualizing Documentary Evidence: Phoenix, Arizona

Based on my research among Central American immigrants in Phoenix, Arizona, I focus on how in-between legal statuses are interpreted, enforced, and experienced on the ground within a context of hyper-enforcement and a multipronged system of immigration laws—federal, state, and local—as immigrants interact with a variety of "document overseers."[32] Individuals in positions of daily, routine contact with immigrants—employers, bank tellers, store owners, car salespeople, apartment managers—attempt to interpret law and implement it to the best of their knowledge, helping to sustain immigration policies through practice.[33] These actors' actions weigh heavily on the lives of immigrants and reveal discrepancies between the law on the books and the law in practice,[34] a particularly salient aspect of life for immigrants who live in the gray area of liminal legality.[35] Immigrants' interactions with those in positions of authority to assess who belongs and is deserving contribute an understanding of how social membership is continually negotiated, produced, and contested. As Claudine Dardy observes, "[Identity] papers are at one and the same time papers of constraint and control, including control by the state, but they are also purveyors of identity."[36]

A study based in the Phoenix metropolitan area may seem to be an extreme case of local immigration enforcement and thus irrelevant elsewhere, and this context may shape the lives of immigrants living in Phoenix in highly specific ways. However, Phoenix is not an isolated case; enforcement, anti-immigrant sentiment, and hostile narratives may simply have received more media attention and exist in more concentrated form in Phoenix, but they are present with various levels of intensity in other contexts as well. For instance, traffic stops in Southern California often surpass those in Maricopa County (Phoenix), and workplace investigations and audits of private businesses suspected of hiring unauthorized workers take place regularly in most other states as well. An examination of this arguably "extreme" case therefore can reveal much about the meanings attached to documents in heightened enforcement regimes. It is precisely this context that allows for theorizing the intersections among expanded enforcement, the racialization of Latino/a immigrants, and the significance of "papers" for these immigrants.[37]

Thus, in certain contexts such as Arizona, proof of status becomes more salient, even vital. In efforts to curb the immigrant population, lawmakers have focused on limiting access to an essential, multipurpose document— the driver's license—which in today's context also signals legal presence and conveys basic rights.[38] Such identity documents acquire particular significance for immigrants who straddle legal statuses and live in "legal limbo" or in "liminal legality," holding temporary permits (but who are unsure whether these permits will be renewed), who are "documented" by virtue of possessing said permits, and who have been granted relief from deportation but are counted among the approximately 11 million unauthorized immigrants in the country because, technically, they are not lawful permanent residents. It is also the case for immigrants who have applied for lawful permanent residence and are still waiting in uncertainty for their cases to be approved. And when these immigrants, like the Central Americans on whom I mostly focus, live in environments like Arizona, where checking documents is routine and Latinos/as live in the path of the radar because they are the quintessential suspects of being "illegal," they experience requests for documents in a pronounced fashion. These presumably extreme cases of immigrant life in heightened spaces of illegality can be particularly rich for understanding how context informs experiences of "papers" on the ground.

Immigrants' encounters with employers, shop owners, or managers of rental housing (or with other individuals who are in positions to determine eligibility for services) impact immigrants' sense of membership in multiple ways. This happens even more acutely when the immigrants are racialized as "undocumented" (or "illegal") and enforcement is expanded. Examining the lives of immigrants who are only temporarily documented (DACA, TPS, those waiting in a queue) can illuminate the experiences of similarly situated immigrants elsewhere, as temporary legal statuses proliferate around the world and more immigrants find themselves in these new legal interstices. As Motomura notes, it is no longer the case that immigrants are expected to become future citizens; the rationale behind temporary statuses is precisely that immigrants will not become full members of society.[39]

Immigrants' Encounters with "Document Overseers"

A growing body of work sheds light on those individuals situated between the law and immigrants who implement immigration policy on the ground—workers in government offices and social service agencies who are charged with making myriad decisions that have profound effects on the lives of immigrants.[40] These "street-level workers"[41] make sense of complex policies on the ground as they deal with competing tensions of policy implementation and cultural abidance, often under demanding circumstances. They ultimately serve as gatekeepers, wielding considerable power and discretion in controlling access to goods and services.[42] As Painter notes, laws are produced "through the myriad mundane actions of officials, clerks, police officers, inspectors, teachers, social workers, doctors and so on."[43] Thus, these actors become de facto immigration enforcers; whether they exercise their discretion to rubber-stamp restrictive policies, to uphold inclusionary ones, or to make culturally or morally informed exceptions, they expand the reach of the state and participate in doing the governmentality work that state agencies normally do.

In the scholarship on immigration there has been attention to this layer of the immigration process, on how the actions of street-level workers might affect immigrants' incorporation and sense of belonging. Some research has focused on the inspectors and officials in the immigration bureaucracy in charge of admission decisions,[44] often facing contradictory mandates as they enforce the law on the ground.[45] Others have examined institutional actors outside the immigration bureaucracy, such as workers in social service agencies and clinics who are positioned to make decisions about deservingness for services,[46] often making their decisions through the lens of race, class, and gender.[47] And it has been noted that immigrants undergo a process of bureaucratic incorporation through their interactions with a range of social service workers.[48] Thus, Jasso notes, everyone with whom immigrants come into contact can affect their life chances.[49]

Thus, I propose an expansion of the group of actors who interpret law on the ground. Although the private actors I examine here are not directly charged with enforcing immigration law, in a context of increased enforcement, their actions regarding the importance of papers become imperative to examine. This becomes even more salient when local laws create penalties not only for the immigrants who are unable to obtain documents but also for those in charge of inspecting them. Examining these interactions from the vantage point of immigrants, I propose, can offer a glimpse into the long-term consequences of these encounters and thus illuminate how these middle-level actors potentially shape membership and belonging as well as life chances for immigrants. These private actors, beyond the state bureaucracy, interpret and implement immigration law as they determine who can make a purchase, rent an apartment, or buy a car, all transactions that are critical for everyday life, and as such constitute markers of social membership. In this light, it is instructive to keep in mind the range of actors involved in carrying out immigration policy on the ground, shaping meanings and practices of belonging.

Documentary Evidence in the Context of Arizona

Asking for and producing documentary evidence does not happen in a social vacuum; indeed, the (social, historical, economic) context largely informs the meanings documents acquire. Arizona recently passed a set of laws that have made documents a central aspect of the lives and identities of the immigrants who reside there. This legal context thus becomes a central factor in understanding how the immigrants in my study see documents and themselves (e.g., the classification and identity aspects) in relation to documentary evidence.

Since 2004, Arizona has seen immigration-related legislative activity every two years on average, with each initiative or piece of legislation progressively encroaching on the lives of immigrants suspected of being in the country undocumented, but with a particular focus on Latinos/as. Given this level of activity, the state currently has a multilayered legal system that touches on almost every aspect of immigrants' lives; many of these laws continue in effect today. The most notorious is, of course, SB 1070, enacted in 2010. Although the U.S. Supreme Court stripped this law of most of its provisions, it left the most controversial in place—the provision requiring police officers to determine the legal status of people with whom they come in contact in the course of routine police activities. Additionally, two years before SB 1070, Arizona passed the Legal Arizona Workers Act (LAWA), which prohibits businesses from knowingly or intentionally hiring unauthorized immigrants and requires businesses to use the E-Verify system to determine employment authorization of all new employees hired after December 31, 2007. Penalties for a first violation of LAWA include the termination of all unauthorized workers, the filing of quarterly reports on new hires, a three-year probationary period, and the possibility of suspension of the employer's business license for up to ten business days; a second violation leads to the permanent revocation of the employer's business license. And although there is evidence that this law is not always enforced,[50] employers worry about the harsh penalties and often invoke this law to fire workers "suspected" of being in the country undocumented, in some cases even firing Latino/a workers holding green cards, "just in case."[51]

Whether or with what degree of intensity these laws are enforced in the course of everyday life in the state does not preclude regular reminders about the law and its enforcement. As is the case of other similarly restrictive laws, SB 1070 and LAWA rely fundamentally on the production of documents for their implementation; both demand that those in positions to assess the legitimacy of an immigrant's presence in the state, and the immigrants whose identity is checked, interact within a context of heightened awareness of the importance of documentary evidence. And both laws have been controversial and ensnared in legal battles and allegations of racial profiling, as both have focused on targeting Latinos/as in the state, even those holding lawful permanent residence or who were born in the United States. It is against this backdrop of heightened state enforcement that I present two aspects of how immigrants relate to documentary evidence in Phoenix.

"The Way You Look" and Comparisons to Other States

One Sunday afternoon in 2013, I stopped by the home of the Bolaños family, a Salvadoran family I have known since 1998. Two adult sons and their mother were home, and we talked about what life was like in Phoenix. Their relatives had just gone back to California after a weekend visit to Phoenix, so the two sons took this opportunity to compare and contrast their experiences as immigrants in the two states. They assured me that life was much easier in California, especially for immigrants in their "situation." Both sons have had TPS status continuously since 2001 and have grown acutely aware of the importance of documentation, as they must renew this permit every eighteen months, a renewal that includes a $495 fee, a clean criminal record, and a form. They have several relatives on TPS in California, and thus they often compare and contrast their experiences. Here is how the conversation unfolded that afternoon.

> MANUEL: Here [in Arizona] is much tougher to live with TPS than in California.

> CM: How so? This permit is the same in every state, no?

> Felipe and Manuel [*laugh in unison*]: Ha ha ha . . . no! We have it tougher in Arizona.

> MANUEL: Let me explain. OK, for instance, here [in Arizona] when your TPS ends, your driver's license also ends so you have to renew your driver's license when you renew your permit. So every eighteen months. But in California they give the license for three or four years, like they do with everyone else in the state, not when your TPS permit ends. See what I mean?

> CM: But here in Arizona licenses are good for many years, like for twenty-five years.

> FELIPE: Exactly. Not the same if you're on TPS. If you're on TPS in Arizona, you don't get the same treatment as other people who live in the state, like in California. One could say that here [in Arizona] we are less than others. Not in California.[52]

Then their mother chimed in, adding that this is why their California relatives have invited them repeatedly to go live in California; life for those on TPS is easier there, the relatives have assured them (and for them the driver's license example is proof). However, the family has roots in Arizona now, the mother owns her own home, they have extended family in Phoenix, Manuel has a U.S.-born daughter whose mother is from Phoenix, and consequently it would be too difficult to uproot everyone and move to the neighboring state.

Importantly, on repeated occasions the immigrants I have come to know in Phoenix have commented that they feel Latinos/as are more scrutinized and more likely to be asked for their papers, and that they feel this is related to the "situation" in Arizona. Adriana, a Mexican woman, and Beatriz, her Guatemalan coworker, assured me that if they "didn't look Latinas" the police would not have followed them closely as they drove, cautiously, observing all traffic signs carefully, on a major street in the east valley. Adriana mentioned—and this has been corroborated by other immigrants—that if stopped she felt it was worse to produce a Mexican *matrícula consular* than nothing at all because that document immediately signals not only that she is Mexican but also that this is the only document she possesses. She felt that being identified as Mexican could translate into worse treatment. Adriana shared an experience with documents that made her cry at the Motor Vehicles Department.

When she accompanied her then-seventeen-year-old, U.S.-born son to obtain his Arizona ID card, the woman at the window not only requested his proof of citizenship, which they had in hand, but asked Adriana to also provide proof of her right to be in the country. The boy did not need his parents' IDs to obtain his own, but Adriana believes that the woman overstepped her authority "because she can; either because she's afraid not to ask for even more proof than one needs or because she wants to make your life hellish because she's racist." Adriana does not speak English, and through this interaction she conferred with her son in Spanish; Adriana thought this signaled to the woman at the MVD window not only that she is Latina but that she is also in the country undocumented. So Adriana produced her Mexican passport. This elicited a reaction that profoundly affected Adriana. "The woman didn't even want to touch my passport. She looked at it with disdain and said, 'that's no good here' and pushed it with her pen toward me. I felt so embarrassed. I wanted to sink and disappear. Why was she treating my Mexican passport as garbage? It was like treating me like garbage because that passport is me, my identity." At this, the clerk said that the son would be unable to obtain an ID. They left, as Adriana says, "in the most embarrassed way possible. So I started to cry right there, in public. I felt so rejected and belittled, right there in public." In Adriana's view, her passport—the document used to classify her as a Mexican national—and her own identity have fused; rejecting her passport constituted a rejection of herself. Adriana believes that the laws in Arizona make it possible for "anyone who wants to make your life difficult. And if you're Latino, you're going to be on the losing side. Here in Arizona that's the law!"

The Bolaños family members concurred that Latinos in general fared worse and are more likely to be asked for their papers because those who need to see their papers often have doubts about either the authenticity of the papers or the immigrants' right to be in the United States. This happens in interactions with street-level workers but also, and importantly, with the expanded cast of actors on whose actions I focus here. For instance, when purchasing a piece of furniture at a store or during a transaction at a bank, Manuel and Felipe agreed that more than one person usually inspects their TPS documents because the first person does not want to run the risk of accepting a document that may not be legitimate. And in the context of Arizona's SB 1070 and LAWA, it seems that people asking for documentary evidence are more watchful about potentially fake documents, even if they are asking for documents in a transaction that is not work-related at all. Manuel explained:

> At the dealer, when I went for the truck, the guy looks at my TPS card and says . . . looks like a *mica chueca* [fake green card]. I said no, this is what you get when you're on TPS. And he says, "what's that? Are you here legally? Do you have another form of ID?" This is all the time. One has to explain what TPS is. No one understands it and they think one is just illegal. And I think people are afraid that if they make a mistake and are not alert to *papeles chuecos* [fake papers] they'll get in trouble because the law [LAWA] right now is tough.

But Manuel also noted, "Oh, but that's because one is Latino. I can bet you if Russian immigrants or some white immigrants were on TPS, the situation would be different. Do you think they'll be asked for several forms of ID if they have blond hair and blue eyes? [*laughs*]."

I was able to get a glimpse of how those in charge of inspecting documents see the papers that immigrants show. I attended a workshop that an organization seeking to educate employees about DACA organized for faculty and staff (but mostly staff) at Arizona State University. I had the opportunity to listen to the questions from the attendees, which largely corroborated the perceptions of the immigrants with whom I have talked, such as Manuel and Felipe above. For instance, several staff members did not know how to differentiate among the various documents that DACA students (or TPS holders) produce as they come to process admissions (or even ask for information), and how these differ from a green card (which, as some workshop attendees noted, is not even green). They expressed concern at the "barrage of documents out there" that exist nowadays, noting especially (correctly) that they were not trained in immigration and legal matters and did not feel qualified to make those "delicate decisions." Often, the staff members noted, they preferred to "err on the safe side" and asked for additional documentation just to make sure they're not breaking the law.[53]

In a climate of enhanced enforcement and a multilayered system of harsh immigration laws and the racialization of Latinos/as as "illegals," those in positions of authority become suspicious of the papers that liminally legal immigrants produce or the documents that the unauthorized can show.[54] In their efforts to "respect the law," not only public employees—such as police and DMV clerks—but also shop owners, clerks, and bank tellers must be watchful. Unschooled in the intricacies of immigration law and fearful of stiff penalties, they must make sure the documentation they see is legitimate.[55] There is also the chance that these workers have their own views about immigration and Latino/a immigrants, and existing laws give them a green light to exercise their biases. The result is what happens when immigration policy is enforced in a racialized climate in which Latino/a immigrants, regardless of their legal status or documentation, are associated with unauthorized status (and images as criminals). In this hostile context, simply being Latino/a signals the likelihood of undocumentedness and thus of not deserving a service.

Enduring Effects

Noting the difficulties of engaging with those who are unfamiliar with the often convoluted set of special permits and temporary protections and accompanying documents, Manuel explained that he is afraid that he might be detained first, and by the time the authorities investigated his record, he might find himself on a plane back to El Salvador. Again, he explained that if it were not for the laws in place ("the sheriff—you know, who hates Latinos and makes everyone do the same") and the suspicion that these laws create, he would not have to be so cautious about his papers. He laughs when he retells the story of his brother being so afraid of misplacing his TPS card that for a while he used to sleep with it under his pillow. "He thought that if there was a break-in in the house, the robbers could take his TPS card! I know, it's funny, but this is how one lives. Always thinking about the papers." Living hyperaware of the law[56] translates into a hyperawareness of their documents that informs almost every aspect of their lives, so that their classification as temporary permit holder (or undocumented) becomes part of their own identity.

Adriana shares this view, only in her case she is unauthorized and cannot produce even a temporary permit. However, her twenty-five years of living in the United States have given her perspective on how laws and their effect on documentary evidence have changed.

> When we came to Arizona more than two decades ago, this was not a problem. I can't believe it myself that I'm telling you this, that me, as a Mexican woman here in Phoenix, didn't really think about my papers when I left my home! I listen to myself and think it's someone else. But yes, that was the case. Yes, of course, papers have always been important, but now it's more than that; now you feel, almost physically, how much they have your hands tied. All these laws and all the fear, and yes of course the sheriff and all that have completely, but really completely, changed life for someone in my position. I used to be able to show without embarrassment my Mexican documents at the bank, at a store, anywhere. And now? If I do that, people immediately think I'm undocumented. Why? Because I'm Mexican, and that's the only identity I have.

Importantly, these experiences have lasting effects. Josefina, who became a lawful permanent resident and later a naturalized citizen during the time I have known her, was always careful to carry her green card with her because she was afraid that she would be questioned and then be sent to detention. In her words, "I fear . . . [that] I will be stopped and deported because now they're deporting even people who are here legally, just because of how you look!" She also mentioned that Latinos are particularly targeted for document inspection on a routine basis. She has had experiences where even supermarket employees have asked her for her documents in the context of making a purchase or when she needs something from the service desk at those establishments, such as purchasing a money order. She remarked that, like the bank tellers and car dealer salespeople in the cases above, employees of commercial establishments also demanded to see an individual's documents, "to make sure you are who you say you are, that you are not going to do something bad." She also added that sometimes those employees ask for extra documentation, "just to make you feel less, to belittle you." She continued, responding to herself, "I am happy to show all my documents because I have everything anyone may want to ask for. I have nothing to fear. My record is clean, so I have no problem. It does not bother me, and in fact I'm proud to show my documents."

Josefina ascribes meaning to her documents that link identity, legal status classification, and deservingness. A coworker and friend of Josefina's who was visiting Josefina's house while I was there, chimed in, "Well, at this point, all those people feel like they have green light to ask for your papers." This then turned into a conversation recounting multiple times when Latino/a employees have demanded to see their documents. They commented, as others in my study also have noted, "Oh, Latinos are the worst. They behave worse than the police." This is likely not the case, but they perceive it as such because it stings to see that "your own people" also act like those in positions of authority, especially in a context like Phoenix, where about 40 percent of the population is Latino/a. Thus, when the exigencies of the legal context focus on documentary evidence on a routine basis, the large presence of co-ethnics, along with expectations of ethnic solidarity, do not necessarily offset the weight of "living with the law." Josefina once used this phrase when explaining the presence of law in her life.

When Josefina applied for and eventually was granted naturalization, her fears did not subside. I accompanied her to the naturalization ceremony and had the opportunity to hear her views immediately after she became a U.S. citizen. There were tables set up for the new citizens to apply for a series of documents, including passports and other benefits. When it came time to apply for her passport she also applied for a passport card, the laminated version of a person's passport. She and other Latinos/as who also had just become naturalized citizens agreed that they had to get those passport cards so that they could carry this new proof of citizenship in their wallets at all times, "just in case." Josefina explained, "When you are so used to making sure that you have your documents with you, when you don't leave the house without your documents because you feel naked if you don't have your TPS card or your green card with you, it's automatic. The thing you think about as you leave the house is, OK, I have my keys and then 'oh, my documents.' I am going to make sure I have my passport card in my purse at all times. It's a habit. It's a good habit to have." Two years later, when I asked her if she still carried her passport card with her in her purse, she replied, "Yes, of course! Wouldn't you, if you lived in Arizona?"

Discussion/Conclusion

The narratives above reflect the climate of insecurity and fear for (mostly Latino/a) immigrants—undocumented, documented, and those with in-between statuses—in an enforcement context where Latinos are racialized as undocumented, as in the Phoenix metro area.

I have discussed the experiences of liminally legal Central American immigrants as well as those of Mexican immigrants who are undocumented, and some immigrants who hold more permanent statuses. This examination provides a window onto the enforcement and implementation of the multilayered immigration regime on the ground,[57] affecting immigrants in a variety of legal and citizenship statuses. In the end, their experiences reveal how the state exerts its power on the immediate worlds of immigrants, present and future, through the creation of multiple legal statuses that shape membership and belonging and must be demonstrated through documentation.

Significantly, the environment in which those who are charged with inspecting documents live shapes how they understand and implement policies to assess immigrants' deservingness. Contexts in which political debates about the undesirability (and undeservingness) of immigrants are conveyed daily through the media mold the frames through which the "document overseers" view immigrants and influence how these overseers interpret and implement policy on the ground.[58] These frames also shape how immigrants evaluate their own deservingness in society.[59] Document overseers must decide what documents are "good" or "legitimate" on the spot, and in order to avoid penalties (written in law), sometimes they prefer to "err on the safe side" and demand more documents, even when these are not needed, and to ask for documents even of U.S. citizens. Employees at car dealerships, banks, stores, or anyone in a position to provide a service are not versed in the complexities of immigration law (and most people are not), but they must assess a person's identity and whether they are eligible for a service. This is how these individuals, situated outside formal state structures, ultimately engage in implementing law; the state exerts its power over immigrants through these overseers. Importantly, as these non-state actors also classify individuals and attach meaning to classifications, documents, and identities, they contribute to linking identities with identifications[60] and as such to producing a modern sense of self predicated on established ties to the state.[61]

The multiplying gray areas of legality today give rise to new forms of negotiating membership. Such areas add a layer of complexity in implementing laws and policies on the ground. Central Americans who hold Temporary Protected Status, immigrants whose applications for permanent status are under review (for years), or immigrants with DACA find themselves in challenging spaces that require explanations and negotiation because their statuses are not easily discernible, and the document overseers, influenced by media messages and politicians' narratives, continue to interpret immigrant legality within the documented–undocumented binary.

In contexts where Latinos/as are racialized, where Latino/a immigrants are equated with unauthorized status, and images of unauthorized immigrants are associated with criminals, determinations of eligibility are made through a lens that reflects this milieu. As immigrants in a variety of legal and citizenship statuses come into contact with document overseers, their experiences illustrate how membership is continually produced and always emergent, and how belonging is negotiated in everyday life.[62] As temporary legal statuses (e.g., DACA, TPS, parole, etc.) proliferate and receiving states discourage permanent settlement, more immigrants are pushed to live in unauthorized spaces or in uncertain predicaments with serious consequences for survival, incorporation, and membership. Research has shown[63] that unauthorized entry and lengthy periods of time in uncertain legality have serious implications for mobility and long-term incorporation and membership, and that such disadvantages accumulate over generations as they are transmitted in different ways to children.[64] This is the case for immigrants who live hyperaware of the law (and of the documents they must produce to show deservingness) for extended, indefinite periods of time.

As the cast of actors who request documentary evidence with the purpose of identifying individuals expands, they contribute to sustaining the disciplinary reach of the state and, ultimately, to the practice of governmentality. In doing so, these actors engage in the concrete practices of "doing citizenship" on the ground; as Torpey observed, "the notion of national communities must be codified in documents rather than merely imagined."[65] Thus, in the course of non-state business, these actors draw boundaries and classifications, and operationalize belongingness, deservingness, and the constitution of the modern self. At the same time, the multiplicity of actors and documents requested and produced may, as Dardy[66] has observed, unsettle the assumed monolithic nature of the state.[67]

Notes

1 Cecilia Menjívar, Andrea Gómez Cervantes, and Daniel Alvord, "Two Decades of Constructing Immigrants as Criminals," in *The Routledge Handbook of Immigration and Crime*, edited by Holly Ventura Miller and Anthony Peguero (New York: Routledge, 2018), 193–204.

2 States also have passed inclusionary laws (sometimes referred to as "sanctuary" laws), and there is a burgeoning literature on the effects of these laws on immigrants and their families, as well as on the factors that propel some states to pass inclusionary and others to adopt more anti-immigrant legislation. See Monica W.

Varsanyi, "Introduction," in *Taking Local Control: Immigration Policy Activism in U.S. Cities and States* (Stanford, CA: Stanford University Press, 2010), 1–27.

3   Karthick Ramakrishnan and Tom Wong, "Partisanship, Not Spanish: Explaining Municipal Ordinances Affecting Undocumented Immigrants," in *Taking Local Control: Immigration Policy Activism in U.S. Cities and States*, edited by Monica W. Varsanyi (Stanford, CA: Stanford University Press, 2010), 73–92.

4   National Conference of State Legislatures, "New NCSL Report Focuses on 2017 Immigration-Related Bills and Resolutions," 2017, accessed October 9, 2017, http://www.ncsl.org/press-room/new-ncsl-report-focuses-on-2017-immigration-related-bills-and-resolutions.aspx.

5   Pia Møller, "Restoring Law and (Racial) Order to the Old Dominion: White Dreams and New Federalism in Anti-Immigrant Legislation," *Cultural Studies* 28 (2014): 869–910.

6   Doris Meissner, Donald M. Kerwin, Muzzafar Chishti, and Claire Bergeron, *Immigration Enforcement in the United States: The Rise of a Formidable Machinery* (Washington, DC: Migration Policy Institute, 2013), accessed November 30, 2013, http://www.migrationpolicy.org/pubs/enforcementpillars.pdf.

7   Møller, "Restoring Law and (Racial) Order to the Old Dominion."

8   Cecilia Menjívar, "Immigrant Criminalization in Law and the Media: Effects on Latino Immigrant Workers' Identities in Arizona," *American Behavioral Scientist* 60 (2016): 597–616.

9   Daniel Alvord and Cecilia Menjívar, "'Illegal' or 'Undocumented' Immigrants? *The Arizona Republic* and the Relational Production of Nativist Media Discourse," forthcoming.

10 Hiroshi Motomura, *Americans in Waiting: The Lost Story of Immigration and Citizenship in the United States* (New York: Oxford University Press, 2006).

11 Jonathan Xavier Inda and Julie A. Dowling, "Introduction: Governing Immigrant Illegality," in *Governing Immigration through Crime: A Reader*, ed. Julie A. Dowling and Jonathan Xavier Inda (Stanford, CA: Stanford University Press, 2013), 1–35.

12 Erik Camayd-Freixas, *Postville: La criminaliación de los immigrantes* (Guatemala City: F&G Editores, 2009).

13 In this chapter I use the term *immigrant* instead of *migrant*, as specified in the introduction to this volume. I do so to underscore the critical role that receiving state power plays in creating the conditions—for those who have moved to that polity—within which documentation acquires the particular meanings I address here.

14 Marie Østegaard Møller and Deborah Stone, "Disciplining Disability under Danish Active Labour Market Policy," *Social Policy and Administration* 47 (2013): 586–604.

15 Steven Maynard-Moody and Michael Musheno, "Social Equities and Inequities in Practice: Street-Level Workers as Agents and Pragmatists," *Public Administration Review* 72 (2012): S16–S23.

16 Jane Caplan and John Torpey, "Introduction," in *Documenting Individual Identity: The Development of State Practices in the Modern World*, ed. Jane Caplan and John Torpey (Princeton, NJ: Princeton University Press, 2001), 1.

17 See Josiah M. Heyman, "Class and Classification at the U.S.-Mexico Border," *Human Organization* 60 (2001): 128–40.

18 Cook-Martín argues that the administrative domain that states developed to control migration became acceptable as part of state formation because states were responding to mass migration. Furthermore, states do not condition migration flows as a constant, but rather develop institutions and administrative domains to do so that can change and have varying regulatory capacities at different historical points. David Cook-Martín, "Rules, Red Tape, and Paperwork: The Archaeology of State Control over Immigrants," *Journal of Historical Sociology* 21 (2008): 82–119.

19 Kamal Sadiq, *Paper Citizens: How Illegal Immigrants Acquire Citizenship in Developing Countries* (New York: Oxford University Press, 2009).

20 Jaeeun Kim, "Establishing Identity: Documents, Performance, and Biometric Information in Immigration Proceedings," *Law and Social Inquiry* 36 (2011): 760–86. There are other ways in which nonfederal workers contribute to doing the work of state bureaucrats, as they can also shape immigrants' eligibility for status regularization; see Sarah M. Lakhani, "From Problems of Living to Problems of Law: The Legal Translation and Documentation of Immigrant Abuse and Helpfulness," *Law and Social Inquiry* 39 (2014): 643–65.

21 See Caplan and Torpey, "Introduction."

22 Heyman, "Class and Classification at the U.S.-Mexico Border."

23 Heyman, "Class and Classification at the U.S.-Mexico Border," 130. Another angle in the link between identification and identity deals with immigrants coming up with ways to respond to bureaucracies that seek to identify themselves by borrowing, renting, and buying identities, which can lead to the creation of flexible identities based on these other forms of documentary evidence; see Ellie Vasta, "Immigrants and the Paper Market: Borrowing, Renting and Buying Identities," *Ethnic and Racial Studies* 34 (2011): 187–206. This is evident when an immigrant who has borrowed a social security card is so used to going by the name on the card that sometimes they will not respond to their own name when called, as happened to one of my study participants in Phoenix.

24 Andrea Gómez Cervantes, Cecilia Menjívar, and William G. Staples, "Humane Immigration Enforcement and Latina Immigrants in the Detention Complex," *Feminist Criminology* 12 (2017): 269–92.

25 María E. Enchautegui and Cecilia Menjívar, "Paradoxes of Family Reunification Law: Family Separation and Reorganization under the Current Immigration Regime," *Law and Policy* 37 (2015): 32–60.

26 U.S. Census Bureau, "QuickFacts: Maricopa County, Arizona," https://www.census .gov/quickfacts/fact/table/maricopacountyarizona/PST045216. The effects of the Latino/a presence in a locality may vary by neighborhood. Research on the effects of the size of the Latino/a population on perceptions of Latino/a immigrants as a threat has found that whereas the percentage of Latinos/as in the immediate blocks where someone lives has no effect, the larger the Latino/a population is in surrounding blocks the greater the perceived threat; Matthew Hall and Maria Krysan, "The Neighborhood Context of Latino Threat," *Sociology of Race and Ethnicity* 3 (2017): 218–35.

27 Cecilia Menjívar et al., "Immigration Enforcement, the Racialization of Legal Status, and Perceptions of the Police: Latinos in Chicago, Los Angeles, Houston, and Phoenix in Comparative Perspective," *DuBois Review: Social Science Research on Race* 15 (2018): 107–28.

28 Cecilia Menjívar, "The Power of the Law: Central Americans' Legality and Everyday Life in Phoenix, Arizona," *Latino Studies* 9 (2011): 377–95.

29 Menjívar, "The Power of the Law."

30 Cecilia Menjívar and Sarah M. Lakhani, "Transformative Effects of Immigration Law: Immigrants' Personal and Social Metamorphoses through Regularization," *American Journal of Sociology* 121 (2016): 1818–55.

31 In 1940, the U.S. Congress passed the Alien Registration Act, a wartime registration designed to identify political enemies for expulsion from the country. Noncitizens were required to register at post offices around the country and be fingerprinted. This requirement was left in place after the war, and a requirement that all registrants carry their registration receipt at all times was added by the Immigration and Nationality Act of 1952. However, as Morawetz and Fernández-Silber observe, "In truth, no such scheme exists. The federal government abandoned comprehensive alien registration shortly after World War II and today's laws exempt vast numbers of nonimmigrant aliens from any obligation to register, carry documents, or both"; Nancy Morawetz and Natasha Fernández-Silber, "Immigration Law and the Myth of Comprehensive Registration," uc *Davis Law Review* 48 (2014): 144.

32 This chapter draws from my extended fieldwork in the Phoenix metro area, where I have been conducting research since 1998. In the interest of space, I will refer readers to other works for data and methods questions. See, for example, Cecilia Menjívar, "Liminal Legality: Salvadoran and Guatemalan Immigrants' Lives in the United States," *American Journal of Sociology* 111 (2006): 999–1037; Menjívar, "The Power of the Law."

33 See Estelle T. Lau, *Paper Families: Identity, Immigration Administration, and Chinese Exclusion* (Durham, NC: Duke University Press, 2006).

34 See Hiroshi Motomura, *Immigration outside the Law* (New York: Oxford University Press, 2014).

35 Menjívar, "Liminal Legality."

36 Cited in Caplan and Torpey, "Introduction," 6.

37 Of course, others have noted the vital importance that papers have for people, including the "papereality" that Dery discusses, where "a world of symbols, or written representations . . . take precedence over the things and events represented"; David Dery, "'Papereality' and Learning in Bureaucratic Organizations," *Administration and Society* 29 (1998): 678.

38 Provine and Varsanyi, this volume.

39 Motomura, *Americans in Waiting*.

40 Although traditionally not considered street-level workers, employers, particularly when they must abide by laws like LAWA in Arizona, also must interpret the law on the ground, and in doing so indirectly but actively contribute to enacting policy.

41 Steven Maynard-Moody and Michael Musheno, *Cops, Teachers, Counselors: Stories from the Front Lines of Public Service* (Ann Arbor: University of Michigan Press, 2003); Maynard-Moody and Musheno, "Social Equities and Inequities in Practice."

42 Lindsey Carte, "Everyday Restriction: Central American Women and the State in the Mexico-Guatemala Border City of Tapachula," *International Migration Review* 48 (2014): 113–43; Caplan and Torpey, "Introduction"; Josiah M. Heyman, "The Anthropology of Power-Wielding Bureaucracies," *Human Organization* 63 (2004): 487–500.

43 Joe Painter, "Prosaic Geographies of Stateness," *Political Geography* 25 (2006): 761.

44 Janet A. Gilboy, "Deciding Who Gets In: Decision Making by Immigration Inspectors," *Law and Society Review* 26 (1991): 571–600.

45 Lisa L. Magaña, *Straddling the Border: Immigration Policy and the INS* (Austin: University of Texas Press, 2003).

46 Natalia Deeb-Sossa and Jennifer Bickham-Mendez, "Enforcing Borders in the Nuevo South: Gender and Migration in Williamsburg, Virginia, and the Research Triangle, North Carolina," *Gender and Society* 22 (2008): 613–38.

47 Natalia Deeb-Sossa, *Doing Good: Racial Tensions and Workplace Inequalities at a Community Clinic in El Nuevo South* (Tucson: University of Arizona Press, 2013). This is not unlike the case in medieval and Renaissance medical and juridical spaces, where gender, skin color, individual description, and identity documents were intertwined but were also in tension. Valentin Groebner, "Describing the Person, Reading the Signs in Late Medieval and Renaissance Europe: Identity Papers, Vested Figures, and the Limits of Identification," in *Documenting Individual Identity: The Development of State Practices in the Modern World*, ed. Jane Caplan and John Torpey (Princeton, NJ: Princeton University Press, 2001), 19.

48 Helen Marrow, "Immigrant Bureaucratic Incorporation: The Dual Roles of Professional Missions and Government Policies," *American Sociological Review* 74 (2009): 756–76.

49 Guillermina Jasso, "Migration and Stratification," *Social Science Research* 40 (2011): 1292–336.

50 See Joe Henke, "Arizona's E-Verify Law Widely Ignored, Rarely Enforced," *Cronkite News*, January 26, 2013, accessed October 17, 2017, http://tucson.com/business /local/arizona-s-e-verify-law-widely-ignored-rarely-enforced/article_5e9f950e -6565-5c21-9531-69b8c8d05dfb.html.

51 Cecilia Menjívar, "Central American Immigrant Workers and Legal Violence in Phoenix, Arizona," *Latino Studies* 11 (2013): 228–52.

52 I corroborated this information: In California, driver's licenses are not paired with the length of time that TPS lasts; if individuals do not get a ticket, they can obtain a license for the same period others do (four years or so). In Arizona (as well as in Texas and other states), TPS holders must renew their driver's licenses every eighteen months, and they must present the actual TPS card; a receipt that simply confirms renewal is not accepted.

53 The Arizona Taxpayer and Citizen Protection Act, an initiative approved by Arizona voters in 2004, made it a misdemeanor for public officials to fail to report applicants for non-federally mandated public benefits who were found to be in

violation of U.S. immigration law. This initiative contained other provisions related to voter fraud, and thus, the initiative was very much predicated on assessing eligibility for benefits or for voting by checking documentary evidence.

54 This regular suspicion of immigrants' documents can be understood as a form of legal violence. See Leisy J. Abrego and Sarah M. Lakhani, "Incomplete Inclusion: Legal Violence and Immigrants in Liminal Legal Statuses," *Law and Policy* 37 (2015): 265–93; Cecilia Menjívar and Leisy J. Abrego, "Legal Violence: Immigration Law and the Lives of Central American Immigrants," *American Journal of Sociology* 117 (2012): 1380–421. I thank an anonymous reviewer for highlighting this connection.

55 By virtue of working in human service bureaucracies, the street-level workers at ASU had access to some information, however limited, on how to recognize legal statuses and what rights such statuses confer. This is likely unavailable to the private-sector employees on whom I focus here.

56 Menjívar, "The Power of the Law."

57 Cecilia Menjívar, "The 'Poli-Migra': Multi-Layered Legislation, Enforcement Practices, and What We Can Learn about and from Today's Approaches," *American Behavioral Scientist* 58 (2014): 1805–19.

58 Menjívar, "Immigrant Criminalization in Law and the Media."

59 Menjívar and Lakhani, "Transformative Effects of Immigration Law."

60 See Heyman, "Class and Classification at the U.S.-Mexico Border"; Robert Pallitto and Josiah Heyman, "Theorizing Cross-Border Mobility: Surveillance, Security and Identity," *Surveillance and Society* 5 (2008): 315–33.

61 Pallitto and Heyman, "Theorizing Cross-Border Mobility."

62 See Roberto Gonzales and Nando Sigona, eds., *Within and Beyond Citizenship: Borders, Membership, and Belonging* (London: Routledge, 2017).

63 Frank D. Bean et al., "The Educational Legacy of Undocumented Migration: Comparisons across U.S.-Immigrant Groups in How Parents' Status Affects Their Offspring," *International Migration Review* 45 (2011): 348–85.

64 Frank D. Bean et al., "Unauthorized Mexican Migration and the Socioeconomic Integration of Mexican Americans," in *Changing Times: America in a New Century*, ed. John R. Logan (New York: Russell Sage Foundation, 2013).

65 John Torpey, *The Invention of the Passport: Surveillance, Citizenship, and the State* (Cambridge: Cambridge University Press, 2000), 6.

66 Cited in Caplan and Torpey, "Introduction, 6."

67 See also Jacqueline Stevens, "Introduction," in *Citizenship in Question: Evidentiary Birthright and Statelessness*, ed. Benjamin N. Lawrence and Jacqueline Stevens (Durham, NC: Duke University Press, 2017), 2–24.

Bibliography

Abrego, Leisy J., and Sarah M. Lakhani. "Incomplete Inclusion: Legal Violence and Immigrants in Liminal Legal Statuses." *Law and Policy* 37 (2015): 265–93.

Alvord, Daniel, and Cecilia Menjívar. "'Illegal' or 'Undocumented' Immigrants? The *Arizona Republic* and the Relational Production of Nativist Media Discourse." Forthcoming.

Bean, Fran D., Susan K. Brown, Mark A. Leach, James D. Bachmeier, and Jennifer Van Hook. "Unauthorized Mexican Migration and the Socioeconomic Integration of Mexican Americans." In *Changing Times: America in a New Century*, edited by John R. Logan. New York: Russell Sage Foundation, 2013.

Bean, Frank D., Mark A. Leach, Susan K. Brown, James D. Bachmeier, and John R. Hipp. "The Educational Legacy of Undocumented Migration: Comparisons across U.S.-Immigrant Groups in How Parents' Status Affects Their Offspring." *International Migration Review* 45 (2011): 348–85.

Camayd-Freixas, Erik. *Postville: La criminaliación de los immigrantes*. Guatemala City: F&G Editores, 2009.

Caplan, Jane, and John Torpey, eds. *Documenting Individual Identity: The Development of State Practices in the Modern World*. Princeton, NJ: Princeton University Press, 2001.

Carte, Lindsey. "Everyday Restriction: Central American Women and the State in the Mexico-Guatemala Border City of Tapachula." *International Migration Review* 48 (2014): 113–43.

Cook-Martín, David. "Rules, Red Tape, and Paperwork: The Archaeology of State Control over Immigrants." *Journal of Historical Sociology* 21 (2008): 82–119.

Deeb-Sossa, Natalia. *Doing Good: Racial Tensions and Workplace Inequalities at a Community Clinic in El Nuevo South*. Tucson: University of Arizona Press, 2013.

Deeb-Sossa, Natalia, and Jennifer Bickham-Mendez. "Enforcing Borders in the Nuevo South: Gender and Migration in Williamsburg, Virginia, and the Research Triangle, North Carolina." *Gender and Society* 22 (2008): 613–38.

Dery, David. "'Papereality' and Learning in Bureaucratic Organizations." *Administration and Society* 29 (1998): 677–89.

Enchautegui, María E., and Cecilia Menjívar. "Paradoxes of Family Reunification Law: Family Separation and Reorganization under the Current Immigration Regime." *Law and Policy* 37 (2015): 32–60.

Gilboy, Janet A. "Deciding Who Gets In: Decision Making by Immigration Inspectors." *Law and Society Review* 26 (1991): 571–600.

Gómez Cervantes, Andrea, Cecilia Menjívar, and William G. Staples. "'Humane Immigration Enforcement and Latina Immigrants in the Detention Complex." *Feminist Criminology* 12 (2017): 269–92.

Gonzales, Roberto, and Nando Sigona, eds. *Within and Beyond Citizenship: Borders, Membership, and Belonging*. London: Routledge, 2017.

Groebner, Valentin. "Describing the Person, Reading the Signs in Late Medieval and Renaissance Europe: Identity Papers, Vested Figures, and the Limits of Identification." In *Documenting Individual Identity: The Development of State Practices in the Modern World*, edited by Jane Caplan and John Torpey, 15–27. Princeton, NJ: Princeton University Press, 2001.

Hall, Matthew, and Maria Krysan. "The Neighborhood Context of Latino Threat." *Sociology of Race and Ethnicity* 3 (2017): 218–35.

Henke, Joe. 2013. "Arizona's E-Verify Law Widely Ignored, Rarely Enforced." *Cronkite News*, January 26, 2013. Accessed October 17, 2017. http://tucson.com/business/local

/arizona-s-e-verify-law-widely-ignored-rarely-enforced/article_5e9f950e-6565-5c21
-9531-69b8c8d05dfb.html.

Heyman, Josiah M. "The Anthropology of Power-Wielding Bureaucracies." *Human Organization* 63 (2004): 487–500.

Heyman, Josiah M. "Class and Classification at the U.S.-Mexico Border." *Human Organization* 60 (2001): 128–40.

Inda, Jonathan Xavier, and Julie A. Dowling. "Introduction: Governing Immigrant Illegality." In *Governing Immigration through Crime: A Reader*, edited by Julie A. Dowling and Jonathan Xavier Inda, 1–35. Stanford, CA: Stanford University Press, 2013.

Jasso, Guillermina. "Migration and Stratification." *Social Science Research* 40 (2011): 1292–336.

Kim, Jaeeun. "Establishing Identity: Documents, Performance, and Biometric Information in Immigration Proceedings." *Law and Social Inquiry* 36 (2011): 760–86.

Lakhani, Sarah M. "From Problems of Living to Problems of Law: The Legal Translation and Documentation of Immigrant Abuse and Helpfulness." *Law and Social Inquiry* 39 (2014): 643–65.

Lau, Estelle T. *Paper Families: Identity, Immigration Administration, and Chinese Exclusion*. Durham, NC: Duke University Press, 2006.

Magaña, Lisa L. *Straddling the Border: Immigration Policy and the INS*. Austin: University of Texas Press, 2003.

Marrow, Helen. "Immigrant Bureaucratic Incorporation: The Dual Roles of Professional Missions and Government Policies." *American Sociological Review* 74 (2009): 756–76.

Maynard-Moody, Steven, and Michael Musheno. *Cops, Teachers, Counselors: Stories from the Front Lines of Public Service*. Ann Arbor: University of Michigan Press, 2003.

Maynard-Moody, Steven, and Michael Musheno. "Social Equities and Inequities in Practice: Street-Level Workers as Agents and Pragmatists." *Public Administration Review* 72 (2012): S16–S23.

Meissner, Doris, Donald M. Kerwin, Muzzafar Chishti, and Claire Bergeron. *Immigration Enforcement in the United States: The Rise of a Formidable Machinery*. Washington, DC: Migration Policy Institute, 2013. Accessed November 30, 2013. http://www .migrationpolicy.org/pubs/enforcementpillars.pdf.

Menjívar, Cecilia. "Central American Immigrant Workers and Legal Violence in Phoenix, Arizona." *Latino Studies* 11 (2013): 228–52.

Menjívar, Cecilia. "Immigrant Criminalization in Law and the Media: Effects on Latino Immigrant Workers' Identities in Arizona." *American Behavioral Scientist* 60 (2016): 597–616.

Menjívar, Cecilia. "Liminal Legality: Salvadoran and Guatemalan Immigrants' Lives in the United States." *American Journal of Sociology* 111 (2006): 999–1037.

Menjívar, Cecilia. "The 'Poli-Migra': Multi-Layered Legislation, Enforcement Practices, and What We Can Learn about and from Today's Approaches." *American Behavioral Scientist* 58 (2014): 1805–19.

Menjívar, Cecilia. "The Power of the Law: Central Americans' Legality and Everyday Life in Phoenix, Arizona." *Latino Studies* 9 (2011): 377–95.

Menjívar, Cecilia, and Leisy J. Abrego. "Legal Violence: Immigration Law and the Lives of Central American Immigrants." *American Journal of Sociology* 117 (2012): 1380–421.

Menjívar, Cecilia, Andrea Gómez Cervantes, and Daniel Alvord. "Two Decades of Constructing Immigrants as Criminals." In *The Routledge Handbook of Immigration and Crime*, edited by Holly Ventura Miller and Anthony Peguero, 193–204. New York: Routledge, 2018.

Menjívar, Cecilia, and Sarah M. Lakhani. "Transformative Effects of Immigration Law: Immigrants' Personal and Social Metamorphoses through Regularization." *American Journal of Sociology* 121 (2016): 1818–55.

Menjívar, Cecilia, William Paul Simmons, Daniel Alvord, and Elizabeth Salerno Valdez. "Immigration Enforcement, the Racialization of Legal Status, and Perceptions of the Police: Latinos in Chicago, Los Angeles, Houston, and Phoenix in Comparative Perspective." *DuBois Review: Social Science Research on Race* 15 (2018): 107–28.

Møller, Pia. "Restoring Law and (Racial) Order to the Old Dominion: White Dreams and New Federalism in Anti-Immigrant Legislation." *Cultural Studies* 28 (2014): 869–910.

Morawetz, Nancy, and Natasha Fernández-Silber. "Immigration Law and the Myth of Comprehensive Registration." *UC Davis Law Review* 48 (2014): 141–205.

Motomura, Hiroshi. *Americans in Waiting: The Lost Story of Immigration and Citizenship in the United States*. New York: Oxford University Press, 2006.

Motomura, Hiroshi. *Immigration outside the Law*. New York: Oxford University Press, 2014.

National Conference of State Legislatures (NCSL). "New NCSL Report Focuses on 2017 Immigration-Related Bills and Resolutions." 2017. Accessed October 9, 2017. http://www.ncsl.org/press-room/new-ncsl-report-focuses-on-2017-immigration-related-bills-and-resolutions.aspx.

Østegaard Møller, Marie, and Deborah Stone. "Disciplining Disability under Danish Active Labour Market Policy." *Social Policy and Administration* 47 (2013): 586–604.

Painter, Joe. "Prosaic Geographies of Stateness." *Political Geography* 25 (2006): 752–74.

Pallitto, Robert, and Josiah Heyman. "Theorizing Cross-Border Mobility: Surveillance, Security and Identity." *Surveillance and Society* 5 (2008): 315–33.

Ramakrishnan, Karthick, and Tom Wong. "Partisanship, Not Spanish: Explaining Municipal Ordinances Affecting Undocumented Immigrants." In *Taking Local Control: Immigration Policy Activism in U.S. Cities and States*, edited by Monica W. Varsanyi, 73–92. Stanford, CA: Stanford University Press, 2010.

Sadiq, Kamal. *Paper Citizens: How Illegal Immigrants Acquire Citizenship in Developing Countries*. New York: Oxford University Press, 2009.

Stevens, Jacqueline. "Introduction." In *Citizenship in Question: Evidentiary Birthright and Statelessness*, edited by Benjamin N. Lawrence and Jacqueline Stevens, 2–24. Durham, NC: Duke University Press, 2017.

Torpey, John. *The Invention of the Passport: Surveillance, Citizenship, and the State.* Cambridge: Cambridge University Press, 2000.

Varsanyi, Monica W. *Taking Local Control: Immigration Policy Activism in U.S. Cities and States.* Stanford, CA: Stanford University Press, 2010.

Vasta, Ellie. "Immigrants and the Paper Market: Borrowing, Renting and Buying Identities." *Ethnic and Racial Studies* 34 (2011): 187–206.

PART III

RESISTANCE AND REFUSALS

If part II of the volume explores the way migrants and advocates engage with the state and submit to its logics, part III examines modes of resistance to bureaucratic inscription. Foregrounding the agency of migrants and their advocates, these chapters remind us that state control is never complete. These chapters show how migrants and their advocates creatively engage with the state and state-issued identifications. Migrants and advocates attempt to disrupt the processes that make migrants legible to the state once they are entered into its bureaucratic systems. They strategically redefine and repurpose state documents; they circulate, borrow, and rent them. In doing so, they refuse the state's monopoly over controlling mobility and defining social membership.

Gomberg-Muñoz highlights the ways that migrants and their advocates explicitly refuse and resist state power, illustrating the way that documents form an important part of this resistance. Indeed, the sanctuary movement in the United States relies on challenges to the legitimacy of state documents. As Gomberg-Muñoz shows, advocates attempt to persuade local law enforcement to refuse to honor federal "detainer requests" asking that they hold unauthorized migrants for apprehension by ICE—requests that have already been ruled unconstitutional by the Ninth and First Circuit Courts of Appeals.[1] Another defense in the arsenal of migrant advocates is developing alternatives to state-issued identifications. Municipal IDs are one form of local-level identity documents that challenge the state's monopoly over defining social membership.[2] Yet Gomberg-Muñoz focuses on informal documents—the know-your-rights cards informing migrants (and officials) of migrants' right to remain silent. Wallet-sized, these know-your-rights cards can be provided to authorities requesting proof of status in lieu of, say, a driver's license (which, in many states, are inaccessible to unauthorized migrants). Thus, know-your-rights cards both substitute for and challenge state-provided identifications.

If Gomberg-Muñoz's chapter highlights how documents figure in resistance to the deportation regime in the United States, Juan Thomas Ordóñez examines how indigenous Ecuadorian migrants strategically evade immigration controls by creatively deploying identity documents. As he points out, Kichwa migrants are not interested in documents in order to lay claims on the state—that is, to access any rights or benefits. They do not fetishize state-issued documents nor the citizenship status they confer. Instead, Kichwa migrants are primarily interested in documents for their *use*. Therefore, Kichwa migrants disassociate passports and IDs from citizenship status; they exchange and circulate them to skirt state controls on their mobility. Importantly, Ordóñez shows that attitudes toward documents are learned within particular contexts. He argues that Kichwa migrants developed their strategic and pragmatic relationship to documents due to their marginal position within Colombia. Here they learned to pool, forge, and rent documents to get through checkpoints and immigration controls—strategies they have then deployed to varying effect in Korea, the EU, and Russia.

Ordóñez's chapter is noteworthy not only for examining the ingenious ways that migrants pool and forge identity documents[3] but also for pointing out that Kichwa practices of identity circulation are abetted by their own illegibility to officials in a variety of states. Kichwa migrants rely on the inscrutability of their indigeneity as a cover for their use of borrowed documents. Authorities in Colombia can't seem to distinguish one Kichwa migrant from another and typically don't see the Kichwa as a category of concern due to their itinerancy. Meanwhile, officials in Europe often don't know where Ecuador is. Echoing the insights of Menjívar, Ordóñez calls attention to the fact that documents mean different things in different contexts due in part to the social position of the bearer. Just as the naturalized Latino citizens Menjívar discusses find themselves fending off repeated requests for documents simply due to their racialized status, Ordóñez's migrants are peculiarly immune to documentary controls because of their "foreignness"—that is, their out-of-place status as indigenous merchants.

In addressing the case of migrants who cross international lines through travel or deportation, these chapters also highlight the uneven and contradictory ways that documents travel (or do not travel). This is an issue that deserves further study. Growing attention has been paid to the way that documents move across jurisdictional lines within a given nation-state. For example, state-issued driver's licenses for unauthorized migrants in the United States must be marked as not valid for federal purposes (such as receiving federal benefits or voting). Indeed, much scholarship documents the contests that unfold between jurisdictions about whether to extend identity documents to unauthorized migrants, as this is ultimately a debate over migrants' social membership.[4] Yet the issue of the equivalency of documents across international lines has been relatively unexplored. As Gomberg-Muñoz suggests, this is a topic that is timely and ripe for analysis, raising issues such as the power dynamics that play out through jurisdictional rifts between states over recognizing documents, and the erasures of identity and rights accomplished by one state's agents purposefully withholding or confiscating documents (such as passports or orders of removal). Ultimately, the Mexican state's lack of recognition of U.S. birth certificates leads to "undocumented Mexicans" in Mexico because migrant parents no longer have access to the bureaucracies of the nation-state from which they were deported.

As both chapters point out, the subjectivities of migrants who have undergone bureaucratic inscription in multiple states are also ripe for analysis. Ordóñez points out that the subjectivities and attitudes toward documents among itinerant Kichwa migrants must be situated in the context of the different states they inhabit. In a similar manner, the subjectivities of deportees—whose attitudes toward documents were forged first in Mexico and then in the United States—are also worthy of analysis. Gomberg-Muñoz points out that deportees must navigate a clash between two different modes of engaging with state bureaucracies. After living in such a way as to avoid paper trails in the United States—working under the table, avoiding contact with local government authorities, staying out of the way of the police—deportees must suddenly demand recognition from Mexican state bureaucracies in order to establish proof of identity and qualify for benefits. They must transition from avoiding the U.S. state and its representatives to proactively seeking the attention of the U.S. and Mexican states. In short, deportees must navigate two very different sets of relationships with the U.S. and Mexican states. Moreover, ironically, their success in remaining invisible in the United States often backfires in Mexico, as they must furnish evidence of their time in the United States—in the form of check stubs and school transcripts—in order to qualify for state benefits for deportees. Gomberg-Muñoz thus helpfully illuminates the erasures of identity and rights generated by the lack of equivalency of documents across international lines.

While raising new avenues of analysis, then, the chapters in part III show how the creative use of documents is fundamental to resisting state control. If states ensnare and entrap migrants through the paper trails they attach to them, the chapters in part III reveal the way that migrants sometimes evade legibility.

Notes

1 Immigrant Legal Resource Center, "Immigration Detainers Legal Update—July 2018," accessed January 16, 2019, https://www.ilrc.org/immigration-detainers-legal-update-july-2018.

2 City of Toronto, "Access to City Services for Undocumented Torontonians," May 7, 2014, accessed May 2, 2017, http://www.toronto.ca/legdocs/mmis/2014/cd/bgrd/backgroundfile-69193.pdf; Center for Popular Democracy, "Promoting Equality: City and State Policy to Ensure Immigrant Safety and Inclusion," October 25, 2016, accessed January 30, 2019, https://populardemocracy.org/news/publications/promoting-equality-city-and-state-policy-ensure-immigrant-safety-and-inclusion; Els De Graauw, "Municipal ID Cards for Undocumented Immigrants: Local Bureaucratic Membership in a Federal System," *Politics and Society* 42 (2014): 309–30; Helen Marrow, "Deserving to a Point: Unauthorized Immigrants in San Francisco's Universal Access Healthcare Model," *Social Science and Medicine* 74 (2012): 846–54; Monica W. Varsanyi, "Interrogating 'Urban Citizenship' vis-à-vis Undocumented Migration," *Citizenship Studies* 10 (2006): 229–49.

3 See also Apostolous Andrikopolous, "Argonauts of West Africa: Migration, Citizenship, and Changing Kinship Dynamics in a Changing Europe" (Ph.D. diss., Amsterdam Institute for Social Science Research, 2017); Sarah Horton, "Identity Loan: The Moral Economy of Document Exchange in California's Central Valley," *American Ethnologist* 42 (2015): 55–67; Madeleine Reeves, "Clean Fake: Authenticating Documents and Persons in Migrant Moscow," *American Ethnologist* 40 (2013): 508–24.

4 De Graauw, "Municipal ID Cards for Undocumented Immigrants"; Marrow, "Deserving to a Point"; Varsanyi, "Interrogating 'Urban Citizenship' vis-à-vis

Undocumented Migration"; Monica W. Varsanyi et al., "Multilayered Jurisdictional Patchwork: Immigration Federalism in the United States," *Law and Policy* 34 (2012): 138–58; see also Provine and Varsanyi, this volume.

Bibliography

Andrikopolous, Apostolous. "Argonauts of West Africa: Migration, Citizenship, and Changing Kinship Dynamics in a Changing Europe." Ph.D. dissertation, Amsterdam Institute for Social Science Research, 2017.

Center for Popular Democracy. "Promoting Equality: City and State Policy to Ensure Immigrant Safety and Inclusion." Center for Popular Democracy, October 25, 2016. Accessed January 30, 2019. https://populardemocracy.org/news/publications /promoting-equality-city-and-state-policy-ensure-immigrant-safety-and-inclusion.

City of Toronto. "Access to City Services for Undocumented Torontonians." May 7, 2014. Accessed May 2, 2017. http://www.toronto.ca/legdocs/mmis/2014/cd/bgrd /backgroundfile-69193.pdf.

De Graauw, Els. "Municipal ID Cards for Undocumented Immigrants: Local Bureaucratic Membership in a Federal System." *Politics and Society* 42 (2014): 309–30.

Horton, Sarah. "Identity Loan: The Moral Economy of Document Exchange in California's Central Valley." *American Ethnologist* 42 (2015): 55–67.

Immigrant Legal Resource Center. "Immigration Detainers Legal Update—July 2018." Accessed January 16, 2019. https://www.ilrc.org/immigration-detainers-legal -update-july-2018.

Marrow, Helen. "Deserving to a Point: Unauthorized Immigrants in San Francisco's Universal Access Healthcare Model." *Social Science and Medicine* 74 (2012): 846–54.

Reeves, Madeleine. "Clean Fake: Authenticating Documents and Persons in Migrant Moscow." *American Ethnologist* 40 (2013): 508–24.

Varsanyi, Monica W. "Interrogating 'Urban Citizenship' vis-à-vis Undocumented Migration." *Citizenship Studies* 10 (2006): 229–49.

Varsanyi, Monica W., Paul Lewis, Marie Provine, and Scott Decker. "Multilayered Jurisdictional Patchwork: Immigration Federalism in the United States." *Law and Policy* 34 (2012): 138–58.

7

KNOWING YOUR RIGHTS
IN TRUMP'S AMERICA
Paper Trails of Migrant Community Empowerment

Bans and Birthdays

On January 27, 2017, just one week after his inauguration as the forty-fifth president of the United States, Donald Trump issued an executive order suspending the entry of temporary visa holders, refugees, and legal permanent U.S. residents from seven Muslim-majority nations. For melodramatic effect, the ban took effect while hundreds of travelers from those nations were in transit, and in Chicago on the evening of the 28th, visa holders from the affected countries were detained upon their arrival at O'Hare International Airport. As the ACLU and other groups hurriedly filed lawsuits to stay the ban, hundreds of protesters began to converge on O'Hare's international terminal, shutting down traffic outside. Inside the airport, a stream of immigration attorneys began arriving to offer pro bono legal services to the detained travelers and their family members. Hours later, a federal judge in New York ordered an emergency stay of the travel ban, dealing the Trump administration its first legal defeat.

I watched this spectacle unfold mostly through live feeds on my cell phone screen. Many of my friends and colleagues had gone to O'Hare that evening, but I decided to make good on a promise to take my son to a birthday party instead. There, in a suburban Chicago basement, surrounded by colorful balloons and giggly six-year-olds, I was not the only one preoccupied by the nearby airport scene and Trump's punitive immigration agenda.

"I am worried that my husband and I will be deported," one mom confided as we discussed the situation in hushed voices. "And what will happen to our children?" I invited her to a know-your-rights (KYR) workshop at Loyola University Chicago the following week, and when she didn't come, I took a packet of KYR materials to her house. This neighborly exchange created yet another locus in a community-generated paper trail that connects members of immigrant communities with immigrant rights advocates, pro bono attorneys, and grassroots organizations. This community paper trail is both different from and in conversation with its formal, bureaucratic counterpart, as it consists of literature that challenges the interpretation and use of governmental paper trails in aggressive policing, detention, and deportation of U.S. immigrants.[1]

As a candidate, Donald Trump promised to take a hard line on immigration, calling for "extreme vetting" of legal immigrants and mass deportations of millions of people living in the United States unlawfully. In the early days of his presidency, the Trump administration took steps to make good on those promises through a series of executive orders that escalated immigrant policing at consulates, borders, and checkpoints, as well as throughout the U.S. interior.[2] And while Trump's agenda has energized and legitimized racist, xenophobic, and Islamophobic movements, it has also given rise to a surge in resistance activities that include local campaigns for "sanctuary," deportation defense networks, pro bono legal aid for detained immigrants, and KYR workshops.

In all of these spaces, documents accumuate and circulate. The executive orders, lawsuits and stays, passports and visas, applications and forms, and KYR materials constitute elements of legal strategies used by government agents, immigrant advocates, organizers, and immigrants themselves across a contested sociolegal landscape. While state agents strategically monopolize the interpretation and statutory significance of legal documents to exercise power over immigrant communities,[3] immigrant advocates attempt to break this monopoly and exercise their rights via community education and document reclamation.[4] This chapter draws on Susan Coutin's (this volume) conceptualization of immigrant advocates' "legal craft" as the expertise involved in deciphering and interpreting documents and records in applications for immigration benefits. Here, I argue that advocates rapidly maneuver their legal craft not only to advance individual cases for immigration relief, but also to mobilize an arsenal of community defense strategies in response to Trump's overtly hostile and aggressive immigration enforcement agenda.

These defensive strategies, such as KYR workshops and campaigns for sanctuary, entail the generation of documentary paper trails that are different from the government's bureaucratic records, but that interface with and contest governmental paper trails used to apprehend and entrap U.S. immigrants. Some of these documents, such as lawsuits and proposed sanctuary ordinances, will ultimately become part of the state's formal legal record, while other types of literature, such as KYR flyers, likely will not and thus constitute a community-generated "gray" literature. The creation and dissemination of a variety of both formal and informal documents—including PowerPoint presentations, wallet cards, signs, flyers, legislative proposals, and lawsuits—are central to contemporary social and political campaigns contesting the policing of immigrant communities.

This chapter traces the circulation and changing meanings of documents in community education and empowerment campaigns in the wake of Trump's 2016 election. In particular, I examine how advocates use community education to create and exploit legal gray areas as they advance competing interpretations and uses of documents in sociolegal arenas. I also explore how local campaigns for "sanctuary" seek to sever paper trails of documents that can expose immigrant community members to federal immigration agencies. Finally, as documents form new paper trails through deportation, I attend to their changing meanings as they travel in new directions, traverse jurisdictional boundaries, and become repurposed for different uses.

The descriptions that I present here are drawn from several sources. Between November 2016 and June 2017, I participated in three campaigns for sanctuary—one each at the level of my university, community of residence, and state—two KYR workshops, and a binational project to ease the community reintegration of "returnees" in Mexico. While the primary purpose of these activities was to effect political change, and not to produce scholarship per se, participation in these campaigns provided insight into the significance and dynamism of documentation strategies in a period of escalating immigrant policing. As a more formal research technique, I also conducted more than thirty semi-structured interviews with community organizers, legal advocates, government officials, and current and former migrants in and around Chicago, Illinois; Mexico City; and Zapotlanejo, Jalisco.

The chapter begins with a consideration of the legal and political contexts of immigrant policing under the Trump administration, then moves on to an examination of how community education campaigns strategically advance particular legal strategies to protect immigrants from removal.

The following section explores how campaigns for sanctuary arise to refuse the authority of documents generated by federal agencies that entrap immigrant community members in the localities where they live. The final ethnographic section follows documents across the U.S.-Mexico border as they accompany people who are deported to Mexico, illuminating inconsistencies in the jurisdictional meanings of documents that are issued in one context and used in another. Together, these sections illustrate not only how state agents wield legal documents to exercise power, but also how members of immigrant communities strategically interpret, reclaim, repurpose, and refuse documents in an attempt to protect themselves from deportation and exercise rights where they live.

The Legal Landscape of Trump's America

At its core, law constitutes a tool of governance that is created and implemented by state agents to uphold the structures of state society. As such, legal policies and practices often disempower, disenfranchise, and regulate non-elite communities, preserving and legitimizing sociopolitical inequalities. Yet marginalized people do not necessarily accept legal subordination passively, and they may undertake a range of strategies to contest it, including deploying legal strategies to their benefit, participating in movements to reform policy, and carrying out radical measures that seek to subvert the state altogether.[5] In advanced liberal democracies such as the United States, this contestation has resulted in prolonged grassroots campaigns to democratize political power, often intertwined with periods of state restriction and repression.[6] In all, while law is theoretically enacted unilaterally from above, its implementation is dynamic and mediated by a variety of actors with diverse interests, interpretations, and responses.[7]

Immigration and citizenship policies legitimize statehood and imbue it with national meaning, mainly by creating legal categories related to nationality. These categories are most directly tied to a person's nation of birth, but they are also shaped by social inequalities related to ethnoracial classification, class status, and gender.[8] Prior to the 1960s, for example, U.S. immigration and citizenship policies were explicitly designed in accordance with racial ideologies that heralded the biological superiority of Northern and Western Europeans.[9] In the post–civil rights era, the racial dimensions of U.S. immigration policy became muted, while exclusionary policies created, then targeted, an unauthorized population consisting mostly of working-class Latin Americans.[10] Today's U.S. population of 11 million unauthorized people is one result of a series of recent policy decisions that have barred the legal inclusion of certain immigrants into the polity and have especially impeded access to U.S. citizenship for working-class Latinos.[11]

As part of this process, state agents maintain a monopoly over the issuance and interpretation of official documents that grant, or, in some cases, strip (see Boehm, this volume) holders of status; state agents' authority over "papers" is a key component of their power.[12] Not surprisingly, members of marginalized communities develop strategies to challenge this monopoly, as people create, collect, exchange, and interpret documents on their own accord.[13] More broadly, legal advocates, community organizers, and activists develop legal strategies to maneuver contradictions and gaps in law: they contest policies such as the travel ban in courtrooms, challenge the jurisdiction of federal documents in local municipalities, and train community members to question the authority of state agents who try to arrest and deport them. These strategies are limited in their scope and effectiveness, but they seek to slow the escalation of U.S. immigration enforcement measures that have increasingly characterized the U.S. immigration system since the 1980s.

Following the passage of punitive immigration bills in 1986 and 1996, exclusionary U.S. immigration practices reached their pre-Trump zenith under the Barack Obama administration (2008–16), which oversaw record high rates of deportations known as removals. In 2013, the U.S. deportation rate peaked at a historical high of 434,015, then declined some as Obama, facing mounting pressure from immigrant rights activists, rolled back aggressive enforcement campaigns and instituted a program known as DACA in 2012, which protected some unauthorized youth from deportation.[14] And while anti-deportation activism was vigorous during the Obama years, it nevertheless constituted a relatively small component of a larger immigrant rights movement mainly focused on pushing for comprehensive immigration reform legislation.[15]

Early indications are that Trump's immigration enforcement agenda involves a return to and expansion of the enforcement regime responsible for mass deportations in the Obama era. During his first five days in office, Trump issued a series of executive orders intended to significantly escalate immigrant policing, detention, and deportation. In addition to implementing the travel ban and "extreme vetting" of visa applicants from select Muslim-majority nations, the orders expand the category of persons in the United States who are a priority for deportation, from those convicted of a serious crime to those who are convicted or charged with a crime, suspected of a crime, or suspected of fraud or being a threat to public safety; in effect, this change renders all of the 11 million unauthorized people living in the United States priorities for deportation.[16] As a result, in the first nine months of 2017, Immigration and Customs Enforcement (ICE) agents arrested three times the number of "noncriminal" immigrants over the same period in 2016.[17] The orders also expand a process known as "expedited removal," in which people who cannot prove that they have lived in the United States for at least two years can be deported by their arresting immigration officer without ever attending a deportation hearing or seeing an immigration judge; they also tighten criteria for asylum, expand the immigrant detention system, and mandate construction of an expanded wall along the U.S-Mexico border. Finally, on September 5, 2017, the Trump administration sought to end the DACA program and remove the limited protections that program had provided for unauthorized youth.

To execute these heightened enforcement priorities, the executive orders require the Department of Homeland Security (DHS) to add 15,000 new enforcement agents to its roster: 10,000 for ICE and 5,000 for Customs and Border Protection (CBP).[18] In addition to increasing the number of federal agents, the orders reimplement and expand two enforcement programs in the U.S. interior, 287(g) and Secure Communities, which enlist local police agencies in the enforcement of federal immigration law. They also target municipal sanctuary ordinances that seek to inhibit such federal–local cooperation.[19] Together, these measures disproportionately target Muslims and Latinos for exclusion and render millions of unauthorized people in the U.S. interior more vulnerable to deportation than ever before.

Resistance to Trump's agenda has been considerable. Indeed, the airport rallies on the night of the travel ban were just one of many instances of mass community protest in the months following the election. For veteran organizers and legal advocates, this surge in both immigrant policing and community resistance has increased demand for their work and compelled them to shift additional resources toward community defense. Community education and empowerment programs constitute an important part of this work, and Chicago-area organizations quickly found themselves overwhelmed by demand for KYR trainings in the postelection period. In response to an uptick in calls to their support hotline, one Chicago immigrant advocacy group doubled their offerings of KYR workshops and increased their training of KYR trainers to multiply their effectiveness in the months after Trump's election. The proximate goal of these KYR workshops is to empower community members to take steps to prevent apprehension by immigration agents, and, if that fails, to better prepare them for deportation.

But as an organizer with Jesuit Migrant Services told me, community education campaigns are not merely defensive; they also constitute both a source of empowerment and a tool of political organizing in disempowered communities. "Information is the biggest thing," she explained. "The one who has the information is the one who has the power." One ultimate goal of community education programs is to expand the political engagement of marginalized community members and effect political change. By focusing on the creation and circulation of documents within and across several sites, including KYR workshops, movements for local sanctuary, and campaigns to assist deportees and their family members in Mexico, the following sections illustrate how legal advocates and organizers use community-generated documents to carve out some autonomy and control from ever more repressive political practices.

Disputing Documents

I arrived at Loyola's first KYR workshop late, having just come from class. I slipped through a back door and squeezed past a row of people standing against the back wall; every seat in the hundred-person classroom was taken. I scanned the room for my neighbor from the birthday party before turning my attention to the presentation, which was led by an organizer with the Illinois Coalition for Immigrant and Refugee Rights (ICIRR) and two Loyola students. A close-up picture of a document filled the projector screen. "This is a judicial warrant," the organizer was explaining, pointing to large red letters at the top of the document that read, "Sample Warrant Signed by a Judge." He pointed out distinguishing features of the document that were outlined in red before moving to the next slide. Another document appeared, this one with the words "Sample ICE Warrant" at the top. "This is an administrative or ICE warrant," the organizer began explaining. As I listened, I picked up some handouts that had been disseminated around the room, including wallet-sized cards, action plan checklists, and illustrated instructions on how to handle encounters with immigration agents.

Such careful attention to documents in immigrant communities is nothing new. Recognizing the power of "papers," those who are denied formal identity documents by the state have long developed documentation strategies of their own.[20] Aurora Chang has called attention to practices of "hyperdocumentation," in which so-called undocumented people accumulate awards, diplomas, accolades, certificates, and other examples of material recognition of their value and social personhood to contest their devaluation and stake claims to sociolegal belonging.[21] These practices of hyperdocumentation are occasionally rewarded by the state, as when criteria for immigration programs require evidence of continuous residence for periods of several years or of "good moral character."[22] Abarca and Coutin have shown how people may gather and store such evidence for years or decades in anticipation of immigration legislation with a path to legalization that would allow them to change their status.[23]

In the wake of Trump's election, the likelihood of immigration reform with a legalization program has dimmed in relation to the possibility of apprehension and deportation, and not surprisingly, migrants' documentation strategies are shifting in response. In the current period, community education campaigns circulate KYR materials and encourage people who are out of status to accumulate and carry documents that can help shield them from deportation (see also Menjívar, this volume). For example, some legal advocates have encouraged clients who are out of status to carry proof of at least two years of continuous U.S. residence on their persons at all times, not to help them apply for immigration benefits, but to help them guard against expedited removal. Anticipating increased racial profiling of Latinos, some advocates have even urged naturalized U.S. citizens to begin carrying identity documents such as passports that prove their lawful presence in the United States.[24]

As intermediaries between the state and the clients they serve, legal advocacy organizations generate and distribute dozens of texts, including PowerPoint slides, posters, flyers, checklists, copies of forms and applications, and wallet-sized cards, all of which are meant to help members of immigrant communities understand and exercise their rights under U.S. law. The small, bright-red wallet cards that we distributed at Loyola's first KYR workshop, for example, describe constitutional rights in Spanish on one side, including the right to keep your door closed to immigration agents, to remain silent, and to decline to sign any documents; it also includes ICIRR's hotline number. The other side is in English and is intended to be handed over to an immigration agent; this side invokes the cardholder's Fourth and Fifth Amendment rights under the U.S. Constitution to refuse to speak with the agent, to deny the agent entry to their home, and to refuse any search of their belongings. The card thus serves the dual purpose of educating the holder as to their rights and invoking those rights to an immigration agent.

While refusing to speak with an immigration agent is unlikely to protect a person against deportation in the long run, stalling and silence are important tactics that obscure migrants' legibility to state agents. Since immigration agents must establish the citizenship of migrants in order to initiate removal proceedings, for example, remaining silent creates a period in which the inscrutability of migrants' citizenship serves as a temporary bulwark against the finality of removal. Advocates also educate members of immigrant communities to interpret and act on the state's own documents. The ability to tell an administrative warrant from a judicial one, for example, empowers a person presented with an administrative warrant to refuse ICE agents entry into their home. When a person refuses to open their door to ICE agents, they reduce the likelihood of imminent arrest and deportation, buying them time to build legal and community defenses against their removal.

Delaying apprehension, obscuring legibility, and contesting the interpretation of legal documents such as warrants are all tactics that erode the monopoly of state agents over processes of immigrant policing. These practices suggest that, much as immigration agents use discretion, control over time, and legal liminality to amplify their power over migrant communities, immigrant advocates likewise use ambiguity, delay, and illegibility to buy time for legal strategizing and create autonomy from immigrant policing efforts.[25] When whole communities participate in these tactics, they may hinder the effectiveness of ICE operations and even compel ICE to adapt their policing strategies. For example, one Chicago-area organizer told me that in Chicago and Los Angeles, ICE agents have reduced the number of home raids they conduct because so many people simply refuse to answer their doors. While additional research is needed to corroborate these reports, community-based responses to policing measures remain a key component of broader advocacy campaigns.

Still, such strategies to prevent arrest are often unsuccessful, and KYR workshops also help people prepare for the possibility of detention and deportation. In particular, the workshops provide guidance on the preparation of family action plans that establish guardianship of children and power of attorney in the event of a parent's removal, as well as on the organization of important documents such as passports, birth certificates, and medical records that need to travel with people wherever they go. As people live their lives in the United States, they inevitably accumulate such papers around them. Some of these, such as documents generated through contact with police, can put people at risk of deportation when they appear in the databases of federal agents. In the next section, I explore how local campaigns for sanctuary seek to block those trails and protect community members from exposure to immigration agencies.

Refusing Paper Trails

On an April evening in 2017, a friend and I pulled into the darkening parking lot of the neighborhood American Legion Civic Center and found it full of vehicles. "How many people are going to come to this thing?" I asked my friend, who had grown up in the area. "Oh, they'll all come out for this," she responded, and the knot in my stomach grew. We were attending a town hall meeting that our village government had organized in order to debate the adoption of a "welcoming," or sanctuary, ordinance. I was scheduled to speak on behalf of the ordinance, along with a few dozen others. More than two hundred residents turned out for the Monday evening meeting; all of the chairs in the large hall were taken, and several dozen people stood in the back of the room. By the end, more than forty people spoke in support of the ordinance, with some two dozen others voicing stiff opposition. And while the audience appeared more or less evenly divided on the issue, I did note that the speaker who drew the biggest applause opposed the ordinance and asserted that our village had become a gateway for drug trafficking, as evidenced by "two Mexicans," he said, who were apparently exchanging something in front of his house. In the end, our village adopted a "welcoming resolution" with the spirit but not the force of the ordinance, joining a bloc of other North Chicago suburbs that pledged to support immigrant residents by refusing to abide by certain paper trails generated by federal immigration authorities.

In the months following Trump's election, campaigns to adopt sanctuary or welcoming policies proliferated in left-leaning municipalities across the United States. These policies vary widely in their content, but they typically limit the cooperation of municipal policing agencies in the enforcement of federal immigration laws. Sanctuary campaigns such as these respond to a transformation in immigrant policing tactics that has increasingly enlisted local police agencies in immigration enforcement measures since 1996. Historically, unauthorized presence in the United States has been considered a civil, not a criminal, violation, and local police agencies in the U.S. interior are not typically tasked with immigration enforcement. But in 1996, a provision of the Illegal Immigration Reform and Immigrant Responsibility Act opened the door for greater local law enforcement participation in immigrant policing through a program known as 287(g).[26] Implementation of 287(g) was slow, sporadic, fraught with problems, and eventually made largely redundant by the Secure Communities program, which accomplished many of the same ends more effectively.

Secure Communities is a data-sharing program wherein the fingerprints of people who are arrested by local police are run through DHS databases.[27] If DHS records have the fingerprints on file for an immigration violation, federal agents can issue a detainer request, which asks local police to hold the arrestee until an ICE agent can arrive and take them into custody. This facilitates the identification and removal of unauthorized people throughout the U.S. interior by linking digital paper trails that are established when people come into contact with federal and then local police. The program also generates a paper trail: detainer requests, which are issued by federal agencies and ask local police to use their jails and policing resources to assist in the deportation of immigrants.

Programs such as Secure Communities and 287(g) extend the reach of federal enforcement efforts far from the borderlands and helped drive up deportation rates during the Obama administration. Eventually, Secure Communities proved too indiscriminate for Obama's tastes, and his administration replaced it with a more "targeted" program in 2014. Trump's executive orders announced the return and expansion of both 287(g) and the Secure Communities programs, and ICE boasts that more than 10,000 "convicted criminal aliens" were removed through the Secure Communities program in the first six months of 2017 alone.[28]

Because Secure Communities and 287(g) rely on the cooperation of local police, local sanctuary policies can inhibit or disrupt the digital paper trails that make them effective. For example, one common component of sanctuary policies directs local police to refuse ICE detainer requests and to discharge people from jail when they are otherwise eligible for release. In this way, sanctuary policies, such as the one I spoke in favor of, use limited local autonomy to undermine the use of federal paper trails in immigrant policing.

Still, while sanctuary policies are designed to reduce the exposure of some community members to the federal government, they also frequently invoke a distinction between people who are undocumented and "real criminals," exposing those with criminal records to ICE.[29] This is the case in Chicago, a "sanctuary city" that routinely shares city police databases with ICE and even partners with ICE officials to police immigrant residents.[30] This contradiction creates another opportunity for organizers to challenge the digital paper trails that are used to surveil and police Chicago immigrants.

For example, the Chicago group Organized Communities against Deportation has partnered with Black Youth Project 100 to call for the elimination of the city's gang database, which is shared freely with ICE and is used to target people for deportation.[31] Chicago police officers can add anyone to the gang database without evidence or charges, a practice that disproportionately criminalizes black and brown men and boys in Chicago.[32] Chicago organizers are mobilizing against the database and advocating for a stronger sanctuary policy that does not expose any Chicago residents to potential deportation—even those with criminal records.[33] By pointing to the ways in which Chicago's gang database disproportionately criminalizes black and Latino youth, these organizers challenge the legitimacy of paper trails created by local police who use racial profiling to perpetuate mass incarceration and mass deportations of people with criminal records.[34]

Both community education and sanctuary campaigns generate literature that encourages noncompliance with certain federal documents such as ICE warrants and detainer requests in order to protect immigrant community members from deportation. Still, the effectiveness of these measures is limited, and indeed, hundreds of thousands of people are deported from the United States each year.[35] When people are deported, many new documents become important, including certificates of deportation and identity documents from the home country that people who have been living in the United States for many years are unlikely to possess. Much as documents constellate around education and community defense strategies in the United States, so too does removal generate a host of distinct paper trails.

Documents with(out) Borders

The civil registry office in Zapotlanejo, Jalisco, Mexico, is housed on the ground floor of a colonial-style municipal building that spans the eastern edge of the town's central plaza. In May of 2017, I went there with two students to follow the bureaucratic trail of birth certificates that accompany U.S.-born children of Mexican parents as they move from the United States to Mexico, often as a result of deportation. The civil registry administrator, Silvia, was trying to explain the "problem of the apostille" to us. She placed a handwritten ledger on the desktop between us and pointed to a numbered list. "Look, I have had sixty-one applications for dual citizenship since January," she said (it was then late May). "How many of these have the problem with the apostille?" I asked her. "Mmm, I would say at least twenty people have had this problem," or roughly a third of all citizenship applications they had received so far this year.

The problem with the apostille, Silvia explained, is that U.S.-born children of Mexican parents are eligible for dual citizenship, but they must provide long-form U.S. birth certificates that have been "*apostilladas*," or have an apostille affixed, within the past year. An apostille is an official acknowledgment of the authenticity of government documents and their accompanying signatures and seals, and it allows the authority of a birth certificate issued in one nation to be recognized in another. Only birth certificates with the apostille are accepted by Mexican government authorities, who can then issue the holders dual citizenship. But the apostilles are only affixed by specified authorities in the U.S. states where the birth certificates were issued—usually in the secretary of state's office. When parents come to the Zapotlanejo registry to apply for Mexican citizenship for their U.S.-born children, many of them are unaware that they need this additional form of authentication. And because the parents are often unable to return to the United States to get it, U.S.-born children in Mexico can go for long periods of time without Mexican identity documents, during which time they may be unable to enroll in school and are ineligible for social services such as health insurance.[36] Without Mexican citizenship, U.S.-citizen children in Mexico are left "without an identity," in the words of one parent, or "illegal in Mexico," in the words of another.

Unable to travel themselves, parents must resort to less secure, and often expensive and prolonged, methods of attaining an apostille. There are "professionals" who leverage their ability to travel internationally to carry documents such as birth certificates to the United States, and they will, for a fee, take the documents to get an apostille affixed. Parents could also mail the birth certificate to trusted family members or friends in the United States and ask them get the apostille, or they could mail the document directly to the secretary of state's office—a process that can take months and may result in lost documents. Understandably, many parents are reluctant to entrust the only proof of their child's citizenship to this process, and they are often unable to afford the fees to have the document professionally couriered. Instead, parents whose U.S.-born children are eligible for Mexican citizenship but lack the requisite documents often feel compelled to buy them fraudulent Mexican birth certificates so they can enroll the children in school and government programs. But the presence of two birth certificates with conflicting information creates a contradictory paper trail for these children and has the potential to jeopardize their ability to take advantage of the benefits of dual citizenship down the road.

As this example shows, when legal documents cross borders, their jurisdictional authority can be undermined, resulting in inconsistencies in the degree to which documents retain their original meanings and purposes. Interestingly, the apostille was created as part of a 1961 Hague Convention to address precisely this problem, as it is meant to simplify the cross-border authentication of legal documents.[37] But cross-jurisdictional reliability is inconsistent: while U.S. birth certificates without an apostille are not recognized by Mexican authorities, other U.S. government–issued documents, such as deportation orders, not only retain their authority in Mexico but become "breeder documents" that allow access to additional documents, such as Evidence of Repatriation (Constancia de recepción de Mexicanos repatriados, or Constancia de repatriación for short), which identify holders as deportees and qualify them for certain government programs.

After our visit to the civil registry, we crossed the plaza and walked to the shaded gazebo in the plaza's center, where Zapotlanejo's Office of Social Programs is housed. From her rounded office underneath the gazebo, a municipal official told us about one 2015 government program that offered deportees modest cash assistance to invest in opening their own business. The problem, she explained, is that their office was only able to identify three residents who met the documentary requirements of the program, even though nearly ten thousand people were deported to the state of Jalisco that year. Other would-be applicants, including those who were compelled to return to Mexico but not formally deported, those who left the United States in an attempt to adjust their legal status and were subsequently barred, or those who merely declined to obtain or keep their deportation documents, were ineligible for the program. Much as onerous documentary requirements prevent many U.S.-born children from accessing Mexican citizenship, so too do eligibility criteria for government programs keep Mexican citizens from accessing social services ostensibly designed for their benefit.

In addition to legal documents such as Evidence of Repatriation, Mexican government programs may demand other types of paper trails. My friend Luis was deported from the United States in December 2016 and returned to his hometown of León, Guanajuato, after fourteen years in Chicago, leaving behind his common-law wife and three U.S.-citizen children. Desperate and depressed, Luis was watching television late one night when he saw a commercial advertising a Mexican government program, Somos Mexicanos (We Are Mexicans), which is designed to facilitate the social and economic reintegration of people returning to Mexico from the United States. Among other things, the program provides job placement assistance for eligible returnees, and Luis had kept his Evidence of Repatriation so he could prove that he had been deported. Even so, when Luis called the Somos Mexicanos hotline, he was informed that he would need his school transcripts, as well as evidence of his U.S. work history, to qualify for employment assistance. Luis had worked at a car wash in Chicago, and "how am I going to get that?" he asked the operator, frustrated that the program would demand documents located in the United States from people who are unable to travel there. With few employment opportunities and no assistance, Luis began selling used clothing at an outdoor market, where he makes about six hundred pesos, or just over thirty U.S. dollars, in a week.

The ability of deportees to retain possession of U.S.-issued documents, such as birth certificates, passports (issued at consulates), and deportation orders, is critical to their ability to receive wired money, find jobs, open accounts, access government services, and in general to reincorporate into Mexican society. Yet research by Daniel E. Martinez and Jeremy Slack found that U.S. authorities routinely seize and fail to return the possessions of deportees, including money, cell phones, and identity documents.[38] And one official with Mexico's Instituto Nacional de Migración (INM) told us that U.S. CBP officers have begun deporting Mexican citizens through border ports of entry where the INM does not have offices, in violation of international agreements. This practice leaves deportees unable to obtain their Evidence of Repatriation, delaying their registration for Mexican identity documents and government services upon their return. U.S. policing practices such as these, which undermine migrants' own paper trails, can have deleterious effects on deportees long after their removal from the United States.

Like their counterparts in the United States, advocates and community organizers in Mexico work to help returnees develop documentation strategies to demand and exercise their rights. And whereas migrants in the United States may benefit from obscuring their legibility, advocates in Mexico stress the need for returnees to make themselves visible to the state. Even as they warn of the limitations of Mexican government services, advocates urge Mexican citizens to register with the government and demand access to its resources. Otherwise, as one legal advocate explained, "You don't exist, you disappear. You have to exist for the state, otherwise you can't invoke your rights." KYR documents put together by Mexican and binational organizations tell returnees, "You need 'papers' in Mexico," and encourage those facing deportation or considering return to register for Mexican identity documents, including dual citizenship for children, as well as public benefits.

For migrants who spent years grappling with stigma and exclusion in the United States, return to Mexico does not signal an end to their marginalization. "The Mexican government doesn't want us," one organizer explained, adding that Mexican politicians seem more interested in protecting their relationship with the United States than assisting Mexican citizens. In the void created by deficient governmental support, non-state actors have emerged to provide assistance and advocacy around deportees' rights—many of them after having experienced deportation themselves. Indeed, deportation as both threat and actuality connects the experiences of transnational communities in the United States and Mexico, clarifying the need to work across borders to connect paper trails of community organizing.

No Ban, No Wall, Sanctuary for All

The morning after the airport protest broke sunny and mild in Chicago, good January weather for an "interfaith walk" organized by the mosque in my community. The mosque's outreach committee had begun planning this event before the election, but Trump's victory and the travel ban, issued only two days earlier, gave it a new significance. My son and I arrived early to find the basement reception room overflowing with people; mosque members ushered us into a quickly filling upstairs room, where we joined hundreds of others getting ready to set out on a one-mile march through the neighborhood. The walk organizers said they were overwhelmed by the turnout: whereas some two dozen participants had attended the walk the previous year, this year nearly a thousand marchers showed up. "No Ban, No Wall!" we chanted as we exited the mosque and stepped into the cold winter sunlight.

The chant, "No Ban, No Wall!," echoed a protest cry from the airport rallies the night before, and it gestured to linkages among community concerns—in this case, the travel ban targeting Muslims and the border wall targeting Mexicans—that became more visible in the wake of Trump's election. Indeed, "the one good thing" to come from Trump's electoral victory "is that more people are involved," one immigrant rights advocate observed. In addition to marches for women's rights and in defense of science, rallies in support of Muslims took place at mosques across the country, and grassroots antideportation networks have developed to train community members to inhibit immigration enforcement activities in numerous U.S. cities.[39]

In the long run, the community-generated paper trails described in this essay will only be as significant as the sociopolitical relationships forged along them. From the attorneys providing pro bono legal counsel to detained travelers, to advocates for sanctuary campaigns, to members of deportation defense networks, the current political crisis has brought more people "out of the woodwork" and onto the front lines of political organizing. It is too early to speculate about the durability or outcomes of such organizing efforts, but one challenge for organizers will be to formulate a long-term agenda beyond resistance to Trump that honestly addresses the structural bases of discriminatory U.S. policies. The community paper trails that weave among organizers and connect their campaigns will constitute a critical piece of these movements for societal change.

Notes

1 In this chapter, I use the term *immigrant* to describe people who were born outside of the United States but have resided in the United States for long periods of time, regardless of their immigration status. This usage is problematic, since the term *immigrant* technically presupposes legal admission to the nation-state, and as De Genova has pointed out, it is inherently nationalist insofar as it reflects the perspective of the destination nation-state. Nevertheless, I prefer *immigrant* to *migrant* because *migrant* evokes a perception of people as mobile or transient. The people I describe here are immobilized and deeply embedded in the social fabrics of their Chicago communities. For them, *migrant* not only mischaracterizes their life situations but can contribute to the misperception that they are socially marginal or transient. Nicholas De Genova, *Working the Boundaries: Race, Space, and "Illegality" in Mexican Chicago* (Durham, NC: Duke University Press, 2005).

2 Donald Trump, "Executive Order: Enhancing Public Safety in the Interior of the United States," January 25, 2017, accessed March 5, 2017, https://www.whitehouse .gov/the-press-office/2017/01/25/presidential-executive-order-enhancing-public -safety-interior-united; Donald Trump, "Executive Order: Border Security and Immigration Enforcement Improvements," January 25, 2017, accessed March 5, 2017, https://www.whitehouse.gov/the-press-office/2017/01/25/executive-order-border -security-and-immigration-enforcement-improvements; Donald Trump, "Executive Order: Protecting the Nation from Foreign Terrorist Entry into the United States," January 27, 2017, accessed March 5, 2017, https://www.whitehouse.gov/the -press-office/2017/01/27/executive-order-protecting-nation-foreign-terrorist-entry -united-states.

3 Miriam Ticktin, "Policing and Humanitarianism in France: Immigration and the Turn to Law as State of Exception," *Interventions* 7, no. 3 (2005): 347–68.

4 Ruth Gomberg-Muñoz, *Becoming Legal: Immigration Law and Mixed Status Families* (New York: Oxford University Press, 2016).

5 See Monisha Das Gupta, *Unruly Immigrants: Rights, Activism, and Transnational South Asian Politics in the United States* (Durham, NC: Duke University Press,

2006); Josiah M. Heyman, "The Inverse of Power," *Anthropological Theory* 3, no. 2 (2003): 139–56.

6   See, for example, Michelle Alexander, *The New Jim Crow: Mass Incarceration in the Age of Colorblindness* (New York: New Press, 2010).

7   Josiah M. Heyman, "State Effects on Labor Exploitation: The INS and Undocumented Immigrants at the Mexico-United States Border," *Critique of Anthropology* 18, no. 2 (1998): 157–80.

8   Evelyn Nakano Glenn, *Unequal Freedom: How Race and Gender Shaped American Citizenship and Labor* (Cambridge, MA: Harvard University Press, 2004).

9   Stephen Jay Gould, *The Mismeasure of Man* (New York: W. W. Norton, 1981); Nakano Glenn, *Unequal Freedom*; Mae Ngai, *Impossible Subjects: Illegal Aliens and the Making of Modern America* (Princeton, NJ: Princeton University Press, 2005).

10 De Genova, *Working the Boundaries*; Douglas Massey, Jorge Durand, and Nolan J. Malone, *Beyond Smoke and Mirrors: Mexican Immigration in an Era of Economic Integration* (New York: Russell Sage Foundation, 2002).

11 De Genova, *Working the Boundaries*; Ruth Gomberg-Muñoz, "The Punishment/ El Castigo: Undocumented Latinos and U.S. Immigration Processing," *Journal of Ethnic and Migration Studies* 41, no. 14 (2015): 2235–52.

12 Ticktin, "Policing and Humanitarianism in France."

13 Coutin, this volume; Gomberg-Muñoz, *Becoming Legal*; Sarah Horton, "Identity Loan: The Moral Economy of Document Exchange in California's Central Valley," *American Ethnologist* 42, no. 1 (2015): 55–67; Madeleine Reeves, "Clean Fake: Authenticating Documents and Persons in Migrant Moscow," *American Ethnologist* 40, no. 3 (2013): 508–24.

14 Migration Policy Institute, "The Obama Record on Deportations: Deporter in Chief or Not?," *Policy Beat*, January 26, 2017, http://www.migrationpolicy.org /article/obama-record-deportations-deporter-chief-or-not; Roberto Gonzales, *Lives in Limbo: Undocumented and Coming of Age in America* (Berkeley: University of California Press, 2015).

15 Gabriela Marquez-Benitez and Amalia Pallares, "Not One More: Linking Civil Disobediences and Public Anti-Deportation Campaigns," *North American Dialogue* 19, no. 1 (2016): 13–22.

16 Trump, "Executive Order: Enhancing Public Safety in the Interior of the United States."

17 Nick Miroff, "Deportations Fall under President Trump Despite Increase in Arrests by ICE," *Chicago Tribune*, September 28, 2017, http://www.chicagotribune.com /news/nationworld/ct-trump-deportations-20170928-story.html.

18 Trump, "Executive Order: Enhancing Public Safety in the Interior of the United States"; Trump, "Executive Order: Border Security and Immigration Enforcement Improvements."

19 Trump, "Executive Order: Enhancing Public Safety in the Interior of the United States."

20 Gray Abarca and Susan Coutin, "Sovereign Intimacies: The Lives of Documents within US State-Noncitizen Relationships," *American Ethnologist* 45, no. 1 (2018): 7–19; Coutin, this volume; Horton, "Identity Loan."

21 Aurora Chang, "Undocumented to Hyperdocumented: A Jornada of Protection, Papers, and PhD Status," *Harvard Educational Review* 81, no. 3 (2011): 508–20; see also Abarca and Coutin, "Sovereign Intimacies."

22 See Gomberg-Muñoz, *Becoming Legal.*

23 Abarca and Coutin, "Sovereign Intimacies."

24 See Joanna Dreby, *Everyday Illegal: When Policies Undermine Immigrant Families* (Berkeley: University of California Press, 2015); S. Sabo and A. E. Lee, "The Spillover of US Immigration Policy on Citizens and Permanent Residents of Mexican Descent: How Internalizing 'Illegality' Impacts Public Health in the Borderlands," *Frontiers in Public Health* 3 (2015): 155; S. Sabo et al., "Everyday Violence, Structural Racism and Mistreatment at the US-Mexico Border," *Social Science and Medicine* 109 (2014): 66–74; and Menjívar, this volume, for discussions of how immigration enforcement affects Latinos regardless of citizenship status.

25 Ticktin, "Policing and Humanitarianism in France"; Ruben Andersson, "Time and the Migrant Other: European Border Controls and the Temporal Economics of Illegality," *American Anthropologist* 116, no. 4 (2014): 795–809; Cecilia Menjívar, "Liminal Legality: Salvadoran and Guatemalan Immigrants' Lives in the United States," *American Journal of Sociology* 111, no. 4 (2006): 999–1037.

26 U.S. Immigration and Customs Enforcement, "Delegation of Immigration Authority Section 287(g) Immigration and Nationality Act," 2017, https://www.ice.gov/287g.

27 U.S. Immigration and Customs Enforcement. "Secure Communities," 2017, https://www.ice.gov/secure-communities.

28 U.S. Immigration and Customs Enforcement. "Secure Communities."

29 Reyna Wences and Ruth Gomberg-Muñoz, "To Create True Sanctuary Cities, We Must End Racist Policing," *Truth-Out*, May 14, 2018, http://www.truth-out.org/opinion/item/44466-to-create-true-sanctuary-cities-we-must-end-racist-policing.

30 Curtis Black, "Gang Database Compromises Chicago's Sanctuary City Protections," *Chicago Reporter*, September 14, 2017, accessed October 10, 2017, http://chicagoreporter.com/gang-database-compromises-chicagos-sanctuary-city-protections/; Andy Clarno, "Chicago Gang Database: Facts and Figures," December 2017, https://docs.google.com/document/d/1Ft_41wtKLU2NVKG SiN2hMHFmHaSRkIS3rNatZVvAnOk/edit; Organized Communities against Deportation, "Groups Announce Rally in Support of a Stronger Sanctuary City Policy in Chicago That Protects All Immigrants," press release, June 7, 2017, http://organizedcommunities.org/groups-announce-rally-in-support-of-a-stronger-sanctuary-city-policy-in-chicago-that-protects-all-immigrants/.

31 Black, "Gang Database Compromises Chicago's Sanctuary City Protections."

32 Clarno, "Chicago Gang Database: Facts and Figures."

33 Organized Communities against Deportation, "Groups Announce Rally in Support of a Stronger Sanctuary City Policy."

34 Black, "Gang Database Compromises Chicago's Sanctuary City Protections"; see also Ruth Gomberg-Muñoz, "Inequality in a 'Postracial' Era: Race, Immigration, and Criminalization of Low-Wage Labor," *DuBois Review* 9, no 2 (2012): 339–53; Sarah Horton, *They Leave Their Kidneys in the Fields: Illness, Injury, and Illegality*

among *U.S. Farmworkers* (Berkeley: University of California Press, 2016); Amalia
Pallares, *Family Activism: Immigrant Struggle and the Politics of Noncitizenship*
(New Brunswick, NJ: Rutgers University Press, 2014).

35 U.S. Immigration and Customs Enforcement, "FY 2016 ICE Immigration Removals," December 5, 2017, https://www.ice.gov/removal-statistics/2016.

36 Dulce Medina and Cecilia Menjívar, "The Context of Return Migration: Challenges of Mixed-Status Families in Mexico's Schools," *Ethnic and Racial Studies* 38,
no. 12 (2015): 2123–39, doi: 10.1080/01419870.2015.1036091.

37 Christophe Bernasconi, "The Electronic Apostille Program (e-APP): Introduction
and Update," 7th International Forum on the e-APP, Izmir, Turkey, June 14, 2012,
https://assets.hcch.net/upload/e-app2012_fo_pres_cb.pdf.

38 Daniel E. Martínez, Jeremy Slack, and Josiah Heyman, "Bordering on Criminal:
The Routine Abuse of Migrants in the Removal System, Part II: Possessions Taken
and Not Returned," Immigration Policy Center, December 2013; also see Boehm,
this volume.

39 For example, Yana Kunichoff, "Sanctuary in Your City, in Your Home, in Your
Church, in Your School, from Detention, from Deportation, from Displacement,
from Police Violence," *In These Times*, May 17, 2017, accessed June 30, 2017, http://
inthesetimes.com/features/sanctuary_cities_movement_trump.html.

Bibliography

Abarca, Gray, and Susan Coutin, "Sovereign Intimacies: The Lives of Documents within
US State-Noncitizen Relationships." *American Ethnologist* 45, no. 1 (2018): 7–19.

Alexander, Michelle. *The New Jim Crow: Mass Incarceration in the Age of Colorblindness.* New York: New Press, 2010.

American Immigration Council. "The 287(g) Program: An Overview." Accessed
March 15, 2017. https://www.americanimmigrationcouncil.org/research/287g
-program-immigration.

Andersson, Ruben, "Time and the Migrant Other: European Border Controls and
the Temporal Economics of Illegality." *American Anthropologist* 116, no. 4 (2014):
795–809.

Bernasconi, Christophe. "The Electronic Apostille Program (e-APP): Introduction
and Update." 7th International Forum on the e-APP, Izmir, Turkey, June 14, 2012.
https://assets.hcch.net/upload/e-app2012_fo_pres_cb.pdf.

Black, Curtis. "Gang Database Compromises Chicago's Sanctuary City Protections." *Chicago Reporter,* September 14, 2017. Accessed October 10, 2017. http://chicagoreporter
.com/gang-database-compromises-chicagos-sanctuary-city-protections/.

Chang, Aurora. "Undocumented to Hyperdocumented: A Jornada of Protection,
Papers, and PhD Status." *Harvard Educational Review* 81, no. 3 (2011): 508–20.

Clarno, Andy. "Chicago Gang Database: Facts and Figures." December 2017. https://
docs.google.com/document/d/1Ft_41wtKLU2NVKGSiN2hMHFmHaSRkIS3rNatZ
VvAnOk/edit.

Coutin, Susan Bibler. *Legalizing Moves: Salvadoran Immigrants' Struggle for U.S. Residency.* Ann Arbor: University of Michigan Press, 2000.

Das Gupta, Monisha. *Unruly Immigrants: Rights, Activism, and Transnational South Asian Politics in the United States.* Durham, NC: Duke University Press, 2006.

De Genova, Nicholas. *Working the Boundaries: Race, Space, and "Illegality" in Mexican Chicago.* Durham, NC: Duke University Press, 2005.

Dreby, Joanna. *Everyday Illegal: When Policies Undermine Immigrant Families.* Berkeley: University of California Press, 2015.

Gomberg-Muñoz, Ruth. *Becoming Legal: Immigration Law and Mixed Status Families.* New York: Oxford University Press, 2016.

Gomberg-Muñoz, Ruth. "Inequality in a 'Postracial' Era: Race, Immigration, and Criminalization of Low-Wage Labor." *DuBois Review* 9, no 2 (2012): 339–53.

Gomberg-Muñoz, Ruth. "The Punishment/El Castigo: Undocumented Latinos and U.S. Immigration Processing." *Journal of Ethnic and Migration Studies* 41, no. 14 (2015): 2235–52.

Gonzales, Roberto. *Lives in Limbo: Undocumented and Coming of Age in America.* Berkeley: University of California Press, 2015.

Gould, Stephen Jay. *The Mismeasure of Man.* New York: W. W. Norton, 1981.

Heyman, Josiah M. "The Inverse of Power." *Anthropological Theory* 3, no. 2 (2003): 139–16.

Heyman, Josiah M. "State Effects on Labor Exploitation: The INS and Undocumented Immigrants at the Mexico-United States Border." *Critique of Anthropology* 18, no. 2 (1998): 157–80.

Horton, Sarah. "Identity Loan: The Moral Economy of Document Exchange in California's Central Valley." *American Ethnologist* 42, no. 1 (2015): 55–67.

Horton, Sarah. *They Leave Their Kidneys in the Fields: Illness, Injury, and Illegality among U.S. Farmworkers.* Berkeley: University of California Press, 2016.

Kunichoff, Yana. "Sanctuary in Your City, in Your Home, in Your Church, in Your School, from Detention, from Deportation, from Displacement, from Police Violence." *In These Times,* May 17, 2017. Accessed June 30, 2017. http://inthesetimes.com /features/sanctuary_cities_movement_trump.html.

Marquez-Benitez, Gabriela, and Amalia Pallares. "Not One More: Linking Civil Disobediences and Public Anti-Deportation Campaigns." *North American Dialogue* 19, no. 1 (2016): 13–22.

Martínez, Daniel E., Jeremy Slack, and Josiah Heyman. "Bordering on Criminal: The Routine Abuse of Migrants in the Removal System. Part II: Possessions Taken and Not Returned." Immigration Policy Center, December 2013.

Massey, Douglas, Jorge Durand, and Nolan J. Malone. *Beyond Smoke and Mirrors: Mexican Immigration in an Era of Economic Integration.* New York: Russell Sage Foundation, 2002.

Medina, Dulce, and Cecilia Menjívar. "The Context of Return Migration: Challenges of Mixed-Status Families in Mexico's Schools." *Ethnic and Racial Studies* 38, no. 12 (2015): 2123–39. doi: 10.1080/01419870.2015.1036091.

Menjívar, Cecilia. "Liminal Legality: Salvadoran and Guatemalan Immigrants' Lives in the United States." *American Journal of Sociology* 111, no. 4 (2006): 999–1037.

Migration Policy Institute. "The Obama Record on Deportations: Deporter in Chief or Not?" *Policy Beat*, January 26, 2017. http://www.migrationpolicy.org/article /obama-record-deportations-deporter-chief-or-not.

Miroff, Nick. "Deportations Fall under President Trump Despite Increase in Arrests by ICE." *Chicago Tribune*, September 28, 2017. http://www.chicagotribune.com/news /nationworld/ct-trump-deportations-20170928-story.html.

Nakano Glenn, Evelyn. *Unequal Freedom: How Race and Gender Shaped American Citizenship and Labor*. Cambridge, MA: Harvard University Press, 2004.

Ngai, Mae. *Impossible Subjects: Illegal Aliens and the Making of Modern America*. Princeton, NJ: Princeton University Press, 2005.

Organized Communities against Deportation. "Groups Announce Rally in Support of a Stronger Sanctuary City Policy in Chicago That Protects All Immigrants." Press release, June 7, 2017. http://organizedcommunities.org/groups-announce -rally-in-support-of-a-stronger-sanctuary-city-policy-in-chicago-that-protects-all -immigrants/.

Pallares, Amalia. *Family Activism: Immigrant Struggle and the Politics of Noncitizen- ship*. New Brunswick, NJ: Rutgers University Press, 2014.

Redclift, Victoria. "Abjects or Agents? Camps, Contests and the Creation of 'Political Space.'" *Citizenship Studies* 17, nos. 3–4 (2013): 308–21.

Reeves, Madeleine. "Clean Fake: Authenticating Documents and Persons in Migrant Moscow." *American Ethnologist* 40, no. 3 (2013): 508–24.

Sabo, S., and A. E. Lee. "The Spillover of US Immigration Policy on Citizens and Per- manent Residents of Mexican Descent: How Internalizing 'Illegality' Impacts Public Health in the Borderlands." *Frontiers in Public Health* 3 (2015): 155.

Sabo, S., S. Shaw, M. Ingram, N. Teufel-Shone, S. Carvajal, J. G. de Zapien, C. Rosales, F. Redondo, G. Garcia, and R. Rubio-Goldsmith. "Everyday Violence, Structural Racism and Mistreatment at the US-Mexico Border." *Social Science and Medicine* 109 (2014): 66–74.

Ticktin, Miriam. "Policing and Humanitarianism in France: Immigration and the Turn to Law as State of Exception." *Interventions* 7, no. 3 (2005): 347–68.

Trump, Donald. "Executive Order: Border Security and Immigration Enforcement Improvements." January 25, 2017. Accessed March 5, 2017. https://www.whitehouse .gov/the-press-office/2017/01/25/executive-order-border-security-and-immigration -enforcement-improvements.

Trump, Donald. "Executive Order: Enhancing Public Safety in the Interior of the United States." January 25, 2017. Accessed March 5, 2017. https://www.whitehouse .gov/the-press-office/2017/01/25/presidential-executive-order-enhancing-public -safety-interior-united.

Trump, Donald. "Executive Order: Protecting the Nation from Foreign Terrorist Entry into the United States." January 27, 2017. Accessed March 5, 2017. https://www .whitehouse.gov/the-press-office/2017/01/27/executive-order-protecting-nation -foreign-terrorist-entry-united-states.

U.S. Immigration and Customs Enforcement. "Delegation of Immigration Authority Section 287(g) Immigration and Nationality Act." 2017. https://www.ice.gov/287g.

U.S. Immigration and Customs Enforcement. "FY 2016 ICE Immigration Removals."
December 5, 2017. https://www.ice.gov/removal-statistics/2016.

U.S. Immigration and Customs Enforcement. "Secure Communities." 2017. https://
www.ice.gov/secure-communities.

Wences, Reyna, and Ruth Gomberg-Muñoz. "To Create True Sanctuary Cities,
We Must End Racist Policing." *Truth-Out*, May 14, 2018. http://www.truth-out
.org/opinion/item/44466-to-create-true-sanctuary-cities-we-must-end-racist
-policing.

JUAN THOMAS ORDÓÑEZ

8

STRATEGIES OF DOCUMENTATION AMONG
KICHWA TRANSNATIONAL MIGRANTS

Sitting in a corner bakery in the south of Bogotá in 2013, I was surprised to hear my friend Lenin, an indigenous Kichwa musician from Otavalo, Ecuador, talking about his recent trip to Russia. I was confused by the names of cities he said he visited, and I almost fell over the stool when he explained that it was so hard to travel to Western Europe on his last trip that he had considered using his cousin's Italian passport to enter the EU. He explained the plan was to go to Turkey via Russia and Georgia and then wait for the passport to come in the mail. After that he would figure out how to cross into Greece or even Italy. How could he be thinking of this? I asked. Was he serious? Don't they check your fingerprints at some point? "They see an 'Indian' when they look at me and really don't care much if it's me or my cousin in the picture," he answered with a shrug. While most Kichwa migrants these days acknowledge that such tactics are probably less successful than they were in the past, Lenin is one of many who use or have considered using other people's identity documents (IDs) to cross international borders.

This chapter explores the documentary strategies that have shaped Kichwa migration networks over the last forty years. I follow the accounts of two generations of Kichwa-Otavalo migrants who have expanded their networks from neighboring countries to far-off places in Western Europe and Russia. I show how Lenin and other indigenous migrants over the years have learned important skills like playing music, brokering partnerships, and bribing different officials by starting their travels in Colombia. My argument here is that the migration strategies of the last decades have been informed by two elements in Kichwa experience. The first is the historical subaltern position of indigenous communities in Ecuador and Colombia, which has shaped a pragmatic attitude toward documents as a way to get around the state. Marginalization and discrimination are part of living memory for most Otavalos, some quite affluent nowadays, and skirting the state, the police, white landowners, and other actors, if not part of everyday life, is still a common trope in conversations. The second element involves stories of migration told by members of previous generations. Past strategies of travel developed under different migration regimes help to shape the possibilities considered by new migrants, who do not always know how the contexts of documentation have changed.

The migrants in this chapter are itinerant merchants who travel to different places in their youth in search of work and adventure. They use their own or others' state-issued IDs, letters of invitation, manufacturing receipts, and other "papers" in order to deal with various state actors, both formally (that is, in "official" capacities) and informally through bribery. These young migrants—usually men—talk about travel as an "adventure" that proves their worth at making a living. While there are clearly historical processes of marginalization that have led to Kichwa migration, adventure and achieving independence to finance trips are central to how young men understand their travels. Such attitudes lead to a high tolerance for uncertainty and risk. It is seldom that women join the groups, at least not until the musicians can travel independently to known places. Most of the men in this chapter started migrating at a young age and belong to families that are not part of a wealthy transnational entrepreneurial "class" that has emerged from migration over the past decades.[1] Rather, they are people trying to gain access to migration networks and to make enough money to become independent entrepreneurs.

Over the years, the activities related to migration among young Otavalos have shifted from textile commerce to street-corner musical ensembles and the sale of CDs, dream catchers, bracelets, and other handicrafts that are easily transported in their luggage. Musicians travel in groups of friends or business partners, hoping to make back their investments in airfare, equipment, and merchandise, and to send some of the profit home for their family or to save it for future trips. In Europe, the groups find profitable street corners and play Andean and New Age music during the spring and summer tourist seasons, and eventually return to Ecuador for the off-season. Thus, migrants are not particularly preoccupied with exactly what the documents they hold mean or allow in terms of rights and elements of citizenship; rather, they use them simply to move around.

Itinerancy, however, is not a constant in a person's lifetime, and some migrants have found places where business is good and have settled permanently or semipermanently over the years. This has resulted in Kichwa enclaves over a vast geographical expanse that covers many European countries, North America, and Latin America in general.[2] Young itinerant migrants like Lenin thus know and might have relations to Otavalos who live abroad, have different nationalities, and are part of the Kichwa diaspora.

Documenting Movement

Documents determine migrants' experience by affecting the ways they move and become inscribed in the logics of the state throughout their lives. How migrants understand and use different documents shapes their perceptions of the social and political environments they inhabit. Thus, what documents allow and how they regulate interactions with state institutions and other social actors, in practice, establishes the contours of social experience and sets the stage for how migrants perceive their social reality. For many migrants, these "documentary realities" are central to how they move, measure risk, and make decisions. Documentary realities include the taken-for-granted ways of being in the world that documents make possible. In truth, the materiality of the state's inscription—that is, the documents themselves—are not the only important element here. Rumors and theories about documents and their effects also play into the equation because migrants' experiences of multiple bureaucracies are inscribed in the arbitrary nature of the outcomes of their use.[3]

It is no surprise, then, that counterfeit and fake documents are common among disenfranchised migrants trying to attain some semblance of belonging.[4] Fake documents, after all, follow the logics of the state through mimetic articulations with its bureaucracy.[5] Along with counterfeit documents come counterfeit documentary processes: scams to get this or that permit or legal status.[6] Thus, bureaucratic inscription opens the doors to "forgery, imitation, and mimetic performances of power."[7] In many instances, papers become markers of citizenship, and "legal" documents are not only hard to distinguish from the "fake," but it is difficult for migrants to grasp which documents really are salient to formal inscription. All sorts of "papers" can thus become highly fetishized things with power in and of themselves—a power that is equated to the status they confer.[8] This means that inscription is not a clear-cut process and that it entails entering the logics of the state rather than its structure.

As others in this volume show (Anderson, Boehm, Coutin, Menjívar), migrants often hoard documents, keeping every piece of paper that could constitute proof of their documentary existence. This is the case for many undocumented migrants living in the rich industrialized nations of the Global North,[9] but is not necessarily the case for young Kichwa musicians and entrepreneurs. Kichwa itinerant migrants have a pragmatic relationship to documents in which the object is to move from one place to another and cross borders more or less unhindered.

It is difficult to pinpoint how states affect these movements, since the men travel from one country to another, and their destinations of choice have shifted over the years. "The state" thus emerges in their accounts through interactions with various institutions and people at different levels, such as the police, immigration officers, and other types of bureaucrats. Gupta has argued for the "importance of disaggregating the state in order to understand the production of arbitrariness"[10] in questioning the problematic notion that it somehow constitutes a homogeneous apparatus. In the accounts that follow, we can perceive the arbitrary effects of using certain documents in interactions at different levels of the state. Thus, from the perspective of these young entrepreneurs, the state is really a set of experiences with bureaucrats and policing agencies. We can thus outline a type of movement that occurs not between discrete political entities, but rather between different institutional and civil regimes.

Many of the Kichwa men in these pages strategically use documents to get around the state, rather than to locate themselves in particular structures of belonging. In a sense, they seem at some level to be traveling from the margins of one state to the margins of another, exploiting the liminality that their illegibility allows. They are a population that has been inscribed historically on the margins of the Ecuadorian state where racism, political repression, and other forms of discrimination were prevalent. This resulted in a long tradition of resisting and subverting the power of the state as embodied in its institutions, bureaucrats, and other officers. In interacting with these representatives of the state in different countries, Kichwa musicians exploit the indistinct and imprecise categories they get inscribed into due to their "foreignness" as indigenous migrants. The ambiguity lies both in their itinerancy (police and others do not perceive them as migrants with the intent to stay) and in shifting perceptions about their ethnicity and place of origin. In other words, their itinerancy and the strangeness of their ethnicity make them hard to classify; they use tourist visas or enter countries without inspection, overextend their stays but rarely settle permanently, and work informally as musicians who appear to be performing music and dances with "cultural" content.

I suggest that by looking at different practices of documentation in these movements through time we can account for the sometimes obscure and dangerous strategies—like Lenin using his cousin's passport—that migrants use in order to travel. Many of these strategies might seem irrational in one migration regime but were feasible in another and are thus taken to be possible. This means the experiences of peers can refer to arbitrary outcomes mediated by past political and legal realities that nonetheless have salience in decision-making processes years later.[11]

Kichwa Migration

Otavalan outmigration from Imbabura started in the early twentieth century, following patterns of textile commerce that emerged in the region during the colonial period, when it was well known for its textile production.[12] After indigenous entrepreneurs established or acquired looms within the limits of towns and cities that had been primarily mestizo,[13] commerce brought indigenous merchants to neighboring Colombia in the 1920s,[14] where they eventually established permanent and semipermanent settlements.[15] Kichwa migration patterns ultimately generated a series of networks through which many Otavalos have traveled transnationally for several generations, reaching Western Europe and North America in the 1970s[16] and establishing permanent settlements in Spain,[17] Belgium, and other countries.[18]

While most research on Kichwa migration has centered on their expansion to Europe and its effects on Otavalo, studies tend to overlook the importance of Colombia in the spread of these networks. However, at least until the 1980s, most Kichwa migrants probably started their travels with short stints in Colombia, where they learned the tricks of the trade and where they established contacts and business relations that directly or indirectly led to further trips to Europe and other places.[19] These "tricks" include engaging with documentary practices that take advantage of legal ambiguities, knowing how to deal with corrupt authorities, and, in general, learning how to skirt state efforts to control movement and informal commerce.

Today, Colombian cities like Bogotá, Medellín, and Cali are still important nodes in the transnational networks. The indigenous council of Kichwas in Bogotá[20]—officially recognized by the city government as one of five urban indigenous councils in 2005[21]—estimates there are between nine and eleven thousand Otavalos in the city at any given time. Only about half live there permanently. The material in this chapter is thus imbricated in the migration flows that cross Colombia, especially its capital, and that have led me to follow migrants back to Imbabura and trace their movements to other countries. Tracing these flows has also allowed me to meet and collect the migration accounts of several older onetime migrants who have settled either in Bogotá or around Otavalo.

William, for example, is a Kichwa merchant and musician in his late twenties who I first met in Bogotá in 2012, about a year after his first truly international trip, which was to Korea. By the age of four, William was accompanying his father to the south of Colombia during school holidays, where he quickly learned how to manage merchandise and money. At thirteen, he took a year off from school and went to Cali, Colombia's third largest city, alone. After a few months he met up with three older brothers who at the time were in their late twenties to late thirties. One of them had just returned from Europe, where he learned to play Andean music to make money from presentations and selling CDs on the street. William thus became a musician traveling throughout Colombia and managed to make almost $200 a day as the only minor in the group on just his first trip.[22]

In terms of his legal status, it seems William's father had established himself long enough in Colombia to get legal residency, and William remembers having papers that said he was a resident. Police or DAS[23] agents—who handled migration at the time—rarely stopped them; in fact, as a child he never crossed the border "officially" because there was no need. William, however, also remembers having papers that said he was a Colombian citizen and cannot really explain why he had both. Based on other migrants' stories, I assume that he was initially included in his father's residency and at a later date was registered as born in Colombia, something quite common because Colombian law allows birth certificates to be issued with only two witnesses to the birth, which can easily be "found" through family and commercial contacts. William never used these papers and never got around to requesting his *cédula de ciudadanía*, the primary ID of Colombian citizens, when he turned eighteen, because he was traveling in Asia.

By the time he was sixteen, William was selling baby clothing with his older sister, a Colombian citizen who was living in Bogotá. Their venture failed and they ended up in debt to partners who had lent them money based on previous deals with their older siblings. Shortly thereafter an older brother called from Ecuador to say he was going to Korea and needed someone who could play music in a group, so William went back to Otavalo and arranged for his first plane ride, a thirty-hour trip to Seoul via Spain. He was seventeen years old and paying his debts in Colombia by traveling to Asia.

When we met, William was twenty-two. He had recently returned to Colombia without inspection and had been selling clothing in Montería (in northern Colombia), where there were numerous police and army checkpoints due to the paramilitary presence. He thus used the *contraseña* of his nephew—close to him in age—at the numerous checkpoints in the area. The contraseña is a temporary ID with a person's ID number, photo, and fingerprint that is issued while the cédula is being made. In this case it was for a *cédula de extranjería*, which identified him as a legal resident allowed to work. This was not the first time he had used someone else's documents. In Korea, as a minor, he had borrowed a friend's passport when going out on the town. In fact, in 2012, William managed all of his commercial activities with other people's IDs—not only his nephew's (until he had to return it), but also his sister's cédula and debit card for banking. He had even used his sister's ID when he was stopped by the army the week before we met!

Coming and going from Ecuador to Colombia is ambiguous in the documentary sense; William is unsure about the status he had as a foreigner or even whether he was a citizen of a country he has called home at different times in his life. (He speaks Spanish with a very distinctive Colombian regional accent.) This might be tied to the porosity of the border between the two countries, yet his descriptions of Korea are not that different. He had some sort of contract under which he could work and get paid—he really never read or worried about it much—but he had to go to China or Japan every three months to renew it. His employer, who spoke Spanish, handled all the paperwork and sent him and others to these countries with the addresses of the Korean consulates written on papers they showed the taxi drivers to get to their destination. As with his papers from Colombia, he had no use for these documents and threw them away after the trip was over. For William, papers are not consistently necessary in order to get by and make a living. For example, he ended his time in Korea as a driver for other music and dance groups his employer managed, even though he had no driver's license. He assumed—correctly—that no one in Korea would think of doing such a thing and he would not likely be stopped.

This attitude is common among many young migrants. Lenin, in his late twenties, was issued a deportation order in Bogotá in 2011 after overextending his stay, which means he was given two weeks to leave the country voluntarily. Two weeks after he got the "pink paper" ordering his deportation, I asked to see it, only to learn he had disposed of it because he saw no purpose in keeping it. He stayed in Colombia almost a year after that. He says that every time border agents tell him he cannot enter the country, he simply avoids the immigration office and takes a bus to Bogotá. At police and army checkpoints he pretends to be asleep. In the few instances they have actually woken him, he pretends not to understand Spanish and repeats the few sentences he knows in Kichwa until they leave him be. "They don't really bother me because I look indigenous," he explained to me in Bogotá in 2017. When all else fails, Lenin simply offers a bribe.

Learning who and when to bribe is central to Kichwa migration accounts across the generations. In fact, both William and Lenin have depended on their bribing ability in recent trips to Russia. In times past, Otavalos managed most interactions with state actors in Colombia through bribery. Don Eduardo, in his late sixties, developed an uncanny ability to bribe officers of different types when he lived in Cúcuta, on the Colombian border with Venezuela, during the 1970s and '80s. His passports from this period have no Colombian visas or stamps, and when I asked if no one ever checked his status he simply referred to checkpoints on the road. These encounters always ended in small bribes to officers who knew most *ecuatorianos* had no papers. Bribery is thus a strategic practice that circumvents documentary interactions in many instances. To reduce the amount of the bribes required, after leaving Ecuador, Don Eduardo used to stop at the border town of Ipiales, where he paid other Otavalos to have a receipt made for his Ecuadorean textiles that "proved" they were manufactured in Colombia. This made police and customs checkpoints easy to navigate, since he was exempt from import taxes with the fake receipt.

Poole has interpreted the shifting and uncertain interactions people encountered at checkpoints such as these—where identification papers stand at the intersection between the guarantees of citizenship and the vulnerability of its absence—as illustrating the arbitrary power of the state in Latin America.[24] Kichwa entrepreneurs, however, developed the ability to navigate such uncertainty through the ambiguity conferred by the double nature of being "indigenous migrants." In fact, there were so many Otavalos on the road between Cúcuta and Bogotá in the 1980s that Don Eduardo once met a down-and-out *paisano*—a fellow Kichwa—who lived off other Ecuadoran indigenous merchants by impersonating DAS agents in order to take bribes for letting them go without the right papers.

Rather than producing the fetishization of documents mentioned above, the arbitrary nature of the state generated a high tolerance for uncertainty among Kichwa migrants. Bribery and ethnicity replaced the need for certain papers, or at least complemented the use of papers like the fake receipts. The ease with which Kichwa migrants navigate these checkpoints is in no way extended to all indigenous people in Colombia, a country where such populations have suffered displacement and other forms of violence for decades. It is rather a function of the ambiguity between being indigenous merchants and foreigners; in fact, for many bureaucrats, police officers and others, they are simply referred to as "los ecuatorianos"—the Ecuadorians—a class of person unto itself, understood to be foreign and, usually, indigenous. Yet as one generation followed another, some Kichwa did "settle" in Colombia. The documentation that emerged created differences between Colombian-born Kichwas and legal residents, and migrants who continue entering the country without inspection and who have great difficulties accessing the universal health care system, education, and other elements to which their Colombian counterparts have access.

People like Don Eduardo, however, spent years in ambiguous relationships to the Colombian state quite successfully. Nowadays there are more controls in Colombia, especially tied to taxes and permits for retail operations, so many merchants are forced either to regularize their status—which until 2013 was very expensive—or to rent papers from established indigenous merchants who have them. They "rent" in the sense that they use the ID numbers and other documents of established Kichwas to register contracts or property, or to manage bank accounts, agreeing to either pay for the favor or share in the profits. Until maintaining legal residency was made cheap for Ecuadorians through exemption from fines and other charges, it was common for people to let these papers expire indefinitely. Having formally settled partners whose documents are "right" and who can sign contracts for the spaces they use to sell their merchandise is important. This is how William has managed to do business in Colombia all his life; he uses IDs, bank accounts, and debit cards issued to his siblings, who all have Colombian nationality.

Shifting Contexts

William and Lenin belong to a generation of Kichwa musicians who travel the world. They see themselves as following their parents' generation, who, as in Don Eduardo's case, started expanding their commercial networks to other countries and continents in the 1970s.[25] As their parents did before them, the young men began by migrating to Colombia and learning important skills and documentary strategies they would use in their travels later. In both cases, William and Lenin learned to play instruments and manage street-corner musical ensembles; they were exposed to wealthier indigenous merchants who could finance trips, and they learned to use the ambiguity of their ethnicity and immigration status in a system where documentation is a means to facilitate mobility. Yet their ability to do this is shaped by the political contexts and immigration regimes that prevail at particular moments. Although the porosity of the Colombia-Ecuador border has not changed much, immigration controls in Europe clearly have.

Initially allowed to enter Western Europe freely, indigenous migrants from Imbabura describe traveling to Spain, the Netherlands, Belgium, and Germany in the 1970s, '80s, and '90s in ways similar to William's and Lenin's accounts of Colombia. Don Eduardo, for example, ended up in the Netherlands in 1994 with one of his sons and a few other friends and learned to play music on the street there. They also had a German friend whom they had met in Ecuador as a tourist and who helped them buy a car (in his own name) so they could drive around. The group explored different cities and fairs where they could sell their merchandise and play music, learning to deal with police. On the road they had to ensure that the driver had an international driver's license, something Don Eduardo had thought of before leaving Ecuador, which made him highly desired by other groups. Chuckling, men of Don Eduardo's generation say no one who stopped them in Europe knew where Ecuador was. "They would ask 'Bolivia?' And we laughed, 'almost,' 'nearby.'"

This generation describe "being deported" as receiving a "black mark" on their passports and being told to leave the country. The effects are similar to Lenin's "pink paper" account in Bogotá. Don Eduardo was told to leave Germany, for example, and ended up back on the street in Amsterdam trying to get himself deported to Ecuador. He and several other people his age say that in the mid-1990s when you had black seals on your passport you simply went to the Ecuadorian consulate and said you had lost your papers in order to get new ones. Another man in Bogotá, Don Francisco, told me that his group, traveling around Italy, came to consider Ecuadorian passports issued in the Ecuadorian consulates of Western Europe more desirable than their domestically issued counterparts. The police recognized countries they knew on the seals and "bothered" less than if they were faced with acknowledging they did not know where or what Ecuador really was.

Other times they had their merchandise confiscated in interactions that could also include police detention, which they dealt with, again, by playing on the "novelty" they represented to Europeans. "On the street," Eduardo adds, "the police usually saw we were indigenous and didn't really check to see how we entered." Authorities usually approached them while they were playing "indigenous" music in different types of "traditional" attire that, during the 1990s, shifted from regional Ecuadorian pants and ponchos to elaborate Native American outfits—*trajes*—inspired by movies, television, and the internet. These trajes improved their showmanship, and the men say they made their performances look more like "cultural shows," which resulted in fewer problems with police. Dressed as Native Americans and playing New Age–inspired versions of Andean music, they say they did not look like common street musicians, but rather like ethnic musical ensembles. Eventually, there were so many of these groups that the novelty dissipated.

But even then, it was hard to return to Europe if you had been deported. Don Eduardo has another son who was able to return twice using other people's passports. "I have a box upstairs with his old papers," he told me in 2016. "There's someone else's cédula[26] in it with his picture," he chuckles. Don Eduardo's son bought a birth certificate from another person in Otavalo and had both a cédula and a passport issued under that name and ID number, but with his own picture and fingerprints, a practice people still talk about today, with which he reentered Europe after being deported.

People across the generations talk about these practices and inevitably conflate the periods in which they were feasible; after all, they are feasible even today, but not in the context of the EU. After the 1990s, the economic and political realities these first migrants encountered in Europe changed. Visa requirements, street sales, and musical performances became more regulated as the economies they did business in shrank.[27] But while entering the EU with his cousin's Italian passport is probably not so easy these days, Lenin's plans are consistent with things he has heard about. In fact, if he managed to enter Italy, he could probably use his cousin's IDs for day-to-day interactions on the street like many other more "connected" migrants do. That friends and relatives can exchange documents, buy them from strangers, or "rent" them emerges then as a key element in how some of these men have expanded their travels abroad.

Other Frontiers

William and Lenin, roughly the same age, first heard about trips to Russia in Bogotá. Although they do not know each other, the similarity of their accounts points to the expansion of Kichwa migration networks to that country over the last decade. In both cases, more affluent indigenous merchants with contacts of some sort in Russia gave them invitations in Cyrillic to show at the embassy in order to request a visa that would allow them to work. This letter cost Lenin $600 and was a lost investment because the embassy did not accept it; for William it was free and—he thought—successful. Neither one knew what the letter said, as they were both traveling as musicians for other people who were financing the trips and claimed to have used similar papers before. William entered the country with what he understood to be a yearlong visa, while Lenin entered as a tourist, no visa required, with the understanding that he could renew his entry once by leaving the country before three months were up. This has been possible since late 2012 when Russia and Ecuador signed a visa-free travel accord. At least until mid-2017, it was the first thing to appear on the web page of the Russian consulate in Ecuador. Trips to Russia point to a strategic response to more stringent controls in the EU, which appear insurmountable for young migrants. Lenin's group was not sure they would be allowed to enter Russia, so he volunteered to go first with only a fraction of the merchandise to see if he could get through customs and immigration. He always laughs when he retells the story of arriving in Moscow at night with only the clothes on his back and bags full of bracelets and other trinkets bought in Otavalo. There was no trouble at the airport, and the others followed a few days later. The total investment was more than $30,000 and involved mortgaging the home of one of the financers.

William's and Lenin's first experiences on the streets in Moscow are also very similar, as they both describe having to learn to manage the police. In William's case they had a contact from Kazakhstan who spoke Russian and dealt with situations in which they had to deal with Russian-speaking officials. Lenin and his group befriended a university student who spoke a bit of Spanish, and they eventually hired her to deal with the police and other problems that had to be handled in Russian. Knowing how much to pay and in what contexts bribes were acceptable determined whether the groups were allowed to stay or asked to move on. They were not always successful, and both men describe being taken to police stations and having merchandise and money confiscated. Both groups had members who had been to Russia before and therefore had access to locals, usually "foreigners from Eastern Europe," who procured cars or vans and helped them buy musical equipment. As in Don Eduardo's generation, the contacts bought vehicles in their own names in neighboring countries where they were cheaper, with the understanding that they could keep them for another season, or rent them to other musicians, once the groups returned to Ecuador. They provided the service as part of a business deal to help the musicians who could not legally own a car due to their migration status.[28] Through this practice, then, the migrants are again "renting" other people's documents in order to guarantee mobility.

Lenin and William had trouble with their original groups, whose investors did not know how to play music and simply danced around imitating Native American performances they saw on the internet. After paying his debt and leaving the original group, William moved in with his brother, who joined him from Ecuador, but he also called other family members on two continents. The new group William organized consisted of himself, two *sobrinos*—a nephew and a niece his own age—with the same visa, and later another sobrino (the one whose cédula he used in Colombia) who, like Lenin, had entered as a tourist and could renew his entry once before three months were up. William also convinced another sobrino with Spanish citizenship to drive to Russia and pick up his estranged brother in Paris. Having spent twelve years as an undocumented migrant in France with little contact with his family, William is not sure what his brother did to cross all the borders from France, but by the time they reached Russia it was obvious to them all that he would have to return to Ecuador, since he did not have the necessary papers to reenter the EU.

Lenin, on the other hand, simply met up with other Kichwas on the street and, thanks to his Russian contact, ended up playing in a private amusement park in Sochi, where they got some sort of contract in the interpreter/friend's name. He does not know what this contract was, but it made it possible to play in a private park with no police interference. Lenin also has a cousin with Italian citizenship who eventually joined him at the end of the trip.[29] It was this cousin whose passport he thought of using to enter Italy. By using their Russian contact's name in the guise of a "manager," they are replicating practices that are similar to those they have used or heard of others using in countries like Colombia.

When both musicians finally made some money, they sent remittances to Ecuador. The cap at Western Union was $1,000 a month, so they had to get local friends (in Lenin's case, the interpreter) to send anything above that sum, or they used documents of other indigenous musicians who had no money to send back. As Lenin's three months were coming to an end, he crossed to Abkhazia,[30] where he thinks he bribed the border officers to do something that was not legal. He never understood what the stamps on his passport meant because he could not understand the officers, but two of his friends later had trouble leaving Russia when they tried to return to Ecuador. At this point in the accounts of both musicians it was quite clear they had traveled across the world and worked in Russia for months with no distinct notion of their legal status, replicating practices familiar to them from other trips and from the accounts they had heard over the course of their lives. Lenin, in fact, told me a few years later that he had crossed to Abkhazia twice on subsequent trips, but he and his most recent travel partner were still not sure exactly what the process was. "They wanted to deport us, didn't they? So we bribed them," commented his partner. "No, that was legal, I think," answered Lenin. My shock is always met with pride and boasting: "That's what it means to be Kichwa, that is what we do." For Lenin, whatever he did worked, and he left Russia in good standing and has returned twice since. William is another story.

William's group worked in different cities for a few months and eventually made their way to the Finnish border, where his Spanish cousin could exit the country and renew his three-month visa, as they understood the situation. William was convinced that he could stay a whole year in Russia, which meant he had more than six months left. The idea was to find a town to wait in with all the merchandise for the cousin to go to Finland. But the region was *"puro bosque"* (just forest) and they were stopped and taken to what he thinks was a military base and checked for drugs. In Murmansk and a bit nervous, the Spanish nephew decided to go to the Norwegian border instead and left William, a niece, and two nephews from Ecuador playing on the street. But this time different police arrested them. William, who had been taken to what he calls "Cold War–style prisons" "like thirty times," assumed the ordeal would last a few hours. After two days, however, he was told in Russian and poor English that they were all illegal immigrants. William's visa was for a year, they said, but that meant that it expired in a year, not that he had a year to be in Russia. He was told that he could be in the country for a total of 180 days and that after the first three months he was supposed to have left for at least three months. At least this is what he understands to have happened. The niece and one of the nephews had the same problem. Only the youngest nephew, the last to arrive and the only one who had not overextended his stay, was left to try to find the cousin who had driven to Norway.

William and the other two sobrinos were sentenced to a month in prison before deportation and asked to sign a document that the very poor interpreter—William thinks was he Cuban—could not explain to them. They refused to sign. The other nephews who were not arrested tried to get them released, but the Spanish one was told he had to leave the country before his initial three months were up or he would have the same problem. Whatever status these migrants had, none of them knew enough about it to question or contest what they were told and reacted to the agents' instructions without corroborating them.

William and his nephew were sent to an "underground prison with small cells and no windows." The niece was sent somewhere else. Knowing they had to be there for a month, they gave up and were quite surprised when, after a week, an older Russian woman who had bought CDs from them on the street appeared on visiting day and gave them a bag of fruit. She had followed the case on the news, knew where the niece was, and said she and other people were trying to get them released on the condition that they would leave Russia of their own accord. They were let go a few days later.

During the whole process, William managed to talk to the Ecuadorian embassy once, explaining their visa types, as he understood them, and asking for help, was told that the embassy could do nothing. "They were typically Ecuadorian," he adds, "they just said 'let yourself be deported' [*déjese deportar*]." His friends in Moscow heard of the problems through his brother and visited the embassy, only to be told the same. William said they even managed to get people in Ecuador to go to the Russian consulate in Quito, all to no avail. In the end it was the older woman and a group of people who had seen them on the street and bought CDs from them who managed to get them released. This group housed them a few days and gave them airfare to Moscow in order to avoid more trouble on the road. William, incredibly, did not return to Ecuador but stayed in Moscow two more months. Like accounts of times past in Western Europe, or Lenin's "pink paper" in Bogotá, William carried his *carpeta de deportación* (deportation folder) back to Moscow but "misplaced it" and decided to stay to make some money with his brother before leaving.

Documentation in Transnational Migration Networks

The documentary realities that Kichwa itinerant musicians inhabit take shape through the migration networks that Otavalos use to travel around the world, as well as the experiences they have had with different migration regimes over the last eighty years. Strategies migrants developed in places like Colombia, where the ambiguous nature of being "indigenous migrants" has aided Kichwa mobility and their ability to skirt state practices of migration control and commercial regulation, are still in place in some nodes of the network, and these inform migrants' actions in places where they are no longer relevant. Through the adventurous and risky undertakings of young indigenous migrants like Lenin and William, Kichwa musicians and entrepreneurs have managed to travel, do business, and settle in different parts of the world. Young migrants trying their luck and trying to make a living have managed to respond to increasing state controls on movement and commerce by finding new destinations where control is more manageable and where documentary processes of inscription can be manipulated or avoided. Strategies like bribery—that ultimately elude or alter documentary exchanges—can be transposed from one context to another, like Colombia and Russia, but are not used in the EU, while others—like renting documents to do business, to sign contracts, or to buy cars—are more pervasive. The attitudes toward documentation that tie these accounts together suggest that these indigenous merchants and musicians are effectively traveling from the margins of one state to the margins of others. They are navigating the gray areas where their own subjecthood is defined or simply addressed ambiguously, playing with the different meanings that being indigenous can have and using the effects of their "foreignness" to their advantage, albeit with a great amount of risk in some cases.

In Kichwa documentation strategies, documents are often distanced from specific individuals to whom they have been issued and affect the experience of others. Multiple inscriptions of the state that recognize the status of his family members have effects on William's daily life and his ability to move and work, for example. Like Lenin and others, he openly ties his ethnicity to his ability to navigate the system, for he says that as an indigenous person [*un indígena*] police, immigration officers, and even bank tellers really do not check (how else could he get by an army checkpoint with his sister's ID? he asks). Other young men whose migration trajectories I have gathered have similar attitudes, in which ethnicity plays an important role in navigating different aspects of identification. Getting around the state and its multiple apparatuses, after all, is a dangerous game these migrants play by using "papers" to "see what happens." In other words, knowledge of the "official" processes or even of the content of the documents—like invitations in a language they cannot read—are not essential to the uses they allow. Rather, the nature of documents can be put to specific uses that must be experimented with in a system of arbitrary interactions with unforeseeable outcomes. Within this system, Kichwa migrants take advantage of assumptions about their ethnicity to conflate the identities represented in certain papers in order to relate to bureaucrats, police officers, and other state actors. Ethnicity, in fact, is also reshaped through this experience. "What being Kichwa" means in many of these accounts includes undertakings and characteristics used in the ascription that have been learned and mastered through migration. For example, William, his brothers, and Don Eduardo, although separated by decades as migrants, all learned to play in "indigenous" musical troupes on their travels.

In the end, that these practices are undertaken without a need to fully understand them can be seen in William's attempt, a year later, to return to Russia. Trying to meet up with his brother, who left in good standing and hence returned the next season, he approached the Russian consulate to see if he would have trouble entering the country after his deportation. Told he was not in the system, he bought a ticket and went back to Russia, only to be denied entry at the airport. Incredibly, he convinced Russian immigration officers to allow him to continue his travels instead of sending him back to Ecuador. He wanted to go to Kazakhstan and enter Russia by land, but his brother, waiting at the airport, bought the ticket to Seoul, where they still knew people. At the airport in Korea he was denied entry "because you have to be deported to your own country," he explains, so they sent him home via Moscow and Amsterdam. When he finally got back to Ecuador, he had traveled the world for almost a week without having exited a single airport.

Notes

1 Sergio Miguel Huarcaya, "Othering the Mestizo: Alterity and Indigenous Politics in Otavalo, Ecuador," *Latin American and Caribbean Ethnic Studies* 5, no. 3 (2010): 301–15; Rudi Colloredo-Mansfeld, *The Native Leisure Class: Consumption and Cultural Creativity in the Andes* (Chicago: University of Chicago Press, 1999).

2 Luz Piedad Caicedo, "Los Kichwa-Otavalos en Bogotá," in *Niñez Indígena en Migración: Derechos en Riesgo y Traumas Culturales*, ed. Alicia Torres (Quito: FLACSO, 2010), 139–226; Angélica Ordóñez Charpentier, "Migración Transnacional de los Kichwa Otavalo y la Fiesta de Pawkar Raymi," in *Al Filo de la Identidad: La Migración Indígena en América Latina*, ed. Alicia Torres and Jesús Carrasco (Quito: FLACSO, 2008), 69–88; Gina Maldonado, *Comerciantes y viajeros: De la imagen etnoarqueológica de "lo indígena" al imaginario del kichwa otavalo "universal"* (Quito: Editorial Abya Yala, 2004); Andrea Ruiz Balzola, "Estrategias, Inversiones e Interacciones de las Mujeres Migrantes Kichwa Otavalo," in *Al Filo de la Identidad: La Migración Indígena en América Latina*, ed. Alicia Torres and Jesús Carrasco (Quito: FLACSO, 2008), 47–68; Rita Sobczyk and Rosa María Miras Soriano, "La Dimensión Étnica de la Identidad: La Diáspora Comercial de Otavalo," *Latinoamérica: Revista de Estudios Latinoamericanos* 60 (2015): 207–37.

3 Veena Das, *Life and Words: Violence and the Descent into the Ordinary* (Berkeley: University of California Press, 2006); Akhil Gupta, *Red Tape: Bureaucracy, Structural Violence, and Poverty in India* (Durham, NC: Duke University Press, 2012); Deborah Poole, "Between Threat and Guarantee: Justice and Community in the Margins of the Peruvian State," in *Anthropology in the Margins of the State*, ed. Veena Das and Deborah Poole (Santa Fe, NM: SAR Press, 2004), 35–66.

4 Juan Thomas Ordóñez, *Jornalero: Being a Day Laborer in the USA* (Oakland: University of California Press, 2015); Josiah M. Heyman, "Class and Classification at the U.S.-Mexico Border," *Human Organization* 60, no. 2 (2001): 128–40.

5 Juan Thomas Ordóñez, "Documents and Shifting Labor Environments among Undocumented Migrant Workers in Northern California," *Anthropology of Work Review* 37, no. 1 (2016): 24–33.

6 Susan Bibler Coutin, *Legalizing Moves: Salvadoran Immigrants' Struggle for U.S. Residency* (Ann Arbor: University of Michigan Press, 2000); Sarah J. Mahler, *American Dreaming: Immigrant Life on the Margins* (Princeton, NJ: Princeton University Press, 1995).

7 Das, *Life and Words*, 163.

8 Sarah Horton, "Identity Loan: The Moral Economy of Migrant Document Exchange in California's Central Valley," *American Ethnologist* 42, no. 1 (2015): 55–67; Ordóñez, *Jornalero*; Liliana Suárez-Navaz, *Rebordering the Mediterranean: Boundaries and Citizenship in Southern Europe* (New York: Berghahn, 2014); Gastón Gordillo, "The Crucible of Citizenship: ID-Paper Fetishism in the Argentinean Chaco," *American Ethnologist* 33, no. 2 (2006): 162–76.

9 Ordóñez, *Jornalero*.

10 Gupta, *Red Tape*, 33.

11 Ordóñez, "Documents and Shifting Labor Environments among Undocumented Migrant Workers in Northern California."

12 Frank Salomon, "Weavers of Otavalo," in *Peoples and Cultures of Native South America*, ed. Daniel R. Gross (Garden City, NY: Doubleday, 1973).

13 Maldonado, *Comerciantes y viajeros*.

14 Elsie Clews Parsons, *Peguche Canton of Otavalo, Province of Imbaura, Ecuador: A Study of Andean Indians* (Chicago: University of Chicago Press, 1945).

15 Caicedo, "Los Kichwa-Otavalos en Bogotá"; Juan Thomas Ordóñez et al., "Migraciones de los Kichwas-Otavalo en Bogotá," *Revista de Estudios Sociales* 48 (2014): 43–56.

16 Maldonado, *Comerciantes y viajeros*; Lynn A. Meisch, *Andean Entrepreneurs: Otavalo Merchants and Musicians in the Global Arena* (Austin: University of Texas Press, 2002); David Kyle, *Transnational Peasants: Migrations, Networks, and Ethnicity in Andean Ecuador* (Baltimore: Johns Hopkins University Press, 2003).

17 Ruiz Balzola, "Estrategias, Inversiones e Interacciones de las Mujeres Migrantes Kichwa Otavalo"; Alicia Torres, "De Punyaro a Sabadell . . . La Emigración Kichwa Otavalo a Cataluña," in *La Migración Ecuatoriana: Transnacionalismo, Redes e Identidades*, ed. Gioconda Herrera, María Cristina Carrillo, and Alicia Torres (Quito: FLACSO, 2005), 433–48; Rita Sobczyk and Rosa María Soriano Miras, "'El indígena tiene que estar siempre innovando': Transformaciones de la etnicidad de

la diáspora comercial de Otavalo," *Revista Española de Antropología Americana* 45, no. 2 (2017): 457–76.

18 Antonio Silva Guendulain, "La Migración Transnacional de los Kichwas Otavalo a la Ciudad de México en Tiempos de la Globalización," *Pacarina Del Sur* 3, no. 12 (2012); Ordóñez Charpentier, "Migración Transnacional de los Kichwa Otavalo y la Fiesta de Pawkar Raymi."

19 Juan Thomas Ordóñez, "Familias transfronterizas: El caso de la migración transnacional otavaleña," *Revista Intellector* 14, no. 28 (2017): 5–19.

20 *Otavalos* is the term used in most of the English-speaking literature, but it is seldom used in Ecuador by this population, who might refer to themselves as Kichwa-Otavalos, Kichwa, or Otavaleños. In Colombia, the settled population tends not to use Otavaleños or Kichwa-Otavalo; rather, they simply use Kichwa in a way that circumvents their "externality" to the nation.

21 Diana Bocarejo, "Emancipation or Enclosement? The Spatialization of Difference and Urban Ethnic Contestation in Colombia," *Antipode* 44, no. 3 (2012): 663–83.

22 Other young musicians with similar experiences usually end up in relations of exploitation with their group mates.

23 The Departamento Administrativo de Seguridad (Administrative Department of Security, DAS) handled immigration issues until 2011, when it was reformed and replaced by Migración Colombia.

24 Poole, "Between Threat and Guarantee."

25 Meisch, *Andean Entrepreneurs.*

26 In this case he is talking about an Ecuadorian cédula.

27 Ruiz Balzola, "Estrategias, Inversiones e Interacciones de las Mujeres Migrantes Kichwa Otavalo"; Sobczyk and Miras Soriano, "La Dimensión Étnica de la Identidad."

28 Critiques of migration network analysis call attention to the fact that the almost hermetic relations based on kinship or region of provenance they describe undercut the importance of such contacts. Fred Krissman, "Sin Coyote ni Patrón: Why the 'Migrant Network' Fails to Explain International Migration," *International Migration Review* 39, no. 1 (2005): 4–44.

29 There are two ways of organizing these musical groups. The first is when Kichwa entrepreneurs and investors hire musicians with little money to travel with them and play the instruments. Here the investors cover the costs of travel and merchandise and take most of the money made. Family groups are better deals, usually, because expenses and profits are distributed more fairly. It is also noteworthy that the size of the groups also affects profit, so while William had many family members at the start of this stage in his account, they broke off into smaller groups and he ended up traveling with only four other people.

30 Officially part of Georgia, Abkhazia is recognized by Russia as an independent country.

Bibliography

Bocarejo, Diana. "Emancipation or Enclosement? The Spatialization of Difference and Urban Ethnic Contestation in Colombia." *Antipode* 44, no. 3 (2012): 663–83.

Caicedo, Luz Piedad. "Los Kichwa-Otavalos en Bogotá." In *Niñez Indígena en Mi-gración: Derechos en Riesgo y Traumas Culturales*, edited by Alicia Torres, 139–226. Quito: FLACSO, 2010.

Colloredo-Mansfeld, Rudi. *The Native Leisure Class: Consumption and Cultural Creativity in the Andes*. Chicago: University of Chicago Press, 1999.

Coutin, Susan Bibler. *Legalizing Moves: Salvadoran Immigrants' Struggle for U.S. Residency*. Ann Arbor: University of Michigan Press, 2000.

Das, Veena. *Life and Words: Violence and the Descent into the Ordinary*. Berkeley: University of California Press, 2006.

Gordillo, Gastón. "The Crucible of Citizenship: ID-Paper Fetishism in the Argentinean Chaco." *American Ethnologist* 33, no. 2 (2006): 162–76.

Gupta, Akhil. *Red Tape: Bureaucracy, Structural Violence, and Poverty in India*. Durham, NC: Duke University Press Books, 2012.

Heyman, Josiah M. "Class and Classification at the U.S.-Mexico Border." *Human Organization* 60, no. 2 (2001): 128–40.

Horton, Sarah. "Identity Loan: The Moral Economy of Migrant Document Exchange in California's Central Valley." *American Ethnologist* 42, no. 1 (2015): 55–67.

Huarcaya, Sergio Miguel. "Othering the Mestizo: Alterity and Indigenous Politics in Otavalo, Ecuador." *Latin American and Caribbean Ethnic Studies* 5, no. 3 (2010): 301–15.

Krissman, Fred. "Sin Coyote ni Patrón: Why the 'Migrant Network' Fails to Explain International Migration." *International Migration Review* 39, no. 1 (2005): 4–44.

Kyle, David. *Transnational Peasants: Migrations, Networks, and Ethnicity in Andean Ecuador*. Baltimore: Johns Hopkins University Press, 2003.

Mahler, Sarah J. *American Dreaming: Immigrant Life on the Margins*. Princeton, NJ: Princeton University Press, 1995.

Maldonado, Gina. *Comerciantes y viajeros: De la imagen etnoarqueológica de "lo indígena" al imaginario del kichwa otavalo "universal."* Quito: Editorial Abya Yala, 2004.

Meisch, Lynn A. *Andean Entrepreneurs: Otavalo Merchants and Musicians in the Global Arena*. Austin: University of Texas Press, 2002.

Ordóñez, Juan Thomas. "Documents and Shifting Labor Environments among Undocumented Migrant Workers in Northern California." *Anthropology of Work Review* 37, no. 1 (2016): 24–33.

Ordóñez, Juan Thomas. "Familias transfronterizas: El caso de la migración transnacional otavaleña." *Revista Intellector* 14, no. 28 (2017): 5–19.

Ordóñez, Juan Thomas. *Jornalero: Being a Day Laborer in the USA*. Oakland: University of California Press, 2015.

Ordóñez, Juan Thomas, Fabio Andrés Colmenares, Anne Gincel, and Diana Rocío Bernal. "Migraciones de los Kichwas-Otavalo en Bogotá." *Revista de Estudios Sociales* 48 (2014): 43–56.

Ordóñez Charpentier, Angélica. "Migración Transnacional de los Kichwa Otavalo y la Fiesta de Pawkar Raymi." In *Al Filo de la Identidad: La Migración Indígena en América Latina*, edited by Alicia Torres and Jesús Carrasco, 69–88. Quito: FLACSO, 2008.

Parsons, Elsie Clews. *Peguche Canton of Otavalo, Province of Imbaura, Ecuador: A Study of Andean Indians*. Chicago: University of Chicago Press, 1945.

Poole, Deborah. "Between Threat and Guarantee: Justice and Community in the Margins of the Peruvian State." In *Anthropology in the Margins of the State*, edited by Veena Das and Deborah Poole, 35–66. Santa Fe, NM: SAR Press, 2004.

Ruiz Balzola, Andrea. "Estrategias, Inversiones e Interacciones de las Mujeres Migrantes Kichwa Otavalo." In *Al Filo de la Identidad: La Migración Indígena en América Latina*, edited by Alicia Torres and Jesús Carrasco, 47–68. Quito: FLACSO, 2008.

Salomon, Frank. "Weavers of Otavalo." In *Peoples and Cultures of Native South America*, edited by Daniel R. Gross. Garden City, NY: Doubleday, 1973.

Silva Guendulain, Antonio. "La Migración Transnacional de los Kichwas Otavalo a la Ciudad de México en Tiempos de la Globalización." *Pacarina del Sur* 3, no. 12 (2012).

Sobczyk, Rita, and Rosa María Soriano Miras. "La Dimensión Étnica de la Identidad: La Diáspora Comercial de Otavalo." *Latinoamérica: Revista de Estudios Latinoamericanos* 60 (2015): 207–37.

Sobczyk, Rita, and Rosa María Soriano Miras. "'El indígena tiene que estar siempre innovando': Transformaciones de la etnicidad de la diáspora comercial de Otavalo." *Revista Española de Antropología Americana* 45, no. 2 (2017): 457–76.

Suárez-Navaz, Liliana. *Rebordering the Mediterranean: Boundaries and Citizenship in Southern Europe*. New York: Berghahn, 2014.

Torres, Alicia. "De Punyaro a Sabadell . . . La Emigración Kichwa Otavalo a Cataluña." In *La Migración Ecuatoriana: Transnacionalismo, Redes e Identidades*, edited by Gioconda Herrera, María Cristina Carrillo, and Alicia Torres, 433–48. Quito: FLACSO, 2005.

Conclusion. **DOCUMENTS AS POWER**

Identification and the Territorial Nation-State

Reading these fascinating chapters, I am struck by the provocative questions they pose. They engage a power nexus between states and people, centered on citizenship and immigration status, materialized in documents, and used for mobility and to cross borders. In doing so, they address production and reproduction, and broach questions about identity and identification. I will touch on the chapters here, but my main aim is identifying key topics and questions that can stimulate new work. What have we learned, and where might we go?

Nandita Sharma's chapter provides a crucial starting point. In the nineteenth-century case of South Asians working in Mauritius, identification documents emerged as a means of designating individuals with temporary work contracts. For the first time, a subordinate group of migrants were designated, documented, and temporally and spatially bounded inside the ostensibly unified polity and market of the British Empire. This was intentional: these workers were brown-skinned colonial subjects. They contrasted with white citizen settlers, freely mobile and freely marketable, but also with bound African slaves, the workforce being superseded. Not only was documentation of the contract important to admission and departure, but only with a contract could these subordinate people cross the novel border in the Indian Ocean between Mauritius and India.

Sharma, together with other historical works,[1] thus provocatively reveals the origins of modern identification: national citizenship, contrasted with temporary denizenhood or illegality, all being legal statuses enclosed by borders and rendered material in documents. These are the central topics of this book. By revealing their normally taken-for-granted existence, these explorations of historical construction provoke us to ask how the world of state identification of individuals might be otherwise. But such legal and social constructs do not come into place only once, and then remain clear and solid. There are ongoing implementations, erosions, and reinforcements, applied to diverse people and situations, that constitute the strange but powerful institutions of individual identification, bounded spaces, and mobility controls. The claims of absolute state sovereignty to know and govern isolated individuals are just claims—admittedly, claims backed by strong coercive power—but subject to incompleteness of many kinds. Historiography and fieldwork challenge us to attend precisely to complex and mutable sovereignties, statuses, and identifications. We thus advocate a contingent, process view of identification. Often, the best way to probe this construction and complexity is through "paper trails," the social life of documentation.

Bridget Anderson's chapter provides several illuminating examples. We are used to thinking of migrants as crossing sovereign borders, but, as she points out, the time period of travel and residence is likewise highly regulated by states. Visitor, temporary worker, resident, and citizen (by naturalization and even by parentage or birth) all imply temporal statuses, and people often slide from one to another. These time dimensions are subject to law enforcement, either positively (changes of status and extensions of time) or negatively, a temporal violation compelling removal. Consistent with Sharma's case of temporary contract workers, Anderson documents a profusion of national-origin (de facto racial) and other, often related (education, class) differences in the duration of stay of temporary visitors, working and not, to the United Kingdom. An illuminating example is the permanent regularization of formerly temporary or unauthorized residents, on the basis of their accumulated time in place and work, such as domestic workers, previously bound to employers, in Anderson's narrative. Even citizens themselves are subject to controls over space and time, as seen in the vague "habitual residence test" for many collective goods. The matrix of differential space and time statuses significantly shapes social inequality, such as freedom or bondage in labor markets and access to publicly subsidized goods.

Just as Anderson offers time as a way to see the complexity and mutability of sovereign documentation, Deborah Boehm points out that documentation has many valences. It provides belonging, temporary or permanent, but it is also used negatively, to exclude and expel. Notably, this modifies the politically useful but not always accurate term *undocumented*. Documentation of an individual as having an order of removal has highly restrictive effects, and in most cases will result in deportation and blocking of future legal entry. Likewise, documentation is crucial to the legal and spatial operations within the detention archipelago, as people shuttle among immigration court and imprisonment sites. Documentation is thus not just a fixed status, but a moment in processes of agency and power. The complexity introduced by Anderson, Boehm, and others opens space for the investigative work of ethnographers on a subject dominated by abstract ideas about central state sovereignty. While the sovereign state–individual relation, embodied in statuses and documents, is indeed crucial, an important range of actors, relations, and documents coexist with that core relation.

Complexity, Contingency, and Multiplicity in Identification

In what follows, I lay out aspects of that complexity. To begin, statuses before the state are often ambiguous and undergoing change. Temporary or transitional statuses are a central concern of this volume. Hundreds of thousands of people in the United States, for example, were granted Temporary Protected Status (TPS), which provided some social and economic integration (depending on their experiences and duration of residence in the country). When Cecilia Menjívar describes instances of misunderstanding and reluctance to accept TPS documentation by businesses and local governments in Arizona, she in fact presents the confused and uneven process of integration, as this novel form of documentation allowed migrants not only to work but also to rent apartments, buy furniture and cars, and so forth. Now, under the Trump administration, the vast majority of TPS holders face revocation in the near future, not just of the TPS status itself but also of these many quotidian activities. Likewise, DACA (Deferred Action for Childhood Arrivals), discussed by Boehm and in Sarah Horton's introduction, requires documentation of unauthorized status before the age of sixteen (and other requirements) in exchange for temporary social and economic integration; it also is threatened with revocation. Both TPS and DACA always were of uncertain tenure, and were built on admission of previous unauthorized presence (with some exceptions under TPS). People waiting on immigration adjudication processes, such as asylum applicants who get temporary work and other authorizations, also fit this pattern. Full regularization (legalization), discussed by Anderson, also involves transformation, though presumably more enduring. Documents involved in these mutations of status—in keeping with Anderson's reminder that such statuses are temporal as well as spatial—are bound up with individual and familial life histories. Indeed, documents often are treasured and presented as evidence of personal histories, as well as being the results of such changes. That life story–document nexus is the object of the legal craft discussed by Susan Coutin. Immigration statuses and the documents that materialize them are mutable, offered and removed, anticipated and foreclosed, tentative and incomplete, with strange contradictions, ambiguities, and lags. They complicate our idea of a sovereign state exercising definitive authority over an isolated person.

Juan Thomas Ordóñez's chapter reminds us of a related point: states are not omniscient or omnipotent (let alone omnibenevolent). Lazy border and immigration officials, often unconcerned with traveling merchants and musicians, and operating with dismissive stereotypes of indigenous peoples as "all the same," misconstrue Kichwa migrants who actually are impressively clever about scaffolding from starter documents[2] in Colombia through various second- and third-stage documents to enable transnational travel and businesses. As a result, they often carry multiple identities and statuses. (Some of this documentary maneuvering has become harder over time, as the United States has pressured other countries to exercise tighter controls, to have less easy transferability, and to use documents with more definitive information about individuals.) The idea of the sovereign state insinuates that it has absolute and perfect control, but actual states are far from that. Combining this point with the one about the changeability of documents opens room for ethnography of lived documentary experience facing uncertainty, risk, opportunity, and change.

Another intriguing dimension of complex sovereignty, also seen in Ordóñez's chapter, is transnationality. I began my commentary, for the purposes of argument, with an admittedly simple and perfect concept of bounded, territorial states that rule over entry from and exit to the outside and that track presence inside via the use of documents. Recent work[3] has noted the extension of sovereign borders outward on behalf of states that are trying to predict, track, and control flows coming toward them. We see this in several chapters with the diffusion of dominant models of documentary identification and controls from the United States and Europe to states elsewhere, and to regional and global organizations. This level of state institutions is important, but transnationality also occurs below it, via the complex movement back and forth across borders of people and the documents they carry. Ruth Gomberg-Muñoz narrates such a case, relating how return migration and deportation to Mexico involve paper trails that originate from a formal transnational institution, but are made complex by their entanglement with life histories and local societies. The apostille, an internationally recognized certification of the validity of a document from one country, enables it to be used for state identification in another country. For example, the U.S. birth certificates of children of Mexican parents require an apostille attached in the previous year to obtain dual citizenship for those children in Mexico. But in the event, this is often complicated and confused, and takes considerable effort and maneuver. Overall, the various forms of nation-state identification (e.g., registering births and certificates thereof) have diffused widely, though not totally and uniformly, around the world.[4] Yet they also have particular national and local inflections. In a complicated but intriguing way, they are transnational institutions and practices of the nationalization of personhood, meriting ethnographic attention.

Just as nation-states connect outward, they also are internally complex. For example, lower-level government units sometimes reinforce, sometimes resist, and often inflect nation-state–individual relations. For example, municipal identification resists federal immigration enforcement by providing documents that can identify individuals without revealing their immigration status (and other matters, such as gender), although their use is circumscribed.[5] A key example in this book is driver's licenses. To understand their complicated scalar ramifications, I will detour to consider the varied kinds of goods and settings in which identification documents such as licenses are used, and then return to discuss that particular document.

Enforcement of immigration status is so intensive, especially at borders but also in the interior, that it tends to deflect attention from other kinds of governmental and private identification processes used to enable access or deny collective goods, often of great importance to people, involving distinctive actors, dynamics, and distributions. For example, in the United States children of all citizenship and immigration statuses, including unauthorized status, are entitled to full K–12 public education, based on the *Plyler v. Doe* Supreme Court decision, but not to higher education, which varies by states, that is, subnational units. This important collective good is distributed by residence in a school district. Access to public K–12 education involves a distinctive, often complicated and dense, set of identification documents— for example, mailing addresses and utility bills. Those documents, and the handling of children and parents or guardians accompanying them, are scrutinized by a distinct group of street-level state bureaucrats—district and school officials, teachers, social workers, and so forth. Each school district and indeed each school site has its own micropolitical setting. While school–immigrant community relations thus vary greatly, interactions tend toward the inclusive rather than exclusionary, as seen in the well-researched fact that unauthorized immigrant parents and children trust schools most among all official institutions.[6] The broad lesson is this: Just as not all statuses and documents are singular and cohesive, the state itself is made up of diverse parts with different attitudes and practices toward immigrants.

There are many other collective goods bound up with specific statuses and identification documents. Some are governed under sovereign state identity, such as authorization to work or, in the United Kingdom, access to the National Health System, others partially so, such as the fragmented U.S. health system, and others not at all, such as access to public transportation (but border enforcers in the United States do search "common carriers" within a hundred miles of the border). There are other collective good–documentation nexuses. Researchers might inquire about a worker's disability (see Horton's work, discussed below), other kinds of disability, retirement, income and food support, and public housing and shelter—and this is hardly a comprehensive list. Each collective good and its relationship—or lack thereof—to various parts and levels of the state merits ethnographic attention, as does the presence (or not) of immigration and citizenship criteria in access to such goods. The web of connections and disarticulations, the kinds of people, statuses, and documents, and the controlling organizations and bureaucrats all need to be studied in their complexity.

To add to this complexity, identification documents and processes are widespread in the private sector. The historical literature on identification has found that the private sector has been important in developing individual documentation and identification records, helping to drive governmental processes by their demands for clear records.[7] Credit ratings are a notable example. More needs to be done on these data traces and documents. Meanwhile, sovereign states often use private data to track mobile people, as exemplified by U.S. Customs and Border Protection collecting social media identities. Menjívar's chapter examines one such interaction, in which nongovernmental street-level workers, such as apartment managers, car salespeople, and furniture salespeople, check official identification documents in order to know who someone is, sometimes not for clear reasons. These hybrid state–private identification processes create confusion and conflict when liminal or temporary statuses (e.g., TPS) are hard for nonexperts to follow. Menjívar studied a time and place, Arizona in the last two decades, of partial hostility and suspicion toward immigrants. Yet in other cases, the private sector or private–local state alliances resist sovereign-state processes of exclusionary identification. Local credit unions and banks, interested in accounts and loans to ostensibly unauthorized immigrants, sometimes support municipal identification documents based only on residence, which is inclusive of undocumented residents, homeless people, and others.[8]

This panoply of identification requirements, evidence, and documents interacts with complex lives. A striking example comes from Coutin's observation of the legal craft of immigration service providers. In one case, a wife who can petition for her husband to obtain permanent residency is prevented by the times he has spent with her in the United States without authorization, reflecting a genuine relation. But if he could not prove the relationship, he might also have been denied. In the other case, a woman who was legalized under a special program, the Nicaraguan Adjustment and Central American Relief Act, had already obtained permanent residency for her husband, without knowing it, through simply naming him in her own application, despite his unauthorized presence. Many kinds of immigration status before the sovereign state depend on specific recognized personal relations. Hence, identification before the sovereign is not always individualizing but often involves life histories and relationships. Non-sovereign identification processes add to the complexity. This opens space for ethnographic inquiry in conversation with political theory.

A distinctive and important illustration of these points comes from Doris Marie Provine and Monica Varsanyi's chapter on political struggles around driver's licenses. Permission to drive, and identification when doing it, is a collective good—indeed, an almost perfect illustration of that concept, since individuals are licensed, upon proper certification and behavior, to access a shared space and activity that cannot be segmented as private property. The core matter at stake in licenses is competence to drive, and thus public safety. This has long been handled by subnational units: state bureaus and state and local police departments. Yet in the 2005 REAL ID Act (with long phased-in implementation), the central U.S. government required of these subnational units increasingly restrictive requirements for identification and issuance of licenses, which effectively deny driving access to unauthorized immigrants or include a mark on their licenses indicating deportable status. This comes from a pervasive drive in the United States to use driver's licenses as de facto national identification documents.

Provine and Varsanyi compare two subnational units, New Mexico and Arizona. Both delayed implementing the federal law, but for different reasons. Arizona already had more restrictive licensing requirements than the federal ones, while New Mexico struggled to keep licenses available for people of all immigration and citizenship statuses. New Mexico to some extent was able to delay and limit the central state capture of licenses. In the United States, with weak public transportation and a culture of automobility, driver's licenses are fundamental to production and extended reproduction (concepts discussed below), and also to intimate social relations, as in the classic Tejano song "Un Mojado sin Licencia."[9] This is the sad tale of an undocumented man who wants to journey to marry his girlfriend Chencha. He easily buys a bad car, but lacks a license; in the end, he is jailed and loses both the car and Chencha. He is not (yet) deported at the end of the song, but Angela Stuesse and Mathew Coleman found that traffic stops were a crucial path to deportation from the interior.[10] It is for these reasons that access to driver's licenses is a central concern of U.S. immigrant communities (personal observation), and that the struggle over documents in New Mexico described by Provine and Varsanyi was crucial. Questions of struggles, goals, and values will conclude this essay, but first I will look at how documents shape ideas and practices.

Identification and Identity

It is well known that identification is not the same as identity: identification is a label placed on a person or group by the dominant social order, such as the sovereign state, while identity refers to interior individual and group notions of self.[11] Keeping this distinction clear is vital, but it is just the first step. The interesting question is, How does identification relate to identity? If immigration statuses are central to the bounded nation-state, and documents materialize them, then how and how much do identification practices shape the subjectivities of immigrant individuals, families, and communities?

Louis Althusser provided an influential understanding of this process, interpellation, in which power "hails" a person as a certain kind of being, and they are thus constituted socially and inwardly as a "subject."[12] Documentary identification is a classic example of hailing. However, ethnographically, what is the hailing process in action, and how much does hailing really constitute subjects? We should address these crucial questions about documents and power. Drawing on the chapters in this book, I propose a continuum from the internalization of citizenship and immigration identifications, through the pragmatic use of documents and statuses without internalization, to active resistance and rejection.

Menjívar provides a case of internalization when she reports that when private salespeople ask for documents, many immigrants do not question them because they have become accustomed to being subjects who *have* to identify themselves according to their immigration status. She also recounts instances when people retain their documents long after they no longer need them, suggesting a deep fear of deportation and a belief that they still need to guard against it. Perhaps not for everyone nor always (Menjívar also reports criticisms of U.S. racism), but on the whole for these Salvadorans, seeking security via identification affects their inner identity. By contrast, the Kichwa described by Ordóñez, an Ecuadorian indigenous people in a commercial diaspora across many countries of the world, take a distinctly pragmatic approach to documents, fluidly adopting useful personal and national identities, while retaining an autonomous sense of their hometown and kin relations. This identity shifting is facilitated by national bureaucracies that view them as inscrutable indigenes. The performance of identification, then, does not shape Kichwa inner worlds.

A third possibility is active rejection of identification statuses, documents, and borders (e.g., destroying or refusing identification documents). That does not occur in this book's chapters, but a less frontal kind of resistance is described by Gomberg-Muñoz concerning know-your-rights documents distributed at trainings by pro-immigrant organizations. These documents do embody a subjectivity of resisting the central state. On the other hand, the rights to which they refer are foundational features of the U.S. state, particularly the Fourth and Fifth Amendments to the Constitution (limits on search and seizure, and thus arrest, and the right to remain silent). The rarity of frontal resistance to documentation deserves further research. Possible motives for choosing inclusion, when possible, over resistance include the desirability of everyday security against arrest, access to collective goods, and pervasive cultural messages of belonging. In the face of state power to track and reward, perhaps "weapons of the weak"[13] are more common, such as evasion and use of altered or transferred documents, seen in Ordóñez's chapter. Likewise, there is need to ask about changes in subjectivity that come from overt resistance, such as knowing your rights, advocating for new documents (municipal identification) and defending old ones (driver's licenses for the undocumented), and collectively advocating for change in immigration statuses (such as the Dreamer movement).[14] The interpellation of subjectivity from identification to identity, then, deserves critical, close ethnographic attention.

A number of chapters here examine individual or large-scale opportunities for changing identification, especially coming in from the shadows after admitting past illegality to the state. As Horton's introduction puts it, the dilemma is whether to gain legitimacy by conceding legibility. Boehm, for example, examines the documentary work involved in temporary legalization in the DACA program. Past illegality vis-à-vis the sovereign state is documented in search of security, albeit temporary and removable. Gaining DACA, she reports, brings a sense of relief from the risk of sudden arrest and expulsion, but also a new fear of exposure to the knowledge of the state (e.g., recording fingerprints). Indeed, the Trump administration's attempts to revoke DACA (currently being considered in various courts) justify their fears, since the DACA applicants have provided identifying information to a now-hostile government. Beyond the difficult present moment, this raises an important point: states are simultaneously threatening—through arrest and removal—and promising, offering collective goods such as driver's licenses, health care, advanced education, and so forth.[15] Because state and private sectors together offer materially and emotionally desirable lives in exchange for submission to identification, the projects of autonomy from governance described by James Scott seem to have largely fallen into abeyance.[16] Powerful attractions to documents, sometimes with ambivalence, are scattered across many chapters in this book, from Boehm's Dreamers to Coutin's heartbroken family petitioners. Processes of documentation, then, provide an important window on attraction, channeling, caging, and empowerment in the contemporary world. They deserve further attention.

Identification, Citizenship Inequality, and Life Chances

Changes in citizenship and immigration status are often desired because they matter to life projects and life chances. Hence, they are critical components of inequality. Citizenship and immigration inequality is relatively understudied, but has been theorized recently.[17] It involves collective effects on life chances brought about by sovereign state–imposed categorical differences in mobility, temporality, vulnerability to expulsion, and access to collective goods.[18] Citizenship inequality intersects in important and largely unstudied ways with other relations of inequality, including race and national origin, gender, sexuality, and class. The topic of citizenship inequality far surpasses this conclusion, but how documentation affects such inequalities merits discussion.

Documentation substantially affects work and compensation—that is, production inequalities. Anderson's chapter, for example, discusses how temporally limited visas shape exploitability in domestic service in the United

Kingdom. Many domestic workers enter the United Kingdom on short-term (six-month) work visas, while bound to much longer-term (five-year) temporary residents. This results in an accumulation of unauthorized domestic workers trapped in service to wealthy households, with alternatives limited by their lack of work documents and deportability. At one point, domestic workers could be regularized if they had been abused by employers, requiring specific kinds of evidence. The change in identification, if they could access it, improved their personal and employment mobility, and offered inclusion in the national insurance and tax systems (production and extended reproduction being linked, as is typical). This brief moment of labor liberation involved both documentation of the past and distribution of documents marking new statuses.

While production is widely understood to shape inequality, extended reproduction is less well explored, though many exceptions can be found. Extended reproduction includes all those processes that renew daily life, such as food, shelter, health, education, and so forth. Inequalities in extended reproduction involve differential access to and outcomes of those processes. As I have already noted, citizenship and immigration statuses enable or block access to collective goods and in some cases even those from the private marketplace (Menjívar). The struggle around driver's licenses (Provine and Varsanyi) mattered precisely because local mobility, or imposed immobility, affected access to workplaces, reproductive goods (health, education, shopping), and even interpersonal relations and emotions (visiting friends and family, not being isolated). In a setting quite near that of Provine and Varsanyi, I found that unequal mobility between unauthorized immigrants and citizens shaped life chances through both access to production, such as job sites, and extended reproduction, such as access to health care.[19]

Documentation itself exacerbates these inequalities. Citizens, reinforced by race distinctions (with whites in the most favorable position) have normalized privileges encoded in the way documents are collected and handled. White citizens in the heavily policed U.S.-Mexico borderlands are unlikely to be asked for documents, because they are less likely to travel routes and move through spaces where the Border Patrol stops people and asks for documents (e.g., not riding buses, not living in peripheral communities). When such people are stopped (e.g., at checkpoints), verbal declarations are accepted at face value or documents are not closely scrutinized. Conversely, unauthorized or liminally documented immigrants of visibly Mexican and Central American origin move around heavily patrolled geographies, are targeted for questioning, and have documents and verbal declarations, valid or false, pointedly interrogated. This increases the likelihood of identification, criminal charges (identity theft, false claim to citizenship, etc.), and deportation. Documents reinforce privilege as much as they illegalize people.[20]

Focused on people at the bottom of the power hierarchy, Horton's ethnography of farmworkers in the Central Valley of California, research that leads directly to this book, shows clearly how documents help create profound inequalities in work and extended reproduction.[21] Unauthorized immigrant farmworkers sometimes borrow identification documents needed to work from authorized residents and citizens. They gain income, in very demanding and injurious jobs, but at a cost. When working on other people's documents, their tax withholding (some of it returnable income), social security (retirement funding), disability funds (important for health care), and so on are diverted to those other people. Some elderly unauthorized workers, Horton found, had been working on legitimate social security identification numbers (given in an era when policy was different) and imagined that they would have savings for their old age. But they were ineligible because of their present status, so they effectively gave away this reproductive effort to the federal government. Nationally, this constitutes a vast transfer of savings from the poor to the state.[22]

Meanwhile, Horton shows that working with borrowed or fraudulent identification renders workers controllable in production regimes because they are vulnerable to denunciation, criminal charges about documents, and deportation.[23] Evasive documentary techniques, such as using borrowed documents, false or borrowed social security numbers, and so forth, involve crimes like false impersonation of a U.S. citizen, identity fraud, and aggravated identity theft. As I write, 114 workers at two garden centers in northern Ohio have been arrested in a mass round-up that began with the arrest of a document vendor. The arrested workers will be deported, but government officials describe their first priority to be prosecuting them for document violations.[24] Such violations occur precisely because of the need to simulate falsely the documentary regime. Rarely are employers charged with these violations, but workers often are. The risk in documentary illegality rests heavily on workers.

Documents thus offer a window on the making and reproduction of social inequality. The core phenomenon is citizenship inequality reinforced by race inequality; those processes exacerbate class relations of exploitation in the workplace and life course inequalities in extended reproduction. Processes deserving of ethnographic attention include inequalities of profiling and scrutiny of documents like licenses, documentary (in)eligibility for individual and collective goods, the attitudes and practices of street workers

(Menjívar) who demand and examine documents from racialized others but let the privileged pass untouched, and ways that internalized subjectivity result in self-limitation or, conversely, empowerment. Such research can speak critically and constructively in struggles for social change.

Identification Struggles and the Political-Ethical Values at Stake

I noted that citizenship and immigration statuses are often liminal or change-able, in part because such statuses are the objects of continual struggle. In these politics, they sometimes freeze into difficult-to-change legal shapes, but at other times they rapidly transform. Documents often are the publicly salient objectives or symbols of those struggles. Because documents and the statuses they convey matter to life projects and life chances, they embody crucial political-ethical values. Struggles over documents *matter*.

The know-your-rights documents described by Gomberg-Muñoz, for example, embody the value that "all persons," in the language of the U.S. Bill of Rights, have rights against the police power of the sovereign state and sub-national states, whatever their immigration and citizenship status.[25] Munici-pal identification cards, discussed in the introduction,[26] embody the value that unauthorized people (and others, such as the homeless) are members of communities with access to collective goods, even if not always full members of nation-states. For example, municipal IDs can be used by parents to identify themselves when visiting public schools, as part of community-oriented teaching, in the context of increasing security controls at schools. And the DACA program, discussed in Boehm's chapter and the introduction, concerns who is included in society and polity. People who came without authorization as children are socialized as members of the society of arrival, so that their legal status and their sociocultural being are misaligned. Full legalization and a path to citizenship for such people would recognize their effective membership, while ending DACA and denying a route to citizen-ship, the goal of struggle in the other direction, would make social person-hood conform to existing legal standards. This policy struggle is fought out, in quite intricate ways described by Boehm, via documents, evidence, paperwork, identification of individuals, and so forth.

Coutin's chapter offers a fascinating and rich study of "legal craft," the skill exercised by staff at a low cost/free immigrant advocacy agency. They maneuver through laws and documents on behalf of some immigrants—some, because not all hopeful applicants can be helped within the status quo. This work does not deviate from the actually existing sovereign citizenship and immigration regime. How then is it a struggle? On one extreme, immigrants with money—some but not all wealthy and privileged—and also corporations pay substantial sums for private immigration attorneys and offices, that is, for their legal craft. On the other extreme, unrepresented immigrants (immigration, being administrative and not criminal law, does not have mandatory public representation) suffer from high rates of failure due to lack of legal craft.[27] So low- to no-cost representation makes potential opportunities in law become real for suitable immigrants. Part of this is knowledge of provisions of the law, but part is literally documentary skill, such as packaging paperwork sent to Citizenship and Immigration Services in specific order and formats. In a documentary and legal process dominated by the power of money, even low- or no-cost legal craft constitutes a daily struggle to obtain a modicum of justice. Such struggles are often quotidian, and on rare occasions dramatic, but they embody crucial political-ethical values about collective inclusion, life projects, and life chances.

The importance of this book is that documents, as materializations of citizenship and immigration statuses before the state, open up important questions for ethnographers, with implications for social theory and social justice. In the face of the apparent monolith of the sovereign state, actual documents involve a wide range of topics, scales, and gradations, and a notable mutability, offering many opportunities for creative and thoughtful research. The relationship between external identification and internal or collective identity is problematic, not automatic, opening doors to interesting ethnography and contributions to fundamental social theory. Documents, and the statuses that they materialize, have profound effects on citizenship inequality through production and extended reproduction, intersecting with many other relations of inequality. It is not only that the undocumented or liminally documented are disadvantaged, but, conversely, naturalized advantage adheres to privileged immigrants and citizens, much of this through normalized access to and handling of documents. The topic of citizenship inequality is in need of critical attention, and documents are a vital way to penetrate it. Documents and related statuses embody political-ethical values, both of the status quo and alternatives to it. They thus constitute arenas of important struggle for both scholarly and engaged/applied anthropologists.

Notes

1 Ilsen About, James Brown, and Gayle Lonergan, eds., *Identification and Registration Practices in Transnational Perspective: People, Papers and Practices* (Houndmills,

UK: Palgrave Macmillan, 2013); Jane Caplan and John Torpey, eds., *Documenting Individual Identity: The Development of State Practices in the Modern World* (Princeton, NJ: Princeton University Press, 2001); Adam McKeown, *Melancholy Order: Asian Migration and the Globalization of Borders* (New York: Columbia University Press, 2011); John C. Torpey, *The Invention of the Passport: Surveillance, Citizenship and the State* (Cambridge: Cambridge University Press, 2000).

2   A starter document is an initial identification of a person from which derive all subsequent documents provided to that person.

3   Didier Bigo and Elspeth Guild, *Controlling Frontiers: Free Movement into and within Europe* (Farnham, UK: Ashgate, 2005).

4   About, Brown, and Lonergan, *Identification and Registration Practices*; Caplan and Torpey *Documenting Individual Identity*.

5   Els De Graauw, "Municipal ID Cards for Undocumented Immigrants: Local Bureaucratic Membership in a Federal System," *Politics and Society* 42 (2014): 309–30.

6   Randy Capps et al., *Implications of Immigration Enforcement Activities for the Well-Being of Children in Immigrant Families: A Review of the Literature* (Washington, DC: Urban Institute, 2015), 22.

7   Edward Higgs, "Consuming Identity and Consuming the State in Britain since c. 1750," in Ilsen About, James Brown, and Gayle Lonergan, eds., *Identification and Registration Practices in Transnational Perspective: People, Papers and Practices* (Houndmills, UK: Palgrave Macmillan, 2013).

8   Robert Heyman, personal communication.

9   Flaco Jiménez, "Un Mojado sin Licencia," Arhoolie ARH00396 (El Cerrito, CA: Arhoolie, 1993). The title is literally translated as "A Wetback without a License," but in Spanish *mojado* is not stigmatizing the way wetback is in English.

10 Angela Stuesse and Mathew Coleman, "Automobility, Immobility, Altermobility: Surviving and Resisting the Intensification of Immigrant Policing," *City and Society* 26 (2014): 51–72; also see Amada Armenta, *Protect, Serve, and Deport: The Rise of Policing as Immigration Enforcement* (Berkeley: University of California Press, 2017).

11 Josiah M. Heyman, "Class and Classification at the U.S.-Mexico Border," *Human Organization* 60 (2001): 130; Caplan and Torpey, "Introduction," in *Documenting Individual Identity*, 3.

12 Louis Althusser, "Ideology and Ideological State Apparatuses (Notes towards an Investigation)," in *Lenin and Philosophy and Other Essays*, translated by Ben Brewster (New York: Monthly Review, 1971).

13 James C. Scott, *Weapons of the Weak: Everyday Forms of Peasant Resistance* (New Haven, CT: Yale University Press, 1985).

14 Walter J. Nicholls, *The DREAMers: How the Undocumented Youth Movement Transformed the Immigrant Rights Debate* (Stanford, CA: Stanford University Press, 2013).

15 Workers sometimes desire nondocumentation because they can move freely to choose better employers, as opposed to legal but constrained, nearly bound temporary contract labor.

16 James C. Scott, *The Art of Not Being Governed: An Anarchist History of Upland Southeast Asia* (New Haven, CT: Yale University Press, 2010).

17 Evelyn Glenn, "Citizenship and Inequality: Historical and Global Perspectives," *Social Problems* 47 (2000): 1–20; Josiah M. Heyman, "U.S. Immigration Officers of Mexican Ancestry as Mexican Americans, Citizens, and Immigration Police," *Current Anthropology* 43 (2002): 479–507; Steffen Mau, "Mobility Citizenship, Inequality, and the Liberal State: The Case of Visa Policies," *International Political Sociology* 4 (2010): 339–61.

18 Josiah M. Heyman, "Unequal Relationships between Unauthorized Migrants and the Wider Society: Production, Reproduction, Mobility, and Risk," *Anthropology of Work Review* 37 (2016): 44–48.

19 Josiah M. Heyman, "Trust, Privilege, and Discretion in the Governance of the US Borderlands with Mexico," *Canadian Journal of Law and Society/Revue Canadienne Droit et Société* 24 (2009): 367–90; Josiah M. Heyman, "The State and Mobile People at the U.S.-Mexico Border," in *Class, Contention, and a World in Motion*, ed. Winnie Lem and Pauline Gardiner Barber (Oxford: Berghahn, 2010); Guillermina Gina Núñez and Josiah M. Heyman, "Entrapment Processes and Immigrant Communities in a Time of Heightened Border Vigilance," *Human Organization* 66 (2007): 354–65; also see Heide Castañeda and Milena Andrea Melo, "Health Care Access for Latino Mixed-Status Families: Barriers, Strategies, and Implications for Reform," *American Behavioral Scientist* 58 (2014): 1891–909; Nolan Kline, "Pathogenic Policy: Immigrant Policing, Fear, and Parallel Medical Systems in the US South," *Medical Anthropology* 36 (2017): 396–410.

20 Heyman, "Trust, Privilege, and Discretion in the Governance of the US Borderlands with Mexico."

21 Sarah Horton, "Identity Loan: The Moral Economy of Migrant Document Exchange in California's Central Valley," *American Ethnologist* 42 (2015): 55–67; Sarah Horton, "Ghost Workers: The Implications of Governing Immigration through Crime for Migrant Workplaces," *Anthropology of Work Review* 37 (2016): 9–21; Sarah Horton, "From 'Deportability' to 'Denounce-Ability': New Forms of Labor Subordination in an Era of Governing Immigration through Crime," *Political and Legal Anthropology Review* 39 (2016): 312–26; Sarah Horton, "Diverted Retirement: The Care Crisis among Elderly Mexican Immigrants," in *The U.S.-Mexico Transborder Region: Cultural Dynamics and Historical Interaction*, ed. Carlos Vélez-Ibáñez and Josiah Heyman (Tucson: University of Arizona Press, 2017).

22 Alexa Fernández Campbell, "Undocumented Immigrants Pay Billions of Dollars in Federal Taxes Each Year: Here's How They Do It," *Vox.com*, May 24, 2018, accessed June 3, 2018, https://www.vox.com/2018/4/13/17229018/undocumented-immigrants-pay-taxes.

23 Horton, "From 'Deportability' to 'Denounce-Ability'"; also see Josiah M. Heyman, "State Effects on Labor Exploitation: The INS and Undocumented Immigrants at the Mexico-United States Border," *Critique of Anthropology* 18 (1998): 157–80.

24 Carma Hassan and Eric Levenson, "ICE Arrests 114 at Ohio Garden Center in Major Mass Raid," CNN, June 6, 2018, accessed June 7, 2018, https://www.cnn.com /2018/06/06/us/ice-undocumented-immigrants-arrests-garden-ohio/index.html.

25 Timothy J. Dunn, *Blockading the Border and Human Rights: The El Paso Operation That Remade Immigration Enforcement* (Austin: University of Texas Press, 2009).

26 Also see De Graauw, "Municipal ID Cards for Undocumented Immigrants."

27 For example, see Transactional Records Access Clearinghouse, "Continued Rise in Asylum Denial Rates: Impact of Representation and Nationality," December 13, 2016, accessed June 3, 2018, http://trac.syr.edu/immigration/reports/448/.

Bibliography

About, Ilsen, James Brown, and Gayle Lonergan, eds. *Identification and Registration Practices in Transnational Perspective: People, Papers and Practices.* Houndmills, UK: Palgrave Macmillan, 2013.

Althusser, Louis. "Ideology and Ideological State Apparatuses (Notes towards an Investigation)." In *Lenin and Philosophy and Other Essays,* translated by Ben Brewster, 127–86. New York: Monthly Review, 1971.

Armenta, Amada. *Protect, Serve, and Deport: The Rise of Policing as Immigration Enforcement.* Berkeley: University of California Press, 2017.

Bigo, Didier, and Elspeth Guild. *Controlling Frontiers: Free Movement into and within Europe.* Farnham, UK: Ashgate, 2005.

Campbell, Alexa Fernández. "Undocumented Immigrants Pay Billions of Dollars in Federal Taxes Each Year: Here's How They Do It." Vox.com, May 24, 2018. Accessed June 3, 2018. https://www.vox.com/2018/4/13/17229018/undocumented-immigrants -pay-taxes.

Caplan, Jane, and John Torpey, eds. *Documenting Individual Identity: The Development of State Practices in the Modern World.* Princeton, NJ: Princeton University Press, 2001.

Capps, Randy, Heather Koball, Andrea Campetella, Krista Perreira, Sarah Hooker, and Juan Manuel Pedroza. *Implications of Immigration Enforcement Activities for the Well-Being of Children in Immigrant Families: A Review of the Literature.* Washington, DC: Urban Institute, 2015.

Castañeda, Heide, and Milena Andrea Melo. "Health Care Access for Latino Mixed-Status Families: Barriers, Strategies, and Implications for Reform." *American Behavioral Scientist* 58 (2014): 1891–909.

De Graauw, Els. "Municipal ID Cards for Undocumented Immigrants: Local Bureaucratic Membership in a Federal System." *Politics and Society* 42 (2014): 309–30.

Dunn, Timothy J. *Blockading the Border and Human Rights: The El Paso Operation That Remade Immigration Enforcement.* Austin: University of Texas Press, 2009.

Glenn, Evelyn. "Citizenship and Inequality: Historical and Global Perspectives." *Social Problems* 47 (2000): 1–20.

Hassan, Carma, and Eric Levenson. "ICE Arrests 114 at Ohio Garden Center in Major Mass Raid." CNN, June 6, 2018. Accessed June 7, 2018. https://www.cnn.com/2018/06 /06/us/ice-undocumented-immigrants-arrests-garden-ohio/index.html.

Heyman, Josiah M. "Class and Classification at the U.S.-Mexico Border." *Human Organization* 60 (2001): 128–40.

Heyman, Josiah M. "The State and Mobile People at the U.S.-Mexico Border." In *Class, Contention, and a World in Motion*, edited by Winnie Lem and Pauline Gardiner Barber, 58–78. Oxford: Berghahn, 2010.

Heyman, Josiah M. "State Effects on Labor Exploitation: The INS and Undocumented Immigrants at the Mexico-United States Border." *Critique of Anthropology* 18 (1998): 157–80.

Heyman, Josiah M. "Trust, Privilege, and Discretion in the Governance of the US Borderlands with Mexico." *Canadian Journal of Law and Society/Revue Canadienne Droit et Société* 24 (2009): 367–90.

Heyman, Josiah M. "Unequal Relationships between Unauthorized Migrants and the Wider Society: Production, Reproduction, Mobility, and Risk." *Anthropology of Work Review* 37 (2016): 44–48.

Heyman, Josiah M. "U.S. Immigration Officers of Mexican Ancestry as Mexican Americans, Citizens, and Immigration Police." *Current Anthropology* 43 (2002): 479–507.

Higgs, Edward. "Consuming Identity and Consuming the State in Britain since c. 1750." In *Identification and Registration Practices in Transnational Perspective: People, Papers and Practices*, edited by Ilsen About, James Brown, and Gayle Lonergan, 164–84. Houndmills, UK: Palgrave Macmillan, 2013.

Horton, Sarah. "Diverted Retirement: The Care Crisis among Elderly Mexican Immigrants." In *The U.S.-Mexico Transborder Region: Cultural Dynamics and Historical Interaction*, edited by Carlos Vélez-Ibáñez and Josiah Heyman, 322–41. Tucson: University of Arizona Press, 2017.

Horton, Sarah. "From 'Deportability' to 'Denounce-Ability': New Forms of Labor Subordination in an Era of Governing Immigration through Crime." *Political and Legal Anthropology Review* 39 (2016): 312–26.

Horton, Sarah. "Ghost Workers: The Implications of Governing Immigration through Crime for Migrant Workplaces." *Anthropology of Work Review* 37 (2016): 9–21.

Horton, Sarah. "Identity Loan: The Moral Economy of Migrant Document Exchange in California's Central Valley." *American Ethnologist* 42 (2015): 55–67.

Jiménez, Flaco. "Un Mojado sin Licencia." Arhoolie ARH00396. El Cerrito, CA: Arhoolie, 1993.

Kline, Nolan. "Pathogenic Policy: Immigrant Policing, Fear, and Parallel Medical Systems in the US South." *Medical Anthropology* 36 (2017): 396–410.

Mau, Steffen. "Mobility Citizenship, Inequality, and the Liberal State: The Case of Visa Policies." *International Political Sociology* 4 (2010): 339–61.

McKeown, Adam. *Melancholy Order: Asian Migration and the Globalization of Borders*. New York: Columbia University Press, 2011.

Nicholls, Walter J. *The DREAMers: How the Undocumented Youth Movement Transformed the Immigrant Rights Debate*. Stanford, CA: Stanford University Press, 2013.

Núñez, Guillermina Gina, and Josiah M. Heyman. "Entrapment Processes and Immigrant Communities in a Time of Heightened Border Vigilance." *Human Organization* 66 (2007): 354–65.

Scott, James C. *The Art of Not Being Governed: An Anarchist History of Upland South-east Asia.* New Haven, CT: Yale University Press, 2010.

Scott, James C. *Weapons of the Weak: Everyday Forms of Peasant Resistance.* New Haven, CT: Yale University Press, 1985.

Stuesse, Angela, and Mathew Coleman. "Automobility, Immobility, Altermobility: Surviving and Resisting the Intensification of Immigrant Policing." *City and Society* 26 (2014): 51–72.

Torpey, John C. *The Invention of the Passport: Surveillance, Citizenship and the State.* Cambridge: Cambridge University Press, 2000.

Transactional Records Access Clearinghouse. "Continued Rise in Asylum Denial Rates: Impact of Representation and Nationality." December 13, 2016. Accessed June 3, 2018. http://trac.syr.edu/immigration/reports/448/.

BRIDGET ANDERSON is Professor of Migration and Citizenship and Director of Migration Mobilities Bristol at the University of Bristol, UK. Dr. Anderson holds a Ph.D. in sociology and her research focuses on the functions of immigration in key labor market sectors. She is the author of *Us and Them? The Dangerous Politics of Immigration Controls* (2013), *Doing the Dirty Work? The Global Politics of Domestic Labour* (2000), and coeditor of *Who Needs Migrant Workers? Labour Shortages, Immigration and Public Policy* (2010, 2012), *The Social, Political, and Historical Contours of Deportation* (2013), and *Migration and Care Labour: Theory and Politics* (2014).

DEBORAH A. BOEHM is Professor of Anthropology and Gender, Race, and Identity at the University of Nevada, Reno. Dr. Boehm is an expert in the areas of mixed-status and transnational families, migration and citizenship, immigration detention, and deportation. She is the author of *Returned: Going and Coming in an Age of Deportation* (2016) and *Intimate Migrations: Gender, Family, and "Illegality" among Transnational Mexicans* (2012), and coeditor of *Illegal Encounters: The Effect of Detention and Deportation on Young People* (2019) and *Everyday Ruptures: Children, Youth, and Migration in Global Perspective* (2011).

SUSAN BIBLER COUTIN is Professor, Departments of Criminology, Law and Society and Anthropology, University of California, Irvine. Dr. Coutin holds a Ph.D. in sociocultural anthropology and focuses on social, political, and legal activism surrounding immigration from Central America to the United States. Her books include *Exiled Home: Salvadoran Transnational Youth in the Aftermath of Violence* (Duke University Press, 2016), *Nations of Emigrants: Shifting Boundaries of Citizenship in El Salvador and the United States* (2007), and *Legalizing Moves: Salvadoran Immigrants' Struggle for U.S. Residency* (2000).

RUTH GOMBERG-MUÑOZ is Associate Professor, Department of Anthropology, Loyola University Chicago. Dr. Gomberg-Muñoz is an expert in the areas of immigration law, unauthorized migrants, labor, and social movements. She is the author of *Becoming Legal: Immigration Law and Mixed-Status Families* (2016) and *Labor and Legality: An Ethnography of a Mexican Immigrant Network* (2011).

JOSIAH HEYMAN is Endowed Professor of Border Trade Issues, Professor of Anthropology, and Director of the Center for Interamerican and Border Studies, University of Texas–El Paso. Dr. Heyman is the author of over one hundred articles and book chapters on borders, states, and bureaucracies. He is coeditor of *The U.S.-Mexico Transborder Region: Cultural Dynamics and Historical Interactions* (2017) and *States and Illegal Practices* (1999), and author of *Life and Labor on the Border: Working People of Northeastern Sonora, 1886–1986* (1991) and *Finding a Moral Heart for U.S. Immigration Policy: An Anthropological Perspective* (1998).

SARAH B. HORTON is Associate Professor, Department of Anthropology, University of Colorado, Denver. Dr. Horton is an expert in the areas of migrant "illegality," health, and labor. She is author of *They Leave Their Kidneys in the Fields: Illness, Injury, and "Illegality" among U.S. Farmworkers* (2016), which was awarded the Robert Textor and Family Prize in Anticipatory Anthropology and was a runner-up for the Society for the Anthropology of North America book prize.

CECILIA MENJÍVAR holds the Dorothy L. Meier Chair in Social Equities and is Professor of Sociology at the University of California, Los Angeles. Dr. Menjívar is the recipient of a Guggenheim fellowship and an Andrew Carnegie Fellowship and author of over one hundred articles on how immigration laws and enforcement policies affect migrants' lives. Her most recent publications include the edited volume *Constructing Immigrant Illegality: Critiques, Experiences, and Responses* (2014), the book *Immigrant Families* (2016), and the coedited volume, *The Oxford Handbook of Migration Crises* (2019).

JUAN THOMAS ORDÓÑEZ is Associate Professor, School of Human Sciences, Universidad del Rosario in Bogotá, Colombia. Dr. Ordóñez holds a Ph.D. in medical anthropology and is author of multiple articles on how unauthorized migrants in the United States engage with documents and the book *Jornalero: Being a Day Laborer in the USA* (2015).

DORIS MARIE PROVINE is Professor Emerita, Justice Studies, Arizona State University. Dr. Provine is an expert on the U.S. legal system and has authored multiple articles on the use of local police to carry out federal immigration enforcement in the United States. She is coauthor of *Policing Immigrants: Local Law Enforcement on the Front Lines* (2016). Her solo-authored books include *Unequal under the Law: Race in the War on Drugs* (2007) and *Judging Credentials: Nonlawyer Judges and the Politics of Professionalism* (1986).

NANDITA SHARMA is Professor, Department of Sociology, University of Hawaii. Dr. Sharma is a leading expert on immigration control and nationalism in the Global North, specifically Canada, and author of the seminal work *Home Economics: Nationalism and the Making of "Migrant Workers" in Canada* (2006). Her latest book is *Home Rule: National Sovereignty and the Separation of Natives and Migrants* (2020, Duke University Press).

MONICA W. VARSANYI is Professor of Geography and Executive Officer of the Earth and Environmental Sciences Program at the CUNY Graduate Center, and Professor of Political Science at John Jay College, City University of New York. Dr. Varsanyi holds a Ph.D. in geography and is an expert on the role of localities in determining migrant membership policy in the United States. She is the editor of the volume *Taking Local Control: Immigration Policy Activism in U.S. Cities and States* (2010) and coauthor of *Policing Immigrants: Local Law Enforcement on the Front Lines* (2016).

Index

CPSIA information can be obtained
at www.ICGtesting.com
Printed in the USA
BVHW051703040322
630607BV00006B/18